"Silk and Bamboo" Music in Shanghai

Other Kent State Titles
in World Musics

The Ethnomusicologist
MANTLE HOOD

Music in the Mind: The Concepts of Music and Musician in Afghanistan
HIROMI LORRAINE SAKATA

The Music of the Bauls of Bengal
CHARLES CAPWELL

Blackfoot Musical Thought: Comparative Perspectives
BRUNO NETTL

The Melodic Tradition of Ireland
JAMES R. COWDERY

Indispensable Harp: Historical Development, Modern Roles,
Configurations, and Performance Practices in Ecuador and Latin America
JOHN SCHECHTER

The Way of the Pipa: Structure and Imagery in Chinese Lute Music
JOHN MYERS

"Silk and Bamboo" Music in Shanghai

The *Jiangnan Sizhu* Instrumental Ensemble Tradition

江南絲竹音樂在上海

J. LAWRENCE WITZLEBEN

韋慈朋著

The Kent State University Press
Kent, Ohio, and London, England

© 1995 by The Kent State University Press, Kent, Ohio 44242
Library of Congress Catalog Card Number 94-9092
ISBN 0-87338-499-7
Manufactured in the United States of America

Some of the material in chapter 2 appeared in an earlier form in
Ethnomusicology 32 (1987): 240–60. I am grateful to the
Society for Ethnomusicology for permission to reprint it here.

LIBRARY OF CONGRESS CATALOGING-IN-PUBLICATION DATA

Witzleben, J. Lawrence (John Lawrence), 1951–
   "Silk and bamboo" music in Shanghai : the jiangnan sizhu
instrumental ensemble tradition / J. Lawrence Witzleben.
      p.   cm. — (World musics)
   Includes bibliographical references (p.   ) and index.
   ISBN 0-87338-499-7
   1. Folk music—China—Shanghai—History and criticism.
I. Series.
ML3746.8.S5W57   1995
781.62'951051132—dc20

94-9092
CIP
MN

British Library Cataloging-in-Publication data are available.

Contents

Preface

Of all the world's major musical cultures, that of China may well be the least thoroughly understood and most often misunderstood by Western scholars and music lovers. The reasons for this are manifold, including the wealth of Chinese historical documents and theoretical treatises (few of which have been translated), the high degree of ethnic and regional diversity, the sheer quantity of genres, styles, and musical instruments, and the apparent paradox of a people who revere the past yet have no qualms about reshaping their artistic legacy to conform with current aesthetics and ideology. In recent decades, much of China has been inaccessible to Western scholars, so the budding field of ethnomusicology—at least those aspects of the discipline in which fieldwork and participant-observation are emphasized—has developed with relatively little input from the music of the world's largest nation.[1]

The problems of complexity and accessibility are augmented by Chinese scholars' longstanding bias in favor of traditions cultivated by the literati and in the courts. Music played on the streets, in teahouses and "pleasure houses," and in ordinary homes has rarely been the subject of scholarly study, even though fiction and autobiographies indicate that informal musical activity has long pervaded daily life in China. Even when traditions embraced by the Chinese people at large have been studied, the focus has rarely been on the musicians themselves or on the processes of music making. Since the early twentieth century, and especially since 1949, the study of non-elite culture and arts has become acceptable and often encouraged. Many scholars have investigated traditions that were previously ignored, but most Chinese musicologists still emphasize musical notation and theory rather than musicians and their musical and social environment.[2]

The present study is a first step toward a comprehensive understanding of one tradition as it exists in a particular locale. The tradition—the instrumental ensemble music known as *Jiangnan sizhu*—is in many respects one that is played and enjoyed by a cult of eccentrics whose musical activities comprise only a tiny part of the cultural life of its primary native locale, the city of Shanghai. Despite this apparent (and misleading) insignificance, an in-depth look at the *Jiangnan sizhu* tradition can reveal much about Chinese musical culture: the music is deeply rooted in ordinary life, and its proponents represent a broad spectrum of Chinese society; it is cultivated as an amateur art, but many of the performers have close ties with the professional musical community; the genre is a regional one, but it has been highly influential in the development of pan-Chinese contemporary solo and ensemble music for Chinese instruments; in recent years, issues of preservation and development have surrounded the tradition, so it provides a fine case study for a look at the contemporary aesthetic and political climate of Chinese music. When we begin to examine *Jiangnan sizhu* in depth, it quickly becomes apparent that many of the polarities that are convenient for discussing Chinese music and society (amateur/professional, popular/refined, insider/outsider, traditional/modern) are in fact continuums.

Although this is a rather specific case study, it also addresses some fundamental aspects of Chinese music that have been relatively neglected by both Chinese and Western scholars. What follows is a multifaceted examination of *Jiangnan sizhu:* the musical sounds and the concepts behind them; the people who play, teach, and learn the music; and the environment in which it is and has been played, heard, and discussed.

BACKGROUND OF THE STUDY

The genesis of this study can be traced to a Chinese variety show in Honolulu in 1979 in which an amateur ensemble, the Wo Lok Music Club, performed several instrumental pieces. The combination of timbres, melodic lines, and rhythms produced sounds which were unlike any Chinese (or other) music I had previously heard live or recorded, yet they were immediately attractive to me. I later learned that this music (listed on the program as "Chinese Classical Orchestra") was from the ensemble tradition called Cantonese Music *(Guangdong Yinyue)*. Subsequently, I began to learn the Cantonese style of playing the *erhu,* two-stringed bowed lute, from Harry Lee, the leader of the group, and to attend their weekly rehearsals.

I found that many Chinese commercial recordings and collections of musical notation for Cantonese Music were available, but written sources in Western languages gave no clue as to how this type of musical tradition fit into the scheme of Chinese musical culture, either past or present. Although substantial information was available on ancient court ensemble musics, few scholars had paid attention to Cantonese Music or any other of China's many living instrumental ensemble traditions.[3]

This situation soon began to change. Musicologists such as Han Kuo-huang (1979) began to write about regional instrumental ensemble traditions, and it became apparent to me that a substantial body of Chinese writings (mostly post-1949 and especially from the late 1970s onward) on these traditions existed. In 1980–81 I spent seven months in Hong Kong researching Cantonese instrumental ensemble Music for my thesis for the M.A. degree in music with a concentration in ethnomusicology at the University of Hawai'i. Although Cantonese music was rarely played as an independent genre in Hong Kong at that time, it formed an important part of Cantonese operatic music and was also frequently included in instrumental performances in which a variety of traditional and modern Chinese musical traditions were juxtaposed.

In the fall of 1981 I was admitted to the Shanghai Conservatory of Music as a research student. Before I went to China, I had little idea of the state of traditional instrumental music in the People's Republic; Elizabeth Wichmann had studied Peking opera in Nanjing, but I was the first American student and one of the first foreign students to be admitted to a music school in China.[4] Thus, when I arrived I had little prior knowledge concerning the state of traditional music or the way it was being taught. My studies during this period were largely exploratory, but given the nature of my previous research and my unexpected but welcome assignment to Shanghai,[5] I was especially interested in the instrumental ensemble music native to that part of China.

I found that this local music, *Jiangnan sizhu,* was regularly played by several music clubs in Shanghai. During that year in China, I was able to hear some of these groups, meet several scholars with some knowledge of the music, and learn to play some of the repertory. The music clubs I heard played *Jiangnan sizhu* almost exclusively, and it was performed as a purely instrumental genre. Somewhat surprisingly (given the long-term Western influence in Shanghai and radical social changes in the city since 1949), the music and the performers seemed to represent musical practices and values that were far more "traditional" and "Chinese" than "revolutionary" or "Western." In 1982, I returned to the United States to begin doctoral studies in ethnomusicology at the University of Pittsburgh. In 1984 I was able to return to Shanghai for fifteen months, this time with the specific purpose of conducting research for a dissertation on *Jiangnan sizhu.*

Li Minxiong in an impromptu drumming demonstration in a park in Wuxi

RESEARCH CLIMATE & METHODOLOGY

At the Shanghai Conservatory, my status was that of a Senior Advanced Research Student, a classification designated by the Chinese Ministry of Education for foreign students engaged in dissertation research. My adviser was Li Minxiong, a scholar-composer-performer who specializes in Chinese instrumental music theory. Li met with me regularly to supervise my work, instruct me in Chinese music theory, and arrange research-related activity outside the school. During my first year in Shanghai, our meetings were devoted primarily to formal analysis of a wide variety of solo and ensemble repertory. During my second stay, we focused more exclusively on analyzing *Jiangnan sizhu* repertory and on comparing early notated source melodies for these pieces with the versions performed today.

I had borrowing privileges for scores and books in the conservatory library; periodicals and phonograph records were available for use in the library but could not be checked out. With few exceptions, the books and recordings to which I had access were of post-1949 vintage; older source materials may still exist in restricted or private collections. As will be discussed, written materials on *Jiangnan sizhu* do exist, but these are mostly brief articles. Bibliographic work was supplementary to other aspects of my research.

Throughout both of my residencies in Shanghai, I studied several Chinese instruments: *zheng* (plucked zither) with Sun Wenyan and He Baoquan, *erhu* with Wu Zhimin, *xiao* (end-blown bamboo flute) with Tan Weiyu, *dizi* (transverse bamboo flute) with Lu Chunling, and *pipa* (plucked lute) with Zhang Zupei, all professors at the conservatory. These lessons were aimed at teaching solo repertory, basic techniques, and the characteristics of various regional styles of playing the instruments. I was able to learn some pieces from the *Jiangnan sizhu* repertory; in addition, my teachers' knowledge of, and emphasis on, musical aesthetics and regional stylistic differences contributed significantly to my research. Li Minxiong also arranged for me to have several special lessons in the *Jiangnan sizhu* style of playing the *erhu, yangqin* (struck zither), and *dizi,* taught respectively by Zhou Hao, Zhou Hui, and Jin Zuli, professional performers and teachers widely recognized as *Jiangnan sizhu* experts. Since the musicians were brought in from outside my "unit" *(danwei)*, considerable bureaucratic red tape was involved, and the lessons were limited to four meetings with each teacher.[6]

Much of my time in Shanghai was spent with the *Jiangnan sizhu* music clubs in the city: listening, taking notes, talking with the musicians, sometimes making tape recordings or taking photographs, and usually playing one or two pieces on the *erhu* with the ensemble. From a Western academic perspective, I was a participant-observer; to most of the *Jiangnan sizhu* performers, I was an apprentice musician. Traditionally, one learns about this music by learning to play it. The "meaning" of the music is intertwined with the "flavor" of the music, and the process of interacting in the musical group is widely viewed as a prerequisite to understanding the music. Thus, despite the atypical circumstances of my background and the ultimate goals of my study, in many ways I was following a tradition, and many of the amateur *sizhu* musicians became my unofficial teachers.[7]

In addition to my work in Shanghai, short research trips to Hangzhou, Nanjing, Wuxi, and Ningbo were arranged by Li Minxiong for the two of us. On these trips, we heard *Jiangnan sizhu* or related genres and met with scholars and musicians. In Hangzhou, a group of performers from the Zhejiang Song and Dance Troupe played for us, and two of the

The Tianshan Music Club (Jin Zuli, *front center*) with the author (*front left*) at the Shanghai Conservatory

musicians from the group (Shen Fengquan and Song Jinglian) lectured on *Jiangnan sizhu* performance, theory, and aesthetics. This was the only *Jiangnan sizhu* I heard outside of Shanghai; although (according to Shen and Song) there are at least two amateur *Jiangnan sizhu* music clubs in Hangzhou, I was not able to obtain enough information to locate them. In Nanjing, Gao Houyong, a well-known scholar of Chinese instrumental music, gave two lectures on *Jiangnan sizhu* for me and the other foreign students from the Shanghai Conservatory, and I was also able to arrange an interview with Gan Tao, a performer and scholar of *Jiangnan sizhu*. In Wuxi, we heard a local genre of Chinese opera *(Xiju)* and two performances of percussion ensemble music, one by an amateur ensemble of workers, the other an accompaniment to a *madeng* "horse lantern" dance. In Ningbo, Li and I had several interviews with Shao Xiaoxian, an accomplished accompanist for the narrative singing genre *siming nanci*, and we heard performances of another type of narrative singing *(Jiaochuan zoushu)* and of local opera *(Yongju)*.

Zhou Hao *(seated)* and his students, seen here at the Shanghai Conservatory

Few musicians in Shanghai who do not participate in the *Jiangnan sizhu* music clubs are aware of the extent and locations of these groups' activities. One could spend years in the city without discovering them, so it is quite possible that there are groups (of which my informants were unaware) meeting regularly to play *Jiangnan sizhu* in Nanjing, Wuxi, Ningbo, or elsewhere in the Jiangnan region. Similarly, I have no evidence concerning the state of *Jiangnan sizhu* in rural Jiangnan. The focus of the present study is *Jiangnan sizhu* music as it is played in Shanghai; the state of the tradition elsewhere in the region is a subject awaiting further investigation.

Near the end of my stay in China, I was asked to present the results of my research to the faculty of Chinese music at the conservatory; my *Jiangnan sizhu* teachers and several representatives from Shanghai's musical community outside the school were also invited. First, I read a paper summarizing my work with Li Minxiong on formal structure (published for internal use by the Conservatory using my Chinese name as Wei Cipeng 1985). Then, I discussed the *Jiangnan sizhu* style of playing the various instruments I had studied and performed brief excerpts on each. The presentation was followed by questions and discussion, which provided me with valuable feedback from knowledgeable and often highly opinionated musicians and scholars in Shanghai.

In my field research, my intention was to understand the music as perceived by the people who make it, and to approach it with as few preconceptions as possible; I made no attempt to apply or validate any particular theory or method from ethnomusicology, anthropology, Sinology, or other disciplines. Little can be accomplished, however, unless a researcher has at least a tentative methodological framework, a list of priorities for which aspects of the music are to be studied, and a set of approaches to be followed in the process of study. Some of the approaches used in the present study and the rationale for choosing them are listed below. To anyone trained in an ethnomusicology graduate program in the United States, this list may seem to be a restatement of the obvious. Most musicologists in China, however, have very different ideas about the aims, emphases, and methodologies of research on music. What follows, then, may be viewed as the cultural, temporal, methodological, and personal biases that have shaped the present study.

1. The primary focus of research has been on the "carriers" of the *Jiangnan sizhu* tradition: those who know it intimately and/or perform the music. The observations of individuals outside the tradition (whether or not they are insiders to the culture or have musical training) have been treated as complementary sources of information.

2. An effort has been made to observe and document what performers and listeners in music clubs actually do and say. During observation, no events or details should be considered insignificant or irrelevant, even if the performers themselves consider them to be so.

3. Careful attention has been paid to discrepancies between what informants or written sources state about the musical tradition and what actually happens in practice. Ideals may contain the most important values held by the performers and listeners; variance between these ideals and performance or behavioral practice may indicate the range of flexibility allowable within the tradition.

4. Considerable time has been devoted to learning to play the music and to performing it with *Jiangnan sizhu* ensembles. Musicians are often much more willing to criticize an outsider to their tradition or an inexperienced performer than they are to fault the playing of an established player; as both an outsider and a beginner, I was thus subject to criticism.[8] This type of negative input may, by implication, reveal some of the positive values held by the musicians. Through performing the music of an ensemble tradition, the researcher can also gain insight into the nature of interaction in the performance process.

5. The learning process itself has been an important subject of study, as it is central to the nature of the music. Attitudes toward memorization, imita-

tion, notation, and learning through intuitive absorption affect the way performers hear and think about the music.

6. In several areas of inquiry, the questions addressed in this study have been
influenced by the work of other scholars and by my own performing background in unrelated musical traditions (particularly Javanese *gamelan* and
Western folk and popular music). While it cannot be assumed that concepts or
values present in one musical tradition are present in another, it can be useful
to attempt to determine if a particular value or characteristic found in one
cultural tradition is also present in another. Comparative inquiry may contribute to our knowledge of musical universals and of the various ways in which a
musical principle or characteristic is manifested in different locales.

SOURCE MATERIALS

Many of the items in the bibliography for this study include the words
"Jiangnan sizhu" in their titles, and other items also contain information
on the genre. However, the quantity of sources is misleading in that
most of these articles or pertinent sections of books are very short (most
are less than five pages long) and many authors have repeated or para-
phrased earlier writings. The most substantial introductions to the
music are found in Jin (1961), Gao (1981), and Li Minxiong (1982). The
later writings, especially Gao's, draw heavily on the earlier essay; this is
not surprising, since Jin's writing was used as teaching material at the
Shanghai Conservatory when he was a professor and Gao and Li were
students. All three scholars provide an introduction to *Jiangnan sizhu*
and discuss the repertory and musical style. Jin discusses each of the
main pieces in the repertory individually, Gao provides many brief musical examples, and Li includes complete analyses of two pieces. Shanghai
Qunzhong (1960)—although he is not credited, the volume was edited
by Xu Qingyan—is primarily a collection of multipart scores; however,
it also includes a brief but informative overview of the tradition, discussions of each of the pieces included in the collection, and explanations of the idiomatic techniques for each instrument.

Jin and Xu (1983) have written the most thorough history of the
music. Although only four pages long and dealing almost exclusively with
the city of Shanghai, this article provides a wealth of detail. Xu Qingyan
(1983) has written on the historical connections between *Jiangnan sizhu*
and the string, wind, and percussion tradition *shifan luogu;* more information on *shifan luogu* and the related *shifan gu* is contained in the
introductory material for Yang Yinliu's compilations of notation for these
traditions (Yang Yinliu 1980; Yang and Cao 1982).

At least two early collections of musical notation (Wu Yuan 1920 and
Zheng Jinwen 1924) contain pieces from the *Jiangnan sizhu* repertory.

Guofeng (1939) is almost completely devoted to *Jiangnan sizhu* repertory, including multiple versions of some pieces. Both Zheng and
Guofeng also include diagrams of the tunings and fingerings for several
instruments. More recently, Shen Fengquan (1982) has published a
compilation of notation that includes all of the Eight Great Pieces
(some in single-line melody, others in two- or three-part arrangement)
and twenty other pieces (mostly in single-line melody) associated with
Jiangnan sizhu. Gan Tao (1985) has compiled a massive (over five
hundred pages) collection of *Jiangnan sizhu* notation including individual parts for many different instruments and multipart scores. This
book includes not only Gan's own arrangements, but also many (some
previously published) by other scholars and performers. Zhou Hui,
Zhou, and Ma (1986) is a collection of multipart scores for all of the
Eight Great Pieces. Jiang and Yuan (1989) consists of multipart scores
for selected *Jiangnan sizhu* repertory. Many collections of notation for
specific solo instruments contain pieces drawn from various regions or
genres, and *Jiangnan sizhu* repertory is sometimes included. Notable
among such collections are Lu Chunling's book of *dizi* notation (1982)
and Sun Yude's method for *xiao* (1977).[9]

In English, overviews of the music are provided in Witzleben (1983b,
1987a). Alan Thrasher has examined structural elements (1985), including several important relationships which Chinese scholars have
neglected, and variation techniques (1993) in *Jiangnan sizhu*. Han Kuo-
huang (1979) and Shen Sin-yan (1979) discuss the larger topic of instrumental ensemble music and *Jiangnan sizhu*'s place in it, while Alan
Thrasher gives consideration to *sizhu* traditions in his writings on the
aesthetics (1980) and sociology (1981) of Chinese music. Among the
studies of other regional *sizhu* traditions are Chen Chien-tai (1978),
Thrasher (1988), Witzleben (1983a), Yeh (1985), Ying-fen Wang (1986,
1992), and Dujunco (1994). All of these contain substantial bibliographies of Chinese and Western sources relevant to these traditions.

Many commercial recordings of *Jiangnan sizhu* exist, and new ones
continue to be produced. A reliable discography is not practicable at this
time; I do not yet have access to many important early recordings, and
many of the recordings I do have are multiple-generation cassette dub-
bings with no discographical information. The problem is augmented by
the widespread practice (notably in Hong Kong) of rereleasing recordings, usually without any information concerning the original recording
and often even omitting the names of performers. A short Selected Discography of commercial recordings of *Jiangnan sizhu* and related
traditions follows the References Cited.

Much of this study is based on interviews, conversations, and personal observations on Shanghai *Jiangnan sizhu* performance practice. Analysis of the music relies heavily on my own field recordings and on several musicians' personal (noncommercial) recordings of their own and their group's playing.

GOALS & SIGNIFICANCE OF THE STUDY

A substantial body of literature in Chinese exists concerning *Jiangnan sizhu* and other instrumental ensemble traditions, and since the late 1970s, Western-language studies of Chinese instrumental ensemble musics have appeared with increasing regularity. Despite this burgeoning scholarship, there are still many aspects of *sizhu* musics which have not yet been given sufficient attention. The present study examines some of these neglected topics, including: concepts of variation, improvisation, and heterophony; aesthetic principles applicable to Chinese ensemble musics and to Chinese oral/aural traditions in general; regionality and regional identity; social context, including interactions among performers and between performers and audience; and urbanization, Westernization, and strategies for preservation and/or development of traditional Chinese musics. All of these issues need to be addressed, not only to attain an understanding of *Jiangnan sizhu* but also to broaden our knowledge of Chinese music as a whole. Obviously, these themes are also cross-culturally relevant.

Although this study leaves many questions unanswered, it is the only monograph on *Jiangnan sizhu* to date in any language. It is also the first book in the field of ethnomusicology that is based primarily on extended fieldwork in the People's Republic of China (PRC).[10]

This study is at once an introduction to the sounds, concepts, and behavior associated with *Jiangnan sizhu* and a series of exploratory essays, with reference to *Jiangnan sizhu,* on selected issues and problems such as those mentioned above. In the course of my research, I have been exposed to the views of ethnomusicologists and Western-trained China specialists, to Chinese musicologists, and to Chinese performers (professional and amateur) from both within and without the *Jiangnan sizhu* tradition. The interplay of these various perspectives, combined with that of my own as a participant-observer, is a recurring theme in this book. Through looking at *Jiangnan sizhu* from these various angles, the outlines of a multidimensional image of the tradition should begin to emerge.

TOPICS FOR FURTHER RESEARCH

The history of *Jiangnan sizhu* is closely tied to that of other musical traditions in the region. Many of the "related genres" mentioned in chapter 1 have been given little or no scholarly attention, and much more needs to be known about their music and historical background before questions such as the nature of "Jiangnan musical style" can be answered. As for *Jiangnan sizhu* itself, the social background of performing arts is a sensitive topic in the PRC, and contemporary writings on music history often steer clear of the subject or treat it with platitudes. However, the social background of early *Jiangnan sizhu* performers, the nature of their musical training, and the cultural milieu in which they have lived need to be investigated if we are to understand the music's place in Chinese musical and cultural history.

For the principal musical instruments in the *Jiangnan sizhu* ensemble, the relationships between Jiangnan solo traditions, non-*sizhu* ensemble traditions, and the *Jiangnan sizhu* style of playing need to be investigated. For the secondary instruments, such as the *sheng* (mouth organ) and *sanxian* (three-stringed plucked lute), the *Jiangnan sizhu* playing style should also be studied in detail. For all instruments, traditional temperament needs to be thoroughly examined. With regard to repertory, many questions remain concerning the relationships between the musical materials used in *Jiangnan sizhu* and related tunes and pieces played elsewhere in China (such as the "Kaimen"/"Baimen" tune complex). The subjects of variation and heterophony are major ones, and the present work barely begins to address them. In particular, the roles of improvisation and spontaneous interaction in *Jiangnan sizhu* need further study. With regard to aesthetics, there is a need for source materials that give the perspective of performers; this is a subject for which sound and video recordings combining verbal explanations with musical examples would be of great benefit. Documentation of *Jiangnan sizhu* has been woefully neglected, and the playing of many of the greatest performers of the music (some of whom are now deceased or barely able to play) was never captured on tape. Comprehensive recording of all the music clubs in Shanghai, especially of older performers and rare repertory, would be of great value to present and future generations.

Acknowledgments

Many *Jiangnan sizhu* musicians in Shanghai shared their music, ideas, and friendship with me. Special thanks are due to my *Jiangnan sizhu* teachers—Jin Zuli, Zhou Hao, Zhou Hui, and Lu Chunling—and to Lu Dehua, Zhang Zhengming, Zhu Wenyi, Ma Huanzhang, Dong Kejun, Pan Lian'gen, Liu Yuehua, Liu Chengyi, Chen Yonglu, Qin Pengzhang, Xu Zhongyi, Gu Jikang, Yang Lixian, and Zhang Pingzhou.

My advisor at the Shanghai Conservatory, Li Minxiong, was unstinting in his devotion to teaching me Chinese music theory, and I was also fortunate to be able to share his ideas and company on our research trips together. I am grateful to all of my teachers at the Shanghai Conservatory of Music for their encouragement and patience, especially Sun Wenyan, He Baoquan, Wu Zhimin, Tan Weiyu, Zhang Zupei, Huang Yunzhen, Jin Jianmin, and Jiang Mingdun. Also at the Shanghai Conservatory, I am grateful to Lin Youren, Dai Xiaolian, Chen Yingshi, Teng Yongran, Huang Xiuying, Zhou Min, and Mercedes Dujunco for their help and friendship. Elsewhere in China, special thanks are due to Shao Xiaoxiang in Ningbo, Shen Fengquan, Song Jinglian, and Zhou Dafeng in Hangzhou and to Gao Houyong, Gan Tao, and Cheng Gongliang in Nanjing.

At the University of Pittsburgh, my dissertation committee members, J. H. Kwabena Nketia, Evelyn Rawski, Deane Root, and James Watson, shared much of their valuable time, expertise, and advice with me, and I am also grateful to Wayne Slawson, Doris Dyen, Rubie Watson, Chan Sau-yan, Afolabi Alaja-Browne, Li Ping-hui, Wang Ying-fen, and Tsao Pen-yeh for their interest in and comments on my work. Ronald Grimes introduced me to the field of ritual studies, and his teaching and writing have been a source of inspiration. Terry Liu and I shared ideas, frustrations, and triumphs not only during my fieldwork, but also throughout the dissertation-writing process, and his encouragement and friendship helped see me through. My far-flung fellow graduate students in Chinese music, Nora Yeh, Fred Lau, and Yu Siu Wah, also encouraged me to persevere.

While at the University of Michigan Center for Chinese Studies (researching music in Chinese fiction on a postdoctoral fellowship from the Center), I had several opportunities to present some of the material in this book to the faculty and students of the China center and ethnomusicology program. I would like particularly to thank Kenneth DeWoskin, Michel Oksenberg, William Malm, Judith Becker, René Lysloff, and Deborah Wong for their valuable feedback. I am also grateful to the members of the Burton Tower Silk and Bamboo Ensemble for their enthusiasm in learning to perform *Jiangnan sizhu*.

Bell Yung, my dissertation advisor, has been encouraging and guiding my research since my first studies in Hong Kong, and his constructive criticism and advice have been a constant source of inspiration. Barbara Smith (who, along with Ricardo Trimillos, Byong-won Lee, and Hardja Susilo at the University of Hawai'i, taught me to be an ethnomusicologist) has painstakingly read and reread the many revisions of this manuscript and provided a wealth of valuable suggestions. Without the two of them, this book would not exist.

My editors at The Kent State University Press have been conscientious and patient in seeing this manuscript through its many revisions, not to mention endless correspondence between Ohio and Hong Kong. Julia Morton, Joanna Hildebrand, and Linda Cuckovich deserve my warmest thanks for a job well done.

Lastly, I would like to thank my parents and my brother and sister and their families for their understanding and support throughout my studies, fieldwork, and writing.

Research in China was supported by two fellowships from the Committee on Scholarly Communication with the People's Republic of China. The final months of my fieldwork and my dissertation writing were supported by two Andrew Mellon Pre-Doctoral Fellowships from the University of Pittsburgh, with additional support provided by the Pitt China Program.

Romanization, Pronunciation, & Translation

The *pinyin* romanization system is used throughout this book, with the exception of a few words (Cantonese, Peking opera, Taoist, Yangtze River) that have become very familiar to Western readers in another spelling. *Pinyin* is the official romanization of the People's Republic of China, and pronunciation corresponds to the national spoken language (based on the dialect of the Beijing area) called *putong hua* (in the PRC), *guoyu* (in Taiwan), or Mandarin (in the West).

Every system of romanization presents problems for the nonnative speaker, and *pinyin* is no exception. What follows is a very brief layman's guide; the interested reader should consult a reliable language textbook such as John De Francis's *Beginning Chinese Reader* (1976) for a thorough explanation of the romanization and of Chinese pronunciation.

The consonants *b, d, f, g, h, j, k, l, m, n, p, r, s, t, w,* and *y* and the combinations *ch* and *ng* are pronounced in a manner that roughly resembles their English equivalents (although linguists distinguish many subtle differences). Vowels change according to the letters preceding and following them, but, with the exceptions listed below, *a, i,* and *u* resemble their Italian equivalents. Other letters and problematic combinations are as follows (quoted material is adapted from De Francis 1976:24–31):

a   in *ian* and *uan:* "a sound between the *an* of *man* and the *en* of *men*"

c   "like the *t's H* in *it's Hal,* but with much more breath and with the tongue farther forward"

e   as an independent syllable or after a consonant other than *y:* "begins as the *e* in *error* and passes quickly into the *o* in *of*"
     in *ie* and *ye,* or after *u:* "like *ye* in *yet*"

en   "like the *en* in *chicken*"

eng   "like the *ung* in *lung*"

i   after *c, r, s,* or *z:* "like the first *a* in *banana*"
     after *ch, sh,* or *zh:* like an *r*
     in *ui:* "like the *we* in *weigh*"

j   "like the *tch* in *itching*"

o   "like the *wa* in *wall*"
in *ao:* "like the *au's* in *sauerkraut*"
in *iao:* "like the *yow* in *yowl*"
in *ong:* "like the *ung* in the German *jung*"
in *ou:* "as in *soul*"
in *uo:* "like the *wa* in *waltz*"

q   "like the *ch* in *cheap*, but with more breath . . ."

u   in *iu:* "close to the *yo* in *yoke*"
in the combination *ue* and after *j, q, x,* or *y:* as *ü* (below)

ü   "like the *u* in the German *über*"

x   "between the *s* in *see* and the *sh* in *she*"

z   "like the *t's* in *it's Al,* but with the tongue farther forward"

zh "like the *ch* in *chew,* but unaspiratied with the tongue tip curled far
back"

All syllables end in a vowel, a diphthong, *n, ng,* or *r.* In current usage for
proper names and terms, two or more syllables are often run together
without a space or hyphen. The first syllable should be assumed to end
with *ng, n, r,* or the last vowel before a consonant. Thus *Jiangnan sizhu* is
Jiang-nan si-zhu and *erhu* is *er-hu.* If there is a syllable change between
n and *g,* before *n* or *r,* or between vowels, an apostrophe is used, as in
Lian'gen, Pu'an, or the city Xi'an (distinguished from the single syllable
xian as in *xiansheng*).

All translations of passages quoted from Chinese sources and of titles,
terms, and expressions are my own unless indicated otherwise. Roman-
ized Chinese terms retained in translated passages are italicized. The
terms "Cantonese Music" and "Modern Chinese Orchestra" refer to specific musical genres described in the text, and are capitalized throughout.

"Silk and Bamboo" Music in Shanghai

Prologue

In the heart of the old section of the city of Shanghai is the Mid-Lake Pavilion, surrounded by a lotus pond and connected to the outside world by the Bridge of Nine Turnings. On certain afternoons, one corner of the upper story of the pavilion is taken over by a group of men playing Chinese musical instruments. Periodically, some of the performers leave their places around a table and are replaced by other musicians. A few non-performers (or performers taking a break from playing) listen intently; other tables are filled by Chinese and (perhaps) foreign tourists, some listening, some talking, some watching the musicians or each other. Attendants bustle around, delivering clay pots of tea leaves and filling or refilling the pots from kettles of hot water.

The music being played is traditionally referred to as *sizhu*, more recently as *Jiangnan sizhu*: "silk and bamboo music" from south of the Chang Jiang (Yangtze) River. Although this music was not played in the Mid-Lake Pavilion until the 1950s, similar musical activity has occurred throughout the city of Shanghai since at least the beginning of this century. Amateur music clubs meet in private homes, theaters, neighborhood committee offices, and teahouses. Meeting places have changed continually, and the combination of musicians may change from year to year or even week to week, but a common repertory, semifixed instrumentation, and a body of shared musical values have combined to form a musical tradition that is unique to the Yangtze delta area and that has flourished most noticeably in Shanghai.

"Jiangnan" is a geographical term, literally meaning "south of the river." The region commonly referred to as Jiangnan is the area along the south bank of the lower Yangtze valley, encompassing parts of the provinces of Zhejiang, Jiangsu, and Anhui and including the cities of Shanghai, Nanjing, Wuxi, Suzhou, Hangzhou, and Ningbo. "*Sizhu*" refers to the ancient organological system in which instruments were classified according to the materials producing their sound. "Silk" (*si*) instruments had silk strings, while "bamboo" (*zhu*) instruments were mostly bamboo flutes. In current usage, silk and bamboo music is played by a string and wind ensemble that often includes small percussion instruments made of wood, wood and skin, or metal. The term "sizhu" has come to imply music of relatively low volume that is usually played indoors; contemporary Chinese musicologists categorize a variety of regional instrumental ensemble genres as *sizhu* traditions.

Thus, *Jiangnan sizhu* means "silk and bamboo music from the south bank of the Yangtze." Musicians in Shanghai have traditionally referred to their music as *sizhu*. In order to distinguish this regional tradition from other ensemble musics native to Guangdong, Fujian, and Taiwan (which musicologists also categorize as *sizhu*), the addition of the prefix *Jiangnan* has become widespread since the 1950s, when it was first used formally (Jin and Xu 1983:30), and the complete name *Jiangnan sizhu* is now widely used by both scholars and performers.

The instruments most commonly played in the *Jiangnan sizhu* ensemble are the *dizi* (transverse bamboo flute), *xiao* (end-blown bamboo flute), *sheng* (mouth organ), *erhu* (two-stringed bowed lute), *pipa* (four-stringed plucked lute), *sanxian* (three-stringed plucked lute), *qinqin* (two- or three-stringed plucked lute), *yangqin* (struck zither), *ban* (clapper), and either a *biqi gu* (small drum) or *bangzi* (woodblock). Other instruments that are occasionally added include the *ruan* (four-stringed plucked lute), *zheng* (thirteen- to twenty-one-stringed plucked zither), various two-stringed bowed lutes larger in size than the *erhu*, and *pengling* (a pair of small bronze concussion bells). As few as two or as many as ten musicians may play together at one time; in special cases, more than twenty players may participate. Generally, only one of each instrument is played. Written sources usually list the *dizi* and *erhu* as the most important instruments in the ensemble; in practice, the leading instrument or instruments vary according to the piece being played and the relative experience and authority of the musicians playing them.

At the center of the *Jiangnan sizhu* repertory are the Eight Great Pieces (*Ba Da Qu*) or Eight Great Famous Pieces (*Ba Da Mingqu*).[1] Other pieces are also performed, but opinions vary among scholars and musicians as to which of them are truly *Jiangnan sizhu*. Some of the repertory frequently played by *Jiangnan sizhu* groups is clearly adapted from other regional genres, and is identified as such by musicians.

In Shanghai, at least twelve *Jiangnan sizhu* music clubs were active in 1985. Jin Zuli suggests that as of 1983 there were about two hundred musicians of note playing *Jiangnan sizhu* in Shanghai (Jin and Xu 1983:28). Large-scale *Jiangnan sizhu* performances are publicized in Shanghai newspapers, and these announcements are sometimes accompanied by articles introducing the music. This type of performance is usually tape-recorded and subsequently broadcast on the radio; commercial recordings of the music are also occasionally broadcast. Nevertheless, most residents of Shanghai would probably not be able to identify the term *Jiangnan sizhu*, and it is doubtful that nonmusicians would be familiar with any of the repertory. Thus, this music belongs to a viable but somewhat invisible subculture in Shanghai, and its role in the city's musical life is much less prominent than traditions such as Shanghai opera *(Huju)*, Western art music, or Western-style Chinese popular song.[2]

In the Chinese musical community, however, *Jiangnan sizhu* occupies a more significant position. Chinese music specialists in China list it as one of the most important types of traditional ensemble music in China and, as such, it is assured a place in almost any overview of Chinese music. Because of the complexity and special features of the formal structure of some *Jiangnan sizhu* pieces, they are often included in textbooks or publications on music analysis (such as Gao 1981:84–97; Li Minxiong 1982:309–21 and 1983:123–35; Ye 1983:175–89; and Li Xi'an and Jun 1985:65–74, 94–97). The genre is also well known for the sophistication of the relationships among the melodic lines in the musical texture and for the relative independence of these lines. Thus, it appears in some discussions of multipart texture in Chinese music (A'erzamanuofu 1962:113–14; Gao 1981:97–101; and Li Minxiong 1982:131–54).

Many performers of Chinese musical instruments know some *Jiangnan sizhu* repertory. There is much overlapping between solo and ensemble repertory in Chinese instrumental music; pieces that were originally solo may be played in ensemble settings, and vice versa. Most collections of musical notation for a given instrument include pieces from ensemble traditions, which may be played by either a soloist or an ensemble. Professional performers throughout China are expected to have some mastery of a variety of regional musical styles, and for some instruments the Jiangnan style of playing is considered to be a major one. To learn this style, a musician studies repertory indigenous to the Jiangnan region, which may include solo pieces associated with the area, *Jiangnan sizhu*, and possibly music from regional opera or narrative singing traditions. For the *dizi*, many collections of notation contain *Jiangnan sizhu* repertory (as in Lu 1982:46–73), and these pieces are widely performed as solos. For the *erhu* and *yangqin*, none of the pieces associated with *Jiangnan sizhu* have become part of the standard solo repertory, but most students of these instruments learn at least one *Jiangnan sizhu* piece, and several of the Eight Great Pieces have been included in recent collections of *erhu* and *yangqin* music (Renmin 1983:1:4–7; 2:9–10; Zhongguo Yinyue 1983:1–2). For the *pipa*, the Eight Great Pieces are relatively infrequently performed as solos, but one important school of *pipa*-playing (the Pudong school) is native to the Shanghai area and closely related to the *Jiangnan sizhu pipa* style. Most *pipa* students are expected to learn some of the repertory and playing style of this school.

Thus, students of Chinese music theory and composition are aware of *Jiangnan sizhu* and are expected to know something about it. Students of musical instruments that are important in *Jiangnan sizhu* are expected to have some expertise in the Jiangnan style and to learn a few pieces central or peripheral to the *Jiangnan sizhu* tradition. Because of this, most scholars, composers, and performers of Chinese music who have studied in a conservatory setting have had some training in *Jiangnan sizhu*.

Overseas interest in *Jiangnan sizhu* has had an impact on the music in recent years, but the long-term effects of this interest on the tradition remain to be seen. My activity as a participant-observer was noted in a Shanghai newspaper and was later the subject of a television feature. An American scholar-performer, Alan Thrasher, visited Shanghai and Hangzhou in 1984 and played the *dizi* in *sizhu* groups, a fact that was repeatedly mentioned to me by musicians in these cities. At a conference on *Jiangnan sizhu* music held in Shanghai in January 1985, both Thrasher and I were cited as evidence of the music's global appeal. In May 1987, a competition for performance and composition of *Jiangnan sizhu* was held in Shanghai. Participants included groups from Singapore and Hong Kong and an ensemble of Shanghai Conservatory students from Australia, England, France, Japan, and the United States, as well as China; this international participation was emphasized in both Chinese- and English-language newspaper articles reporting the event (Renmin Ribao 1987; Qiao and Kong 1987).

As in some other Chinese traditional arts, appreciation by foreigners may well lead to a renewed appreciation within China. More specifically, this international interest provides moral support for the practitioners of the music and may even cause record companies or travel agents to recognize a commercial potential in the music's appeal to foreigners. It is questionable, however, whether the interest of people overseas will have a significant effect on the Chinese musical community at large.

ONE

Historical Background &
Intergenre Relationships

*J*iangnan sizhu is a young tradition by Chinese standards, but string
and wind ensembles have played an important role in Chinese music
for over two millennia. Moreover, *Jiangnan sizhu* music is closely linked
to other instrumental and vocal genres in the Jiangnan region.

ANTECEDENTS

Silk and bamboo are two of the materials among the "eight sounds"
(bayin) used to classify musical instruments in the ancient Chinese
organological system first outlined in the Zhou Dynasty (1122–255 B.C.)
in the *Zhouli* [Rituals of Zhou] (Li Minxiong 1982:35). The best-
documented ancient Chinese ensembles were comprised of a variety of
instrumental types, including bronze bells, stone chimes, and other
loud percussion instruments. String and wind instruments may have
been emphasized in certain pieces or passages (since no musical notation from this period survives, we can only speculate), but they were
certainly not the dominant instruments—in volume, at least—in these
ensembles.

At some point in China's early musical history, the idea of a small ensemble featuring strings and relatively soft wind instruments became
valued as an aesthetically desirable musical combination. Archaeologi-
cal evidence from the Zenghouyi tomb, which was sealed in 433 B.C.
(DeWoskin 1982:25), indicates that such ensembles were already in existence at that time. In addition to the set of bronze bells for which this
tomb has become famous, many other instruments were also unearthed:
"The coffin of the Marquis was found in the eastern cell which is
thought to be the bed room. In this room, a silk and bamboo chamber
orchestra was found. It contains ten pieces [*sic*] of wind, plucked string
and percussion instruments" (Lee 1980:3). Thus, in addition to the

large orchestras that played for ceremonial and ritual events, string and wind instruments were combined for music making on a smaller scale and of a more intimate nature.

One ancient tradition often cited as a precedent for later *sizhu* developments is that of *xianghe ge*, "harmonious songs." These were songs with *sizhu* accompaniment and were developed from folk songs of northern China as early as 200 B.C. (Yang Yinliu 1981:114); instrumental preludes to the singing became an important part of this tradition (Yeh 1985:65). Although little is known about the actual music of these songs or their accompaniment, they represent the earliest specifically named genre known to have featured a *sizhu* ensemble.

In the Sui-Tang period (A.D. 581–907), the genre known as *qingshang yue*, which the Japanese scholar Shigeo Kishibe has described as "popular songs of the Han dynasty" (1960–61:14), prospered. Nora Yeh has summarized the findings of Chinese music historians concerning this music: "During the fifth and sixth centuries . . . the folk music in both northern and southern China came to be known as "qingshang yue." . . . [it] came to be regarded as one of the music departments (known as *jiubu ji* or *shibu ji*) in the imperial court. It used mainly the silk-bamboo instruments" (1985:66). *Jiubu ji* were the "nine kinds of music" established in the reign of Emperor Yang (605–17), which included not only Chinese traditions but also musics from Korea, India, and various parts of the regions that later came to be known as Chinese and Russian Turkestan, and were used for "various feasts and festivals in the court" (Kishibe 1960–61:15, 16). *Shibu ji* were the "ten kinds of music" established in A.D. 640–42. In both of these genres, fixed sequences were established for performing the nine or ten musical types (ibid.:17).

He Changlin (1985) suggests that another form of music dating from the Tang Dynasty, *chashan douyue* ("*dou* music from the tea hills"), was at least in part an early type of *sizhu* ensemble music.[1] A special grade of tea was grown in the area to the west of Lake Tai, near the border between present-day Zhejiang and Jiangsu provinces. A tradition was established of presenting tea to the emperor, and a festival was held each year when the tea was picked, tasted, and graded. The festival lasted about twenty days, with both court specialists and amateur folk musicians taking part in performing various types of music and dance. In describing the festivities, the late-Tang poet Cao Song refers to a "tea hills *sizhu* festival," and, according to He's interpretation, Cao's poem suggests that music making would already be in progress while participants were still on board the boats bringing them to the event (ibid.:43).

The predecessors of the bowed and plucked lutes so prominent in contemporary *sizhu* musics came to China from central Asia at relatively late dates. Based on the visual evidence from frescos in the Mugao caves at Dunhuang in Gansu province, the *pipa* was included in entertainment orchestras as early as A.D. 642 (Han 1979:3, 5), while the bowed lutes became assimilated by the fourteenth century during the Yuan Dynasty, 1279–1368, whose Mongol rulers were accustomed to hearing similar instruments and looked with favor upon their use in court circles.

"*Sizhu,*" in addition to its literal organological meaning, came to be used as a euphemism for music in general, usually implying a music played indoors. The term has been in use at least since the Han Dynasty (206 B.C.–A.D. 220), where it is found in the *Jinshu* [Book of the Jin (dynasty)] (Li Minxiong 1982:35). The term "*sizhu*" was later used by writers of poetry and prose for affective purposes. A famous example is found in the Tang poet Bai Juyi's "Changhen Ge" (Lament everlasting), which refers to "slow songs, leisurely dances, crystallizing string and reed" (Levy 1971:1, 137) played in the emperor's chambers.

Another common term related to *sizhu* (also found in the *Jinshu*) is *guanxian*, "winds and strings." While this expression refers to the manner of sound production rather than materials used to make the sounds, the connotations of *guanxian* may be considered to be essentially the same as those of *sizhu*.[2]

During the Ming Dynasty (1368–1644), Chinese opera underwent considerable development, culminating in the genre that came to be known as *Kunqu*, "songs of Kun," which originated in the Kunshan region of Jiangsu province. *Kunqu* is a genre in which elements of the northern *zaju*, "miscellaneous plays," and the southern *nanxi* ("southern plays," later called *chuanji*, meaning "marvel tales") were integrated. The rise of *Kunqu* is associated with Wei Liangfu and a small circle of associates, who "devised" the new tradition "during the years 1540–66" (Dolby 1976:91). It is widely assumed that the northern style emphasized string instruments while the southern style favored winds; however, Yang Yinliu (1981:902) believes that such distinctions were rarely rigid and, by the fourteenth century, southern repertory came to be accompanied by the *pipa* and *zheng*, and the *dizi* could be used to accompany northern repertory. By the late Yuan period, northern and southern dramatic music were combined in "song-sets" (Dolby 1976:74); eventually, the standard accompanying ensemble included both string and wind instruments. Although documentation on *Kunqu* is extensive, specific information on the instruments used and style of accompaniment is relatively scarce, and the detailed accounts that are available may be highly idiosyncratic rather than typical (Yang Yinliu 1981:901). According to one source from 1559, the accompaniment featured *dizi*, *pipa*, and *guan* (a double-reed wind instrument) at that time (Xu 1959:3, 242).[3] Another source (Mackerras

1972:7) also mentions the *xiao* and *yueqin* ("moon stringed-instrument," a plucked lute with a round body and a short neck), and other scholars have added *sanxian* and *sheng*. Yang Yinliu believes that the essential accompanying instruments are percussion, *dizi*, and *sanxian*, with the most common auxiliary instruments including *sheng*, *xiao*, *pipa*, *yueqin*, and *huqin*, the generic term for two-stringed bowed lutes (1981:905).

The 1814 collection of musical notation *Xiansuo Beikao* [A reference appendix for strings], now more often referred to as *Xiansuo Shisantao* [Thirteen pieces for strings], is intended for a string ensemble supplemented by winds (Yang Yinliu and Cao 1979 is an annotated edition of this collection). The notation contains parts for up to six instruments and may either document existing ensemble style or be arrangements by the compiler, Rong Zhai. Four of the musical lines are specified for *pipa*, *sanxian*, *zheng*, and *huqin*. The other two lines may be played by any combination of *xiao*, *dizi*, *sheng*, and *tiqin*, a low-pitched two-stringed bowed lute (Han 1979:7). Thus, the complete ensemble was one very similar to that of contemporary *Jiangnan sizhu*. This manuscript is also significant in that several of the pieces contained in it are still played by *Jiangnan sizhu* music clubs.

Two closely related traditions from the Wuxi area of Jiangsu province that include both a *sizhu* ensemble and a percussion ensemble are probably the most direct antecedents of *Jiangnan sizhu*. These string-wind-percussion genres are *shifan gu* and *shifan luogu* and will hereafter be referred to collectively as *shifan* music.[4] Although various explanations exist for the meaning of the names, *shifan* can best be thought of as meaning "ten times," with the sense of "many changes" (Yang Yinliu 1981:992). *Shifan gu*, "*shifan* drums," music is played by a string and wind ensemble plus a drum, a clapper, and a gong chime; *shifan luogu*, "*shifan* gongs and drums," music adds a large percussion ensemble of various gongs and cymbals to this basic instrumentation (Li Minxiong 1982:76). Yang Yinliu believes that despite the apparent similarities, *shifan gu* and *shifan luogu* should be treated as two distinct genres and that they are "two kinds of music which are obviously different and not interrelated. Not only are the types and playing techniques of the percussion instruments considerably different, but the tunes [*qupai*] used in the wind and string music are also different" (1981:993).

In the 1950s the Central Conservatory of Music undertook a large-scale research and collection project that resulted in annotated collections of notation of *shifan luogu* (Yang Yinliu 1980) and *shifan gu* (Yang Yinliu and Cao 1982). *Shifan* musical activity in Wuxi dates from at least the late eighteenth century, when it was documented in the 1795 book *Yangzhou Huafang Lu* [*Yangzhou painted pleasure-boat record*] (Yang

Yinliu and Cao 1982:1). The instruments used in *shifan* music's *sizhu* section (*dizi, xiao, sheng, huqin, pipa,* and *sanxian*) are among those found in the contemporary *Jiangnan sizhu* ensemble. The only significant difference in instrumentation is the occasional presence of a small *suona,* a double-reed wind instrument, and the absence of a *yangqin* in *shifan* music; *Jiangnan sizhu* almost always includes a *yangqin,* but never a *suona.* None of the *shifan* repertory included in Yang's books is identical to that of *Jiangnan sizhu,* but the musical styles of *Jiangnan sizhu* and the *sizhu* portions of *shifan* music are similar, although the texture of the former tends to be more heterophonic.[5]

Outside of Jiangnan, other regional *sizhu* traditions have developed, especially along the southeastern coast of China. The most influential of these are *nanguan* ("Southern pipes"), also called *nanyin* ("Southern sounds"), from Fujian and Taiwan, and *Chaozhou xianshi* ("Chaozhou string poetry") and *Guangdong Yinyue* ("Cantonese Music") from Guangdong province. Other traditions sometimes classified as *sizhu* are *errentai paiziqu* from inner Mongolia and *baisha xiyue* from Yunnan province.[6] In addition to these genres which have become widely recognized as *sizhu* musics, many types of dramatic music, narrative singing, and dance music include instrumental segments played by *sizhu* ensembles. Li Minxiong (1982:35) mentions *Shandong qinshu, Sichuan yangqin, Guangxi wenchang, Henan quzi,* and *siming nanci* (from Zhejiang) as examples of dramatic or narrative genres having important *sizhu* components. Published sources on the instrumental repertory of these traditions are scanty; some information on *siming nanci* was obtained during fieldwork, and this tradition will be discussed later in this chapter.

THE DEVELOPMENT OF *JIANGNAN SIZHU* IN SHANGHAI[7]

Wuxi has been the center of *shifan* music's development, while *Jiangnan sizhu* is most strongly associated with Shanghai. However, both of these genres have been widespread throughout the Jiangnan area. Jin Zuli acknowledges the influence of *shifan* music on the development of *Jiangnan sizhu:* the link between the two traditions can be found in "Luogu Sihe" (Gongs and drums, four together), a piece from the western suburbs of Shanghai played by an ensemble of "*dizi* with drums and gongs" (1983:28). It represents a branch of *shifan* music specific to the Shanghai area, and several of the piece's sections are musically related to some of the Eight Great Pieces of *Jiangnan sizhu.*

As of the mid–nineteenth century, *Jiangnan sizhu* had not yet become a distinct musical genre, but about that time musical groups known as *qingke chuan* became active in the Shanghai area. These were groups of musicians who got together to play for weddings, funerals, and temple fairs. Unlike *xiaotangming* (professional ritual specialists), they were not paid for performances but were treated as guests (and presumably fed) by the hosts of these events. Occasionally, several groups would perform at the same event, and "each [group] would display their ability in a kind of competition; one could often witness occasions of brilliant performances" (ibid.). A similar mixture of self-cultivation for the performers, entertainment for listeners, and competitiveness among groups is characteristic of *Jiangnan sizhu* music to this day. Although Jin does not mention the instruments played by the early *qingke chuan*, he describes their repertory as consisting of "the widely popular folk instrumental pieces 'Lao Liuban,' 'Sanliu,' 'Sihe,' and a few popular *xiaodiao* [a type of urban song] such as 'Huanle Ge,' 'Wuxi Jing,' 'Liuqing Niang,' and 'Shanghai Matou'" (ibid.). All the Eight Great Pieces of *Jiangnan sizhu* are either derived from or closely related to the first four pieces on this list.

Other writings on *Jiangnan sizhu* do not reveal any more about these *qingke chuan*, but the *xiaotangming* have been more fully discussed by the *Kunqu* singer and scholar Ch'ung-ho Chang Frankel, who explains that these groups were made up of poor, illiterate boys taught by a retired *Kunqu* singer:

> [They were] hired to perform at family celebrations. They sang and played their instruments sitting around a table in a corner of the room, not in a conspicuous place. Their performances were intended as background music only, while the guests continued to eat and drink, to converse, and to congratulate their hosts on the festive event. The music performed was always *k'un ch'ü* [*Kunqu*] . . . the money paid for a performance went not to the boys but to their manager; the boys only got a good meal, but of course they did not sit with the guests. (1976:82)

When the boys reached the age of about eleven, those who possessed "good voices and good looks" joined professional troupes, but those lacking these attributes might continue to participate in the *xiaotangming*: "Those who were not chosen could stay on. They would still be called *hsiao t'ang ming* [*xiaotangming*]. But this was not an honorable nor a well-paid profession. If it was said of a singer that his style was *t'ang ming kung* [*tangmin gong, gong* meaning a cultural activities center], this was not a compliment. The *t'ang ming kung* system came to an end about 40 years ago" (ibid.:83).

Jin says that *xiaotangming* "played wind instruments," but he makes no mention of singing, so the term may have somewhat different connotations in different contexts. In any case, they are contrasted with the *qingke chuan* who were treated as "honored guests." He goes on to stress the higher status of these latter groups: "Because the musicians in *qingke chuan* wore long robes (unlike the ritual artists in *xiaotangming*), they were respectfully addressed as 'sir' [*xiansheng*]. Up to the present, Shanghai *sizhu* musicians address each other as 'sir' when they meet; this is a kind of tradition" (1983:28).

Qingke chuan, which are clearly differentiated from the lower-status *xiaotangming*, are viewed as the direct predecessors of *Jiangnan sizhu* ensembles; however, *Jiangnan sizhu* is also differentiated from more elite traditions:

> Shanghai's folk *sizhu* music can be divided into the two streams of "refined" and "popular." The refined stream consists mainly of performing classical *qin* and *pipa* pieces and adaptations of ancient music for string ensemble, and is considered to be the "orthodox school of national music" dating from after the Ming and Qing Dynasties. The popular stream is mainly folk ensemble string and wind music, and is in fact *Jiangnan sizhu* . . . (Ibid.)

Since both of these "streams" have often been developed and performed by the same musicians and ensembles in Shanghai, they are closely interrelated. Jin Zuli (like most contemporary *sizhu* scholars and performers) places *Jiangnan sizhu* in a social and artistic middle ground, as a kind of sophisticated folk tradition.

In 1911, a *Jiangnan sizhu* organization began to meet weekly at a Shanghai teahouse. From this time on, *Jiangnan sizhu* organizations began to spring up throughout the city, and by the 1920s a gathering of *sizhu* musicians attracted over two hundred participants. A cigarette advertisement from the Shanghai newspaper *Shenbao* dating from 1927 (figure 1.1) suggests several things about the music and the term as used at that time. The text of the ad reads: "China's *sizhu* is peaceful and harmonious and is deemed superior;[8] Old Mill [literally "red room"] brand tobacco is blended together uniformly and resembles it" (*Shenbao* January 28, 1927). The use of the term *"sizhu"* in an advertisement implies that it was widely known to the populace at that time; the text shows that the aesthetic principles associated with the music—"harmonious," "blended"—are consistent with those often expressed today, and the illustration shows that the instruments used at that time (*dizi, xiao,* and *erhu*) are those found in the contemporary *Jiangnan sizhu* ensemble. In addition, the Shanghai colloquialism *jian chang* ("is deemed superior") sometimes has a negative connotation and may imply that the music seems to go on endlessly (Bell Yung, personal communication). This interpretation suggests that long, expanded pieces were already played at that time and/or that a typical performance was rather long in duration.

FIGURE 1.1 Newspaper advertisement depicting *sizhu* musicians

Many of the early *Jiangnan sizhu* music clubs also played other types of music, including ensemble arrangements of *pipa* suites, new compositions, and various types of narrative singing and dramatic music. With the blossoming of the New Culture Movement in the 1920s, the term "National Music," *Guoyue,* came into vogue throughout China, and many of the Shanghai groups identified themselves as "National Music Clubs," *Guoyuehui.* It is interesting to note the prominence of *pipa* players in many of these early *sizhu* groups. The scholar-performer Lin Shicheng has compiled a "lineage" of the Pudong school of *pipa* playing (1982:66), and many of the individuals included in this lineage appear as leaders or participants in the Shanghai music clubs whose histories Jin outlines. These include Chen Zijing, who first notated and taught the piece "Luogu Sihe"; Wang Yuting, *pipa* teacher in the Datong club; Li Tingsong and Sun Yude, leaders of the Xiaozhao club; Chen Yonglu, leader of the Yunhe club; Wei Zhongle, leader of the Zhongguo club; Qin Pengzhang, later an influential conductor and arranger for the Modern Chinese Orchestra; Ma Shenglong and Lin Shicheng, who have made numerous recordings of *Jiangnan sizhu;* and Jin Zuli, who has participated in many of the influential *sizhu* clubs including the Datong, Yuelin, Yunhe, Zhongguo, and Tianshan ensembles.

The adaptation of *pipa* solos for *sizhu* ensemble has long been an important part of *Jiangnan sizhu.* Such pieces are sometimes distinguished as "refined" *(ya)* or "classical" *(gu* or *gudian),* as opposed to the "popular" *(su)* or "folk" *(minjian)* stream of *sizhu* ensemble music. Jin and many others believe that the popular-folk stream is what should be referred to as *Jiangnan sizhu.* However, the influence of the *pipa* performers and repertory of the Pudong school cannot be ignored in tracing the history of *Jiangnan sizhu,* and many of these *pipa* pieces are still frequently played in ensemble arrangements by Shanghai's *Jiangnan sizhu* clubs.

Early-twentieth-century *sizhu* clubs apparently played a wide variety of musical genres; some groups also took an interest in finding new directions for Chinese music and encouraged composition, rearrangement of traditional pieces, introduction of Western staff notation, formation of large-scale ensembles with a conductor, conscientious rehearsals, and revival of ancient musical instruments and musical types. The activities of the Datong, "Great Togetherness," Music Club (founded in 1920) are exemplary in this regard. The leader and founder, Zheng Jinwen, had studied Confucian ceremonial music and took an interest in reconstructing ancient music and instruments. Since Zheng was also concerned with the poor quality of materials and sound found in many of the traditional instruments being made at that time, Datong became involved in instrument manufacture. Zheng published a history of Chinese music and a collection of melodies for *dizi* and *xiao* containing several of the Eight Great Pieces of *Jiangnan sizhu*. In addition, the group adapted *pipa* solo pieces for *sizhu* ensemble, including the transformation of "Xunyang Yeyue" (Xunyang river, moon and evening) into the widely popular "Chunjiang Hua Yueye" (Spring, river, flowers, moon, and evening) and the reshaping of traditional materials into the five-movement "Guomin Dale" (Great happiness for the nation's people).[9] Although Zheng is often criticized today for his backward-looking and conservative artistic perspective (see Wang Yuhe 1984:47) and for his association with the Nationalist government, many of his group's endeavors anticipated some of the most important later trends in Chinese music. Improving the quality of traditional instruments became a major concern after 1949, and adaptations of *pipa* pieces for ensemble and radical reshaping of traditional music played an important part in the early development of the Modern Chinese Orchestra.[10] More recently, there has been renewed interest in re-creating ancient court instruments, and by the mid-1980s music and dance extravaganzas featuring reconstructions of ancient Chinese instruments were performed widely in China and overseas.

In 1937, China entered into the War of Resistance against Japan, which was followed by the Civil War between the Communists and the Nationalists (1945–49). Despite the turbulence of this period, *Jiangnan sizhu* was still played, and it was "around 1941," according to Jin, that the concept of the Eight Great Pieces came into being (1983:30). In the early days of the People's Republic, *Jiangnan sizhu* and other traditional musics flourished. New music clubs were formed, Chinese music departments were established in the conservatories, and collections of *Jiangnan sizhu* notation and recordings were issued. One important collection (Shanghai Qunzhong 1960) included multipart notation for "Luogu Sihe" and several of the Eight Great Pieces. According to Jin, it was in this collection that the expression *"Jiangnan sizhu"* was first "formally" used (Jin and Xu 1983:31).[11]

During the Cultural Revolution (in a broad sense, 1966–76) *Jiangnan sizhu* and most manifestations of traditional Chinese culture were suppressed. While some musicians met clandestinely in private homes, public activity of the music clubs effectively ceased. In 1977, radio broadcasts of traditional music were resumed, and in 1979 some of the music clubs began to hold regular meetings. Since that time, new groups have been formed, and large-scale festivals in which many groups participate have become regularly recurring events.

The development of *Jiangnan sizhu* reflects the changes that have taken place in China during the past century, most noticeably the rapid growth of some cities and the reshaping of the nation into a secularized and, in theory, classless society. The preeminence of a small ensemble of relatively low volume is consistent with urban space restrictions and a need to alleviate unnecessary noise. It is fitting that this music has flourished in the city that has become China's largest.

The ritual uses of the music documented above for the early *qingke chuan* groups have become almost nonexistent. Informants state that in the earlier part of this century *Jiangnan sizhu* was particularly prominent in wedding celebrations, and the titles of two of the pieces still indicate this. "Xingjie" (Street procession) was played by strolling musicians to accompany the sedan chair of the bride through the streets, and some of the older musicians still preserve the street style of playing the *dizi* for the piece (Zhou Hui, personal communication).[12] "Sihe Ruyi" (Four together, as you please), also known as "Qiao" (Bridge), was played at wedding banquets, often in a special treatment called "Shuang Qiao" (Double bridge) in which two of each melodic instrument were used. In "Shuang Qiao," paired instruments were placed opposite each other along a long table, and several sections of the piece featured overlapping duets played by these pairs of instruments, which were arranged so that the solo passages moved along the table. The name "Qiao" has been explained variously as referring to the linear arrangement of the instruments, the overlapping of the solo or duet passages, and the linking of four tunes in the piece.[13] The title is also a homophone in the Shanghai dialect (though not in Mandarin) for a bride's sedan chair, *jiao.* This piece still occupies a special place in the *Jiangnan sizhu* repertory, and, even in ordinary performances of the piece by Shanghai music clubs, an attempt is made to gather a full contingent of ten musicians before beginning to play. At a midautumn *Jiangnan sizhu* festival in 1985, "Shuang Qiao" was played (according to some musicians, this was the first time in nearly twenty years that this version of the piece had been played); although the ritual physical arrangement of instruments in pairs was not followed, the significance of the event was indicated by the presence of the head priest of the Baiyun Guan Taoist temple acting as percussionist for the performance.

While a "deritualization" of traditional music may be a common response to a growing and changing urban environment, it is not an inevitable one. In Hong Kong, for example, religious and other ritual activities incorporating music are still common. Political and ideological changes in the PRC have had a significant influence on the development of *Jiangnan sizhu.* Elaborate wedding celebrations have negative connotations of waste and extravagance, and traditional wedding ceremonies are associated with "superstition" and other "feudal" remnants. Despite ostensible freedom of religion, Taoist music and rituals in Shanghai were curtailed from 1949 until the early 1980s; the secularization of *Jiangnan sizhu* must be seen, at least in part, as a way of allowing the tradition to survive by emphasizing its healthy "folk" elements and shedding potentially embarrassing extramusical associations. However, since such secularization also occurs in societies without ideological pressure, contextual changes in *Jiangnan sizhu* should not be attributed solely to socialist policies.

RELATED GENRES

Relationships among Chinese musical genres can be said to exist when traditions share historical origins, performance contexts, repertory, instrumentation, or musical style. Any two genres may be related in one or more of these senses, and the intimacy or strength of such relationships may vary considerably. The various musical traditions indigenous to the Jiangnan area can be thought of as comprising a "regional musical system" sharing historical relationships and stylistic characteristics. Although there has been little study of intergenre relationships in a geographical area, the idea of a regional musical system, analogous to the economic and administrative "regional systems" studied by G. William Skinner (1977) and to the concept of linguistic dialect areas (such as the Wu dialect in Jiangnan), is an important aspect of Chinese musical culture (see Witzleben 1989).

Some historical connections between *Jiangnan sizhu* and other genres have been explored earlier in this chapter, and the relationships linking *Jiangnan sizhu* to *Kunqu*, *shifan* music, and the Pudong school of *pipa* music can be referred to as "genetic" in nature. When distinctly different genres are performed in the same venue, the relationship can be referred to as a "contextual" one. At present, *Jiangnan sizhu* is not consistently played in conjunction with any other genre.[14]

Musicians and scholars often refer to connections between *Jiangnan sizhu* and other traditions from the same part of China. These connections may refer to instrumentation, repertory, style for playing a specific instrument, ensemble playing style, or other factors. The connections may be weak or strong, and a variety of expressions are used: *you guanxi*, "has a relationship"; *xiangtong*, "similar" or, depending on context, "identical"; *hen xiang*, "resembles very much"; *wanquan yiyang*, "completely the same"; and so on. Any of these expressions may be strengthened or qualified through the addition of appropriate adverbs.

Many of these intergenre relationships cannot be clearly defined as genetic or contextual: the early history of *Jiangnan sizhu* has not yet been clearly established, and information on many of the traditions discussed below is even more sketchy. Long-term contextual juxtaposition may create new genetic relationships, and in the absence of a comprehensive musical history of the Jiangnan region, it is impossible to determine which of two traditions influenced the other, or whether both were influenced by a third genre. Given these ambiguities, some of the "relationships" discussed below might better be thought of as "similarities," the origins of which are subjects for further research.

Regional Opera

Kunqu opera, discussed earlier in this chapter, is accompanied by a type of *sizhu* ensemble, sometimes augmented by percussion. Although *Kunqu* and *Jiangnan sizhu* do not at present share any common repertory, the styles of playing the *dizi* and *sanxian* in the two traditions are somewhat similar, and the combination of instruments used in *Kunqu* may have served as a model not only for *Jiangnan sizhu* but also for the many regional operatic traditions that developed in the Jiangnan area. In recent years, the musical style for many regional operatic traditions has changed dramatically, and most contemporary performances feature a large ensemble containing both Chinese and Western instruments. Most professional opera troupes include one or more composers who write new music or new arrangements of traditional repertory. Thus, typical modern performances reveal little about the traditional style of many of these genres, but several types of opera from the Jiangnan area are said to share stylistic characteristics with *Jiangnan sizhu*.

Huju is the operatic genre native to Shanghai. In all the performances I have heard, both live and on radio, the accompaniment has been a large ensemble including many Western instruments. The music used in such performances has no discernible relationship to *Jiangnan sizhu*. However, at least one *Jiangnan sizhu erhu* player (Liu Chengyi, personal communication) believes that in the past, the style of playing this instrument was very similar in the two genres, an assertion supported by evidence from older recordings.

Xiju is the operatic genre native to Wuxi. According to Li Minxiong, the heterophonic musical texture in the accompaniment for *Xiju* is similar to that of *Jiangnan sizhu* (personal communication). Although further research is needed, evidence from live performances, a lecture-demonstration (accompanied by a small ensemble of Chinese instruments), and brief interviews suggests that the styles are somewhat similar, but not strongly so.

Yongju is the operatic genre native to Ningbo. Like *Xiju*, the heterophonic texture is said to be similar to that of *Jiangnan sizhu*. None of the live or recorded performances of *Yongju* I have heard are in the traditional style, so I have no basis for commenting on the strength of this similarity.

Shadow Theater

The Chinese term for shadow theater is *piying xi*, literally "leather shadow theater." I saw and heard Shanghai shadow theater music on only one occasion and have not found any commercial recordings of this tradition. However, the musical accompaniment consists of a *Jiangnan sizhu* ensemble with an expanded percussion section. The leading instrument is the *dizi*, and the player of this instrument in the puppet orchestra, Du Lian'gen, is also a well-known performer of *Jiangnan sizhu*. At the performance I attended, "Sanliu" (Three six) was played as an overture; it sounded like a typical *Jiangnan sizhu* rendition of the piece. None of the music used during the actual play was recognizable as *Jiangnan sizhu* repertory, although the style and texture of the accompaniment were quite similar. A piece from the puppet theater repertory called "Piying Diao" (Leather shadow melody) is often played by the Tianshan Music Club in Shanghai (whenever I heard them perform this piece, Du Lian'gen played the *dizi*), and performers in that group believe that "Piying Diao" is stylistically very similar to the standard *Jiangnan sizhu* repertory.

Narrative Song

These genres combine song and speech; sometimes called "storytelling" traditions in English, in Chinese they are known as *shuochang*, "speech-song," or *quyi*, "song arts."

Pingtan, also called *tanci*, is native to Suzhou and is popular throughout much of the Jiangnan area. The accompanying instruments are the *pipa* and *sanxian*, and the style of playing these instruments is similar to that used in *Jiangnan sizhu*. In addition, some of the instrumental pieces played before the singing begins in a storytelling performance are also played in *Jiangnan sizhu*. In particular, the version of "Sanliu" called "Tanci Sanliu," a popular "overture" for *pingtan*, is structurally identical to the *Jiangnan sizhu* piece, and although there are some differences in the rhythm and melodic outline, anyone familiar with one version can immediately perceive its close relationship with the other.

Siming nanci is a genre native to Ningbo. Its traditional accompanying instruments are *xiao, erhu, pipa, yangqin*, and *sanxian*, which also make up an ideal small ensemble for *Jiangnan sizhu*. The style of the instrumental playing is quite similar in the two genres, and the independence of the melodic lines and complex heterophony are also similar. Shao Xiaoxian, a well-known accompanist for *siming nanci*, believes that it may well have influenced *Jiangnan sizhu* ensemble treatments of pieces from the solo *pipa* repertory. He claims that radio broadcasts of *siming nanci* were common in Shanghai in the 1930s and may have influenced the style of *xiao* playing popularized by Sun Yude and other Shanghai musicians influential in the development of *Jiangnan sizhu* (personal communication). In any case, *siming nanci* is the only Jiangnan-area tradition in which the *xiao* is the leading melodic instrument, and the *siming nanci* style of playing that instrument is highly admired by some Shanghai *xiao* players, including my teacher, Tan Weiyu, a long-time student of Sun Yude.

As in *pingtan*, instrumental pieces used as preludes for *siming nanci* performances include some of the pieces played in *Jiangnan sizhu*. These include a version of "Sanliu" that is very close to the *sizhu* version and a version of "Sihe Ruyi" that is rather different.[15] Another piece, "Jiangjun Ling" (The general leads his troops), has been adapted for *Jiangnan sizhu* ensemble under the title of "Wen Jiangjun" (Refined *jiangjun*), and some Shanghai musicians believe that this version is in the authentic *Jiangnan sizhu* style.

Folk Song

Melodically, *Jiangnan sizhu* has much in common with the folk songs of the stylistic area known as Jiangzhe (a contraction of the province names Jiangsu and Zhejiang). Miao Jing and Qiao Jianzhong, in their study of *difang secai*, "local color," areas of folk-song style, have defined Jiangzhe as including "southern Jiangsu, Shanghai, most of Zhejiang, and part of southern Anhui" (1987:101). The folk-song melodies tend to be pentatonic and conjunct with occasional wide leaps providing contrast, and they are described as "like mountain streams, winding, many-faceted, and rich in variation" (ibid.: 107). All of these characteristics can also be found in *Jiangnan sizhu* melodies. Some Zhejiang folk songs also share the *taoqu* (suite) and other formal elements with *Jiangnan sizhu* (ibid.:113).[16] However, despite the stylistic links with *Jiangnan sizhu*, recent researchers of folk song from the same area make no mention of a *sizhu* ensemble or any other instrumental music accompanying or being played in conjunction with the songs they heard (Schimmelpenninck 1990).

Religious Music

The performance of traditional Chinese religious music was strongly discouraged after 1949, and Shanghai Taoists did not resume performance of their ritual music until the mid-1980s. After a gap of more than thirty years, it is difficult to say how closely the music corresponds to that performed in the past. At present, at least one type of Taoist ritual music features a *sizhu* ensemble, with *dizi, erhu, sanxian,* and *sheng* being the most important instruments. Although some melodic fragments played in ritual performances sounded familiar to my ears, none of the pieces I have heard in Shanghai Taoist music are identical to any currently performed *Jiangnan sizhu* repertory.[17] The overall musical style, especially the *dizi* playing, owes much to *Kunqu*. However, the connection between this music and *Jiangnan sizhu* is deserving of further study. The leading Taoist musician in Shanghai, Jin Minggao, is also a well-respected performer of *Jiangnan sizhu,* and the head priest of the Baiyun Taoist temple, Chen Liansheng, while not a regular performer in the music clubs, is familiar with *Jiangnan sizhu* to the extent that he played the percussion for the performance of "Shuang Qiao" at the 1985 midautumn festival performance. His son, an *erhu* teacher, believes that there is a Taoist "school" of playing *Jiangnan sizhu* that differs from the style played by most other performers (Chen Dacan, personal communication), but I have not had an opportunity to hear *Jiangnan sizhu* performed by an ensemble made up exclusively of Taoists.

The connection between *Jiangnan sizhu* and Buddhist music is more tenuous, and I have not heard any live performances of Buddhist music that use any of the instruments found in *Jiangnan sizhu.* However, some musicians in Shanghai have obtained notation for Buddhist instrumental pieces and have experimented with reconstructing this repertory for performance and made a commercial recording *(Zhongguo Fanyue).* The leading musician in this undertaking, Dong Kejun, is an important figure in Shanghai *Jiangnan sizhu* circles, and the instrumentation used by this group of musicians is drawn from the *Jiangnan sizhu* ensemble. Their recordings of this newly reconstructed Buddhist music are stylistically similar to *Jiangnan sizhu,* but it is not clear if this similarity results from the performers being well-versed in *Jiangnan sizhu* or if it indicates a historical relationship between the two traditions.

Chuida Music

Chuida means "blowing and striking," and musics categorized as *chuida* traditions feature wind and percussion instruments. In contrast to *sizhu* musics (relatively soft, usually played indoors), *chuida* is usually loud (gongs, cymbals, and double-reeds are common) and often played outdoors. *Shifan* music is one type of *chuida* music from Jiangnan; *Zhedong luogu* from eastern Zhejiang province should also be mentioned. Like *shifan* music, it combines *sizhu* and percussion sections, and the style of the *sizhu* portions of the music is somewhat similar to that of *Jiangnan sizhu*. Although I have found no repertory that is directly shared by the two traditions, "Wen Jiangjun" was originally a *Zhedong luogu* piece that was adapted as an overture for *siming nanci* and later played as *Jiangnan sizhu*. On our research trip to Ningbo, Li Minxiong and I found no evidence that *Zhedong luogu* is still performed in that locale today.

The Solo *Erhu* Tradition

Solo *pipa* repertory is often adapted for *Jiangnan sizhu* ensemble, and many of the influential *pipa* artists of recent decades have had a strong background in *Jiangnan sizhu*. Although the solo *erhu* tradition is a twentieth-century development, and no *erhu* solo pieces belong to the *Jiangnan sizhu* repertory, *erhu* music has been strongly influenced by the *sizhu* and other traditions of the Jiangnan area.

Liu Tianhua (1895–1932), whose ten compositions for *erhu* are the cornerstone of the modern solo tradition, was a student of the *Jiangnan sizhu* master Zhou Shaomei. The tuning chosen by Liu (which has become standard for the instrument) is that used in *Jiangnan sizhu*, and Liu's choices of tuning and thickness of strings were probably influenced by Zhou (Yu 1985:72). In addition, the manner in which Liu's pieces incorporate nonpentatonic scale degrees (often perceived as innovative or Western-influenced) is in some cases quite similar to the modal shifts found in traditional *Jiangnan sizhu* melodies (ibid.:42–43).

Hua Yanjun (1893–1950), more commonly referred to as A Bing, or "Blind A Bing," was a composer-performer whose *erhu* pieces have also had a strong influence on the development of the solo tradition. He was a native of Jiangsu province and was trained in the Taoist music of his hometown, Wuxi, and in other regional traditions. The extent of his direct contact with *Jiangnan sizhu* is not clear, but stylistic similarities to *sizhu* are evident in his playing. According to my *Jiangnan sizhu erhu* teacher, Zhou Hao, A Bing's recordings contain many techniques of ornamentation and bowing that are idiomatic to *Jiangnan sizhu*. Virtually every *erhu* student learns at least one of A Bing's three *erhu* pieces, and many also learn *Jiangnan sizhu* repertory, but few performers apply these *sizhu* techniques to A Bing's compositions. According to Zhou, this is a serious oversight, since proper execution of some *Jiangnan sizhu* stylistic devices is essential for bringing out the true flavor of A Bing's music (personal communication).

Modern Chinese Orchestra

Links between *Jiangnan sizhu* and the emergence of the Modern Chinese Orchestra in the 1930s are well established. More recently, the Shanghai Chinese Orchestra produced a series of recordings of *Jiangnan sizhu* during the 1950s and 1960s. Some of the featured players were expert *Jiangnan sizhu* performers, and these recordings are widely regarded as "authentic" *Jiangnan sizhu*. The orchestra has also recorded new compositions that are identified as *Jiangnan sizhu* but which have met with less acceptance among *Jiangnan sizhu* musicians. Although no current performers in the orchestra are active in the amateur *Jiangnan sizhu* music clubs, members of the Shanghai Chinese Orchestra do participate in *Jiangnan sizhu* festivals, and their own concerts occasionally feature one or more *Jiangnan sizhu* pieces.

TWO

Jiangnan Sizhu in Shanghai, 1981–1985

In 1985, the amateur groups in Shanghai specializing in playing *Jiangnan sizhu* included the Aihaozhe ("Music Lovers"), Chunjiang ("Spring River"), Hezhong ("United"), Hudong (the name of a part of the city), Jiangnan, Jinling (the old name for the city of Nanjing), Tianshan ("Heavenly Mountains," a mountain range in western China), Xinsheng ("New Sound"), and Zhongguo ("China") music clubs.

THE WORLD OF *JIANGNAN SIZHU*

Of the nine clubs I visited (all of the above except Xinsheng, plus one group which at that time had no name), four met in public teahouses, one in an auditorium, one in a "neighborhood committee" office, one in the former Confucian temple, and two in private homes. In some clubs, the membership is somewhat exclusive: the same players meet week after week, and the rapport built up over a long period of time is highly valued. In others, different players are present at each meeting, and anyone who wishes may participate in the music making; some musicians are active participants in several different music clubs. Each club meets once or twice a week, with a fixed day and time, in the afternoon or, less commonly, evening. Approximately two hundred musicians participate in Shanghai's *Jiangnan sizhu* clubs with some regularity; given that Shanghai is the largest city in China, they can be viewed as a rather small subcommunity, and most of the regular musicians know each other well. A few professional musicians who make their living performing or teaching Chinese music belong to this community. However, their participation in the *Jiangnan sizhu* music clubs is amateur in nature and entirely separate from their professional musical work.

A typical afternoon session lasts about three hours. Shortly before two o'clock, musicians begin to arrive; the musical instruments, which are usually collectively owned, are brought out from a back room where they are stored. One musician tunes the *yangqin* to the pitch level of the *sheng* or one of the flutes; others may make adjustments to the instruments, such as changing strings, replacing the reed membrane on the *dizi*, or fine-tuning the reeds of the *sheng*. Performers sit around a table, usually rectangular, with the *yangqin* placed at one end and the percussion instruments at the other. Arrangement of the other instruments varies, but the *erhu* and *pipa* players often flank the *yangqin* to the left and right, respectively.

Anyone can suggest which piece is to be played, but most often the *dizi* player or the club leader chooses a selection. The percussionist sets the tempo by playing two pulses; if there is no percussion, the *pipa* player provides these pulses by plucking a string which has been damped to produce an unpitched clicking sound. On the third pulse, all the melodic instruments enter. Informants say that the percussionist or *pipa* player is responsible for controlling the tempo throughout a piece; in practice, another musician (most often the *dizi* player) may regulate or alter the tempo through head motions or stomping of the foot. Usually, a particular combination of musicians will play a set of two pieces, after which most of the players get up and either yield their places or switch to another instrument. In general, musicians play in approximately the order they arrive until all have had a chance to play, although an older musician, one who is particularly famous, or an out-of-town visitor may be asked to play before his or her turn as a special honor. It is customary for all to decline to play until prodded repeatedly by other musicians.

No admission is charged by any of the music clubs, but in public teahouse settings, patrons are expected to pay a nominal charge for a pot of tea; some musicians bring their own jar of tea leaves and add hot water, which is free. A fairly high noise level is pervasive in the teahouse environment, and patrons are not expected to keep quiet so others can hear the music. Some of the non-performers may actually be listening carefully, but others relate to the music as a background for conversation. Thus, the typical audience includes both "listeners" and "hearers."[1] In a *Jiangnan sizhu* music club, the only location from which one can hear all the instruments clearly is a seat at the table with the musicians. These seats are customarily reserved for performers, so one must be playing the music to hear it in its totality; this is an indication of the highly participatory nature of the music. Since many of the listeners are also players who are not playing at the moment, there is no clear separation of "performer" and "audience."

The sessions are informal, and some musicians may join or leave the ensemble in the middle of a piece. One club, Tianshan, conscientiously rehearses—starting and stopping, repeating trouble spots—but in general, pieces are played all the way through without pause. The number of pieces played in a session may vary considerably depending on the length of the repertory chosen and the duration of pauses between pieces. The size of the ensemble is flexible; *erhu*, *pipa*, *yangqin*, and either *dizi* or *xiao* make up a core ensemble. A session often begins with four or five play-ers, with the size of the ensemble gradually increasing. No prescribed order determines the selection of pieces; however, if relatively soft pieces (featuring the *xiao* and using neither *dizi* nor percussion) are played, this usually occurs toward the end of a session when most patrons have de-parted and the noise level has abated somewhat; also, if "Sihe Ruyi" is played, it is almost always the last item of a session. This piece contains short solo passages for each instrument, and, as mentioned in the previ-ous chapter, an attempt is usually made to round up a full group of ten players before starting the piece.[2] In the past, the order of pieces played may have been more fixed. According to *pipa* player Lui Pui-yuen, in a typical *sizhu* gathering in the 1950s "Zhonghua Liuban" was "invariably" the first piece played (Yu 1989).

Applause or verbal approval generally does not occur and is not ex-pected at the end of a piece. However, the two pieces that are very long and end in a very fast tempo, "Xingjie" and "Sihe Ruyi," are often followed by applause and shouts, a response that is more an expression of collective exuberance than an indication of a particularly memorable performance. A visiting musician, a new participant, or a foreign student may also be honored or encouraged with applause that has little to do with the quality of their performance; when other musicians stopped calling attention to my own playing by applauding, I felt that I had finally been accepted as a true participant in the musical culture. Musical notation is rarely used during performance, although it is acceptable for beginners to read music for any piece and for any number of musicians to read music if the piece played is not a common one. The ability to play without notation is highly valued, and a musician must dispense with it before being able to interact with the other players and to vary his own interpretation of a piece. Since such variability is encouraged, "internalization" is a more appropriate term than "memorization" for describing the process of moving away from dependence on musical notation: a player eventually knows a piece so well that he does not even think about losing his place and naturally makes slight changes in each performance of it.

Parts or all of the Eight Great Pieces are based on melodies known throughout China, but in their current form they are associated pri-marily with *Jiangnan sizhu*. The repertory is by no means limited to these eight pieces, but most music clubs in Shanghai spend the bulk of their time playing them, and a single piece may be repeated as many as five times during one session. From the *sizhu* performer's perspective, even though a piece may be played many times, its realization in each performance is unique. Each musician plays the melody somewhat differently from every other musician, and all of my teachers believe that an individual should vary his playing with each rendition of a piece. In the words of my *erhu* teacher, Zhou Hao, "improvised ornamentation is re-composition." The performer is a creative participant in the music, constantly challenging himself to bring fresh ideas and feelings into a familiar piece. Thus, both individuality and the submerging of one's individuality for the good of the collective whole are characteristic of *Jiangnan sizhu*: too little individual expression will result in blandness, while too much will result in musical chaos. Some music clubs favor a relatively homogenous sound, while others encourage more divergence among the musical parts.

To a musician not intimately familiar with the music of *Jiangnan sizhu*, the differences among individual performers and among a single performer's various interpretations of a piece are not readily apparent. An outsider to the tradition can identify a technically brilliant or an incompetent musician, but the subtle differences among *Jiangnan sizhu* musicians in general are not easily perceived. For this reason, outsiders often find the music to be tedious. Unable to appreciate the differences which make each performance unique, they find it difficult to understand how *sizhu* aficionados can derive so much pleasure from the continual repetition of an extremely small body of music.

On one occasion when I was present, members from two clubs from the suburbs visited another club in the city center. For most of the afternoon, two pieces, "Zhonghua Liuban" and "Sanliu," were played over and over. In this context of mutual exchange and appreciation, the most familiar pieces were chosen and the unique nuances in each performer's interpretation revealed. A *Jiangnan sizhu* expert is able to identify individual players heard from a distance or on a tape recording; on several occasions, in order to test my progress in learning about their music, musicians quizzed me about who was playing on a recording unfamiliar to me.

The phenomenon of subtle changes providing an endless source of pleasure is a common one in Chinese culture, but is usually associated with literati traditions such as landscape painting, in which a connoisseur can readily distinguish one painter's rendering of a pine tree from another's. In Chinese music, written discussions of aesthetics are also mostly concerned with traditions of the literati, such as *qin* (seven-stringed zither) music and *Kunqu* opera. However, performers of many instruments and genres commonly labeled as "folk" arts also have a highly developed system of aesthetic principles with very stringent standards. Such systems or standards have traditionally not been written down but are passed on orally, through aphorisms or technical instruction, and aurally, through listening to and imitating other musicians. As will be discussed further in chapter 8, the attention to detail and the ability to discern subtle distinctions found among *Jiangnan sizhu* musicians provide ample evidence of the existence of a sophisticated system of aesthetics.

JIANGNAN SIZHU & THE PROFESSIONAL MUSIC WORLD

Most music clubs in Shanghai identify themselves by a proper name followed by the term *"Guoyueshe"* or *"Guoyuehui"* both terms meaning "national music club" or "association," such as Chunjiang Guoyueshe (Spring River National Music Club). All the clubs play *Jiangnan sizhu* almost exclusively, yet their names imply a broader scope of musical activity. The constitution or set of regulations (*tuanzhang*) for one club (translated in appendix A) indicates that their purpose is to play classical music, dance music, Chinese opera, folk music, *Jiangnan sizhu*, "revolutionary music" from the May Fourth Movement (1919) onward, and foreign "music of the people." The scope of activities to be pursued includes instrumental and vocal performance, composition, the study of orchestration (Chinese, Western, or a combination), music criticism, research on music theory and aesthetics, reform of musical instruments, and the study of conducting.[3] In actuality, this club played a total repertory of ten pieces, all *Jiangnan sizhu*, over the course of the numerous sessions I attended. While some time was spent in comparison and criticism of individuals' playing, the other activities outlined in their self-description were not observed on any of my visits.

A "constitution" is an official statement of purpose, and should therefore be acceptable to the Chinese Musicians' Association and other governing and regulating bodies. In contemporary China, officially sanctioned activity of any organization should ideally be healthy, progress-oriented, and patriotic. A commitment to playing only the pre-revolutionary music of one small region of China might seem eccentric to many Chinese, but hardly dangerous or subversive. Nevertheless, putting such a purpose in print could invite criticism of both the club members and those who approved their organization. All the "national music" clubs I visited in Shanghai concentrate on playing *Jiangnan sizhu*. Other pieces that could be described as "folk" or "classical" are played occasionally and, on rare occasions, new compositions are performed, but I heard only one vocal performance and no dance or foreign musics. The discrepancy between the musical purposes stated in the group—

regulations which I have no reason to assume are atypical—and actual practice should not be construed as an indication of duplicity. Besides having to negotiate a potentially tenuous politically correct course, the *Jiangnan sizhu* community is in some senses still recovering from the suppression endured during the Cultural Revolution. Furthermore, since the late 1970s, many young people have become more interested in Western-influenced Chinese popular song than in any form of Chinese traditional music. If the number of talented players increases, the amateur music clubs might well begin to play a greater diversity of music.

The Shanghai branch of the Chinese Musicians' Association (*Zhongguo Yinyuejia Xiehui*) has expressed considerable interest in promoting and developing *Jiangnan sizhu*, and it sponsored a day-long festival on January 11, 1985, in which over twenty groups participated.[4] The festival performances were later broadcast on the radio and were followed by two symposia and the publication of an entire issue of the Musicians' Association's journal, *Shanghai Yinxun* (1985, no. 1), devoted to discussion of the present status of and future prospects for *Jiangnan sizhu*. Much of the verbal and written discussion focused on the need for progress and development in the music: improving performance skills, expanding the repertory, and making the genre more accessible to a national and international audience. The participating musicians and scholars found much of value in *Jiangnan sizhu* and were proud of its local origins and regional flavor, but they repeatedly expressed distress at the music's failure to attract a large audience. Although performers often emphasize the regional nature of their music, they do not find it inconceivable that someone from another part of China could learn to play it well; however, no one pointed to an example of such an individual or group. In fact, few Chinese musicians from outside the Jiangnan area express interest in becoming adept at playing *Jiangnan sizhu*, although events such as an international competition held in Shanghai in 1987 may provide an impetus for wider interest in this music.

Among the music clubs in Shanghai, *Jiangnan sizhu* is strongly associated with a sense of regional ethnicity. The Shanghai dialect is spoken in the clubs and, although virtually all of the musicians can understand Mandarin and most speak it, Chinese visitors not conversant in the Shanghai dialect may feel somewhat out of place.[5] Provincialism is certainly a factor to be reckoned with, and it is quite understandable that musicians from other parts of China would be intimidated from trying to study a style in which the local flavor is so strongly emphasized. What is perplexing is the lack of interest in *Jiangnan sizhu* among professional performers, educators, and music students who are native to Shanghai or other parts of the Jiangnan area. One Shanghai Conservatory professor of *dizi* performance, Lu Chunling, is the leader of one amateur *sizhu* club and frequently visits other clubs, but he is the only person from the conservatory who has regular contact with the *Jiangnan sizhu* community.[6] Many of the conservatory's teachers and some of the students can play a few *Jiangnan sizhu* pieces, but students often complain that the music is difficult to memorize and quite monotonous.[7]

Professional performers, or intended professionals, such as conservatory students, must master a large repertory of technically demanding pieces; the traditional learning method of *Jiangnan sizhu*, summarized by one player (Zhou Hao 1985:38) as *duo ting duo he*, "listen more, [play] together more," requires a major time commitment. In addition, the semi-improvisatory and nonpresentational manner of performance in amateur *Jiangnan sizhu* clubs contrasts with the professional environment, in which strict adherence to notation and an outwardly expressive playing demeanor (often including exaggerated "emoting" using head and body movements and facial expressions) are the norm. To participate in amateur *Jiangnan sizhu* music making, a professional must modify his accustomed approach to performing or feel conspicuously out of place. Since mastering *Jiangnan sizhu* offers few tangible rewards, there is little incentive for the professional musician to spend considerable time in a potentially uncomfortable environment in order to acquire such mastery.

In 1984, a student group from the Shanghai Conservatory began performing versions of two traditional *Jiangnan sizhu* pieces rearranged by the head of the conservatory's Chinese composition department. These arrangements, which include some functional harmony, are almost universally disliked by players in the amateur music clubs; although the amateur *sizhu* experts respect the technical expertise of the young performers from the conservatory, they also criticize the lack of feeling and "flavor" in their playing. However, most conservatory students find these new arrangements far more attractive than the "unimproved" music played by amateur groups. Many performers and scholars in professional circles feel that the amateur *sizhu* musicians are hopelessly conservative, unable to appreciate anything new, and unwilling to see their music develop. Actually, many amateur musicians intellectually support the idea of new composition for the *Jiangnan sizhu* ensemble but believe that few successful pieces have been written. This problem is a complex one: few professional composers of Chinese music are well versed in *Jiangnan sizhu* music, while few of those who are skilled in playing *sizhu* have the training and/or inclination for composition.[8]

On two occasions while I was in Shanghai, I heard a new piece entitled "Jiangnan zhi Chun" ("Spring in Jiangnan"), composed by a professional performer, Shi Quan, who is an active participant in amateur *Jiangnan sizhu* circles. My first hearing was at the 1985 *Jiangnan sizhu* festival. Musicians who discussed the event with me spoke favorably of the composer as an individual and as a performer but felt that this piece was not very successful. Several months later, I heard it played in a teahouse, where it was introduced by the club leader as a new piece possessing the authentic "Jiangnan flavor." The performance was applauded enthusiastically. I, too, found the second hearing to be far more appealing than the first; the sympathetic teahouse environment was undoubtedly a factor, but the musicians also seemed to have begun to internalize the piece (some were playing without musical notation) and were less hesitant about contributing their own ideas to it. Even if this particular piece is ultimately a failed experiment and soon to be forgotten, the event is significant in that it shows the possibility for absorption of new music into the amateur environment.

THE MUSICIANS

The music club environment is one that minimizes demarcations based on education, status, or wealth. A club member is judged by his or her expertise in the music and ability to interact equally with other musicians. A professional performer must wait his turn to play like any other musician, and it is rare to see a musician trying to curry favor through flattery of a famous or well-connected individual. Although some professional musicians have played on numerous recordings of *Jiangnan sizhu*, their playing is as subject to criticism as anyone else's, while several players with menial jobs are among the *Jiangnan sizhu* musicians most highly regarded by both amateurs and professionals. Although disdain for the professional musician has a long history in Chinese society, it does not appear to exist in present-day Shanghai *sizhu* circles. Teaching in a conservatory or performing in a Modern Chinese Orchestra are highly respected occupations. Many of the more prominent performers and teachers among the elder generations are former amateur "folk artists"; some of these musicians maintain their ties with amateur performers, and those who now live elsewhere in China often sit in with *sizhu* clubs when they have occasion to return to Shanghai. Thus, at least among the older generations, no rigid line separates amateur and professional musicians. The music club is an example of a subculture whose membership is achieved rather than ascribed, and is based on common interest rather than on common background or social position. Economic status is not a determinant of who is able to participate; instruments are commonly shared, and equal opportunity—although not equal ability or competence—would seem to be a principle underlying many of the conventions found in *Jiangnan sizhu* performance.

Of the musicians active in the *Jiangnan sizhu* music clubs, the majority are retired, but a large minority are in their thirties and forties; several who are in their twenties are already recognized as experts in the tradition, and young children studying the music occasionally participate. In general, clubs that meet in the evening tend to have more younger players, many of whom work during the day and cannot attend afternoon sessions.

Despite the age spread of the musicians, it is widely lamented that there is a shortage of younger performers of *Jiangnan sizhu*. Almost all the accomplished players in their twenties are sons of performers, and all are amateurs. The obvious training ground for future professional musicians in the Jiangnan area is the Shanghai Conservatory, but few students at that institution have shown any inclination toward becoming experts in the *sizhu* tradition. However, *Jiangnan sizhu* evolved and has been maintained largely through the efforts of amateurs, and at present, two music clubs are dominated by younger players. One group, Aihaozhe, is formed around two generations of two families who live near each other; when they rehearse, the elders are active participants, but when they perform in public only the younger musicians play. The other youth-oriented group (still unnamed when I left Shanghai) has been organized by Dong Kejun, a professional musician in his early forties who is committed to developing and disseminating *Jiangnan sizhu*.

Only two women (one a German) were active in *Jiangnan sizhu* music clubs during my stay in Shanghai. There are no apparent sanctions against female participants; both of these women players were actively encouraged by other musicians, and female professional musicians who visit the clubs are urged to play. In recent centuries, most Chinese instrumental ensemble music has traditionally been played by males; although this has changed radically in professional circles, it has done so only marginally among amateur music clubs. The reasons for this need further investigation, but the search for younger performers to carry on the *Jiangnan sizhu* tradition will be much more difficult if only a very few women participate in the music making.

Musicians who are active in the music clubs are a diverse group. Factory workers are numerous, but there are also retail clerks, engineers, doctors of Chinese medicine, and retired farmers. Virtually all are literate, yet I have met none who would indisputably be called "literati." In their homes, musical instruments, cassette tapes, photographs, calendars, and flowers are often in evidence, but I saw no scholars' libraries or impressive artworks. Typically, the objects a musician would bring out to show with greatest pride would be handwritten musical notation, a treasured concert program or photograph, or a tape recording of a departed master. Although the *Jiangnan sizhu* musicians I know are generally free from pretensions, like many musicians in China (and elsewhere) they tend to have strong opinions about other players and often believe that certain characteristics make their own playing or that of their group special. Visual or sonic memorabilia are a way of indicating such specialness that might not be recognized by society at large but that could be highly meaningful to those knowledgeable about their musical tradition.

LEARNING & TEACHING

In former times, *Jiangnan sizhu* in Shanghai was much more widespread than it is today. Informants state that as recently as the 1950s most neighborhoods had people who played together regularly, so virtually everyone in the city would have had some contact with the music, even if only hearing it in passing. Many musicians say that they heard *Jiangnan sizhu* played in their home or neighborhood as a child. Since the core repertory is small, over the course of many years the same pieces were heard hundreds of times; by the time an individual made a conscious decision to learn the music, he had already begun to internalize it. *Jiangnan sizhu* activity (along with most amateur music making) almost completely ceased during the Cultural Revolution; people now of college age did not grow up hearing the music around them, which may explain in part why relatively few young people feel an affinity for the tradition.

Once one acquires the technique necessary to play an instrument, the step to playing along with a group is not intimidatingly large. In this type of ensemble music, the presence of a beginner is not necessarily an interference: while total incompetence is irritating to everyone, losing one's place temporarily does not necessarily disrupt the flow of the music, and dropping out entirely is acceptable unless one is playing one of the leading instruments. It is thus possible to enter the performers' circle as a beginner; further progress from beginner to expert is a matter of ability, sensitivity, guidance, practice, and time. In the past, some music clubs invited well-known performers to teach their members; now, individuals usually seek out a teacher on their own. The decision of whether or not to accept a student is based largely on the seriousness of the student. The desire to pass on the music and one's personal style of playing it is often expressed. Students are likely to bring up the names of their teachers; teachers are less likely to mention their students and, when questioned, may even disown former students who have not mastered the music to their satisfaction.

Most of the older musicians can play several instruments, and a few can play all the instruments in the ensemble. It is common to have studied each instrument with a different teacher, less common to have more than one teacher for the same instrument. Familiarity with several instruments contributes to the close musical interaction among the players; however, in both amateur and professional circles, musicians are becoming increasingly specialized. Thus, mastering a small body of music on several instruments is giving way to learning a large repertory on one instrument.

Musical notation is rarely used while playing in an ensemble setting, but it is often used for learning. Teachers write out their own version of a piece for their students, and published collections of *Jiangnan sizhu* repertory have existed at least since the 1920s. Cipher notation—called *jianpu*, "simple notation"—is most commonly used at present, although earlier manuscripts were written in *gongchepu* notation, a system in which Chinese characters represent scale degrees, and some recent publications are in Western staff notation.

Whatever notational system is used, the amount and kind of detail contained in it varies according to its intended purpose. A melody intended to be commonly shared by all instruments must be rather general, giving only the skeletal framework, whereas one for a specific instrument may be much more detailed. In instrument-specific notation, fingering and phrasing may be indicated; for wind instruments, breath marks may be included, while for stringed instruments, indications for the use of stopped or open strings and the direction of bowing or plucking are common. Sometimes notation represents a middle level of specificity and is intended for a group of related instruments. The Tianshan Music Club, for example, has three sets of notation for each piece, one set each for plucked strings, bowed strings, and wind instruments. The *yangqin* uses the plucked string notation. The percussion part is not notated and is, in fact, rarely written out in *Jiangnan sizhu* music. Although the percussion player may have considerable responsibility for controlling the tempo of a piece, percussion serves mainly as a marker of the strong and weak beats and is not considered to be a technically difficult part. From the tempo and meter of the piece, an experienced musician should be able to realize the percussion line.

Notation for a piece or arrangement that is not widely known is closely guarded by teachers and students alike, and hand-copied notation is considered to be a meaningful gift when presented to a student or friend. The implication is not so much that these manuscripts contain secret information, but rather that they are something of great value and not to be given away lightly.

In recent years collections of solo pieces for individual instruments have been published nationally, and some of these collections include *Jiangnan sizhu* repertory. The most obvious effect of this mass availability of *Jiangnan sizhu* notation is that musicians outside the Jiangnan area can learn to play the music, as can those who live in the area but have no direct contact with *sizhu* clubs or teachers. However, a gap still exists between what is written and what is heard, particularly with regard to timbre and ornamentation. The increased availability and specificity of musical notation results in the aural component of the learning process—listening and imitating—becoming less essential than in the past, but it is still impossible for a musician to become a true carrier of the *Jiangnan sizhu* tradition through notation alone.

Sound recordings can bring the student one step closer to the music. Commercial recordings and broadcasts of *Jiangnan sizhu* have been accessible for many years, and in some cases these recordings have been highly influential on other musicians. In recent years, cassette recorders have become affordable to an ever-larger segment of the population and are very much in evidence in Shanghai. Individually or collectively owned tape recorders are used by some music clubs for recording their own performances, both for documentation and self-improvement. Some of the younger musicians have also begun to use tapes for practicing and learning, and one can anticipate that this type of activity will become increasingly widespread.

Notation and sound recordings are potentially important learning aids, but a performer who merely plays a memorized and unchanging variant of a piece will not be considered an expert in *Jiangnan sizhu* circles. Most *sizhu* musicians stress the importance of improvisation (at the relatively "micro" level of ornamentation and embellishment). A player should not stick to a fixed version of a piece but should vary it subtly with each rendition, eventually developing a unique style of playing. The importance of this is emphasized by my *Jiangnan sizhu erhu* teacher, Zhou Hao, who stated that "if you play this exactly like me, it's wrong." This statement indicates that notation serves as a guideline rather than as a rigid prescription and that individuality is preferable to slavish imitation of one's mentor.[9] Such an attitude is fairly typical of *sizhu* musicians, but it is in strong contrast to that most commonly found in professional Chinese music circles, where notation is often treated as an absolute standard from which any deviation is a "mistake."

In a sense, all performers within the *sizhu* tradition achieve their individuality within a framework of aesthetic values shared by all. In another sense, there are almost as many sets of aesthetic criteria as there are performers—that is, a musician's tolerance for stylistic differences may be fairly broad, but his actual preferences may be much narrower. Since *Jiangnan sizhu* is ensemble music usually played in an informal and amateur context, maintaining one's preferences to the point of refusing to play with another musician would be unthinkable, and once actual playing begins, the expectation is that all involved will overcome their differences in taste in order to produce a harmonious collective musical result.

In this multiplicity of aesthetic standards, the advantages of having a teacher are obvious: since it is perfectly acceptable for a beginner to mimic his teacher's playing, in the early stages of the learning process a student can concentrate on learning a specific version of a piece without having to worry about making stylistic choices. He can imitate the teacher's style in all respects at first and, when the period of apprenticeship is finished, can then selectively retain or alter what has been learned. Although my own learning process was less straightforward, some of the problems faced were ones all students of the music must solve. I began by learning versions of several *Jiangnan sizhu* pieces in the context of studying *erhu* solo performance. The playing of my teacher at the conservatory, Wu Zhimin, was highly regarded by the amateur musicians, but the arrangements I studied were intended for solo playing and were too "busy" to work well in an ensemble: for example, the trills often featured in an *erhu* solo belong more appropriately to one of the flutes in a *sizhu* ensemble. Thus, I had to begin the process of simplification, largely through trial and error. Players in the music clubs would help by pointing out sections that needed changing and by instructing me to listen carefully to a musician who was playing the piece as it should be played. This process of listening critically to oneself and others and of imitating, deleting, and adding bit by bit is a common one in *Jiangnan sizhu*. Ideally, it eventually leads to establishing a personal style which still reveals traces of one's teachers or models.

Although I was eventually able to study with several *Jiangnan sizhu* specialists, my own learning process continued to be atypical in several ways. Most importantly, as an ethnomusicologist, playing the music was not an end in itself but was a means of reaching an understanding of the music that would ultimately be expressed through words and notes on paper, rather than through sounds. In addition, I was more interested in examining the diversity of playing styles than in choosing one to emulate. As an apprentice performer, this led to the problem of diversifying before a center was established and receiving large quantities of often contradictory advice. However, as a researcher, the lack of allegiance to any one group or teacher caused me to be welcomed by many different music clubs, each of whose members hoped that I would become a convert to their own musical worldview.

A musician's choice to gravitate toward a single music club may be influenced by factors such as convenience of location, the presence of relatives or teachers in a certain group, age of the participants, or preference for one group's repertory or style. However, whether an individual's participation in one club is circumstantial or intentional, participating in their activities fosters a sense of individual and group identity.

Instruments

The performance style and some playing techniques idiomatic to *Jiangnan sizhu* are unique to the Jiangnan region, but the instruments themselves are not. Within the *Jiangnan sizhu* tradition, the actual instruments played may vary considerably in dimensions, shape, materials, and appearance. Information on the organology, history, and playing techniques of Chinese instruments is readily available in both English and Chinese.[1] The focus here is on idiomatic playing techniques and style of playing the instruments in *Jiangnan sizhu*, especially those of the *dizi, erhu, pipa,* and *yangqin,* which are generally considered to be the most important instruments in the ensemble;[2] instruments occasionally added but not normally considered part of the *Jiangnan sizhu* ensemble (such as the *zheng* and *ruan*) will not be discussed.

Traditional *Jiangnan sizhu* uses a heptatonic scale that resembles the Western diatonic major scale, but with slightly higher fourth and lower seventh scale degrees (the exact intervals vary from instrument to instrument and, especially for the flutes, from key to key). Most of the skeleton melodies are pentatonic, with the fourth and seventh degrees occurring in melodic realizations, embellishments, passing tones, or temporary modal shifts. The usual key for the Eight Great Pieces is D, but the absolute pitch may vary, especially when only one or two instruments are played. Pieces adapted from the *pipa* repertory or other genres may be in other keys, such as G. The *dizi* and *xiao* have a pitch vocabulary that includes some notes outside of this basic heptatonic scale. The *pipa* played today is chromatic, but "reformed" chromatic models of the *yangqin* and *sheng* are not usually played in *Jiangnan sizhu*. The *erhu* and *sanxian* can sound all pitch gradations within their range. Modern musical notation for *Jiangnan sizhu* is almost invariably written in the cipher system, with "1" corresponding to D. However, when discussing their music or singing brief excerpts, most *Jiangnan sizhu* musicians use the French solfège syllables (*do, re, mi,* etc.) rather than numbers or pitch names. Here I will use the expression "scale degree" with the understanding that D is the first scale degree unless otherwise stated. Grace notes (either individual notes or part of a more complex ornament) played a scale degree above or below a melody note are a common embellishment for most *sizhu* instruments. Depending on which scale degrees are involved, these grace notes may be a major second, a minor second, or a non-equal-tempered second away from the melody note.

WIND INSTRUMENTS

Two types of bamboo flutes (the *dizi* and *xiao*) and a mouth organ *(sheng)* are played in *Jiangnan sizhu*. At least one of the flutes is almost always included and is one of the leading instruments in the ensemble. The *sheng* is less essential but is still considered to be an important instrument in *Jiangnan sizhu*.

Dizi

The *dizi*, also called *di* or *qudi*—*(Kun)qu dizi*—is a side-blown (transverse) bamboo flute (figure 3.1; the instrument is usually held to the right, but the performer here is left-handed). On the top of the instrument there are six fingerholes, a blowing hole, and a hole covered with a membrane. On the bottom there are two "string holes" which shorten the effective length of the instrument and through which a string, sometimes decorative, may be looped to hang or carry the instrument. The best membrane is made from the pliable inner skin of a reed. A square piece of membrane is first crumpled and then stretched across the hole with the grain of the membrane running parallel to the length of the instrument. The membrane is attached with a water soluble adhesive such as a gum made from peach sap. The surface around the membrane hole is moistened with water, a small chunk of the hardened sap is rubbed over the wet area, and the membrane is stretched and adjusted with the thumbs. Small wrinkles running perpendicular to the length of the instrument are formed in the membrane through this stretching and adjusting process.

The *dizi* played in *Jiangnan sizhu* has a fundamental pitch of a; in the past some musicians preferred an instrument with the fundamental a semitone higher, but these are rare today.[3] The highest note played is usually a^2; a few *Jiangnan sizhu* performers play b^2, and modern solo repertory may include even higher pitches. Equal-tempered instruments are now standard in professional circles, but most *Jiangnan sizhu* musicians prefer the more traditional arrangement of equidistant spacing between the finger holes. Equidistant spacing does not, of course, produce inter-

FIGURE 3.1 *Dizi* and *pipa* played by Lu Chunling *(left)* and Lu Dehua in the Zhong-guo Music Club

vals of equal size (see Thrasher [1978] and Mark [1983] for measurements of the intervals produced on various traditional *dizi*).

Several types of ornaments are characteristic of the *Jiangnan sizhu* style of *dizi* playing. To play a *dayin*, "struck note" (example 3.1a),[4] a finger quickly flicks the hole corresponding to the note a scale degree lower than the primary note. When played before a note, *dayin* sounds like a very quick grace note of indefinite pitch. When played in the middle of a sustained note, it gives a sense of a pulse subdividing the long note (rather than a lower neighbor grace note) and functions more as a rhythmic than as a melodic device. *Yiyin*, "leaning note," is a short note played before the beat, usually a step higher than the on-beat note (example 3.1b). *Chanyin*, "shaking note," is a trill; a short trill consists of the addition of a single occurrence of an upper neighbor note followed by a return to the main note (example 3.1c), while a longer trill, not as commonly played, consists of many oscillations between a note and its upper neighbor (example 3.1d). *Zengyin*, "presenting note" (example 3.1e), is an upper neighbor note added to the end of a sustained note. It is played lightly and quickly and, when executed correctly, gives the sense of an upward turn in the note's shape rather than a movement to another pitch. My teacher, Jin Zuli, cautioned me that *zengyin* should be used sparingly and that overuse of this technique is a serious (and, unfortunately, a common) stylistic error. In the *Jiangnan sizhu* style of *dizi* playing, the timbre should be mellow and rich (*chunhou*), and breaths should be coordinated with the melodic line so that the musical phrases are clear and bright (*qingxi*).

EXAMPLE 3.1 *Dizi* ornaments

Example 3.2, the opening of "Zhonghua Liuban," illustrates the use of these ornaments, including *dayin* (measures 4 and 5), *yiyin*, and *zengyin* (both in measure 3). Example 3.3, the opening of "Xingjie," uses *yiyin* and *dayin* (both in measure 1) and short trills (measures 2 and 3). Example 3.4 is an excerpt from the fast portion of "Xingjie." In such passages, long streams of sixteenth notes are common, and ornaments are used more sparingly. An exception is the use of long trills on the highest note (a²), which may in some cases be sustained for several measures. Long sustained trills are especially characteristic of "Xingjie" and are said to represent the style of *dizi* playing formerly used in street processions (Zhou Hui, personal communication). Often the finger executing these trills does not actually touch the instrument but oscillates over the hole producing a wavering sound. When played in this manner, it is called a *xu*, "empty" or "false," *chanyin*. Whether or not the trilling finger touches the

Adapted from Jin Zuli (unpublished)

EXAMPLE 3.2 "Zhonghua Liuban" (*dizi*)

Adapted from Lu (1982:54)

EXAMPLE 3.3 "Xingjie" (*dizi*)

flute, in a trill on a² the additional note is a lower rather than an upper neighbor because producing a b² requires a complex change of fingering and embouchure.

Adapted from Jin Zuli (unpublished)

EXAMPLE 3.4 "Xingjie" *Kuaiban (dizi)*

Xiao

The *xiao*, also called *dongxiao* ("hole" *xiao*), is an end-blown bamboo flute (figures 3.2 and 3.5). Although often referred to as a "vertical" flute, it is usually held at an angle. The preferred playing position varies from about a forty-five-degree angle to near-horizontal. The *xiao* used in *Jiangnan sizhu* has a fundamental pitch of d and a range of two octaves (to d^2) is used, although, like the *dizi*, higher pitches can be played. There are five fingerholes on the top of the instrument, a thumbhole on the bottom, a notched blowing hole at one end, and two string holes at the other end. Instruments with equidistant finger and thumbholes are preferred by *Jiangnan sizhu* musicians. An equal-tempered *xiao* with two additional fingerholes, derived from the *qinxiao*, which is designed to play duets with the *qin*, is standard in Shanghai professional circles.

FIGURE 3.2 *Xiao* and *erhu* played by Song Jinglian *(left)* and Shen Duomi in the rehearsal room of the Zhejiang Song and Dance Troupe, Hangzhou

Although some *Jiangnan sizhu* musicians are accomplished at playing this so-called "eight-hole *xiao*" (the blowing hole and string holes are not counted), they rarely play it in *Jiangnan sizhu* ensembles.

The *Jiangnan sizhu* style of *xiao* playing emphasizes small ornaments, including *yiyin, dayin,* and short trills. Longer trills and *zengyin* are rare. When played solo or in a duet with the *erhu,* the key of B♭ or C is often preferred to D (fingerings, not the instrument itself, are changed). As example 3.5 (in B♭) illustrates, *yiyin* are liberally added, including those using intervals as large as a fourth. This key also results in some large intervals in the melody, such as leaps from the fundamental d to the c¹ a seventh above (not seen in this excerpt).

Adapted from Sun (1977:71)

EXAMPLE 3.5 "Zhonghua Liuban" *(xiao)*

Sheng

The *sheng* is a free-reed aerophone. The instrument consists of a blowing chamber (formerly made from a gourd, now of wood or metal) and a circle of thin bamboo pipes of graduated sizes that protrude upward from the blowing chamber (figure 3.3). Each pipe contains a free metal reed and has a hole near the bottom. The reed sounds only when this hole is covered with a finger or thumb, and two or three of the pipes are usually sounded simultaneously. There are seventeen pipes on the *sheng* most commonly played in *Jiangnan sizhu.* Four of the pipes are silent (added for symmetry and balance); the sounding pipes are tuned a¹, b¹, c², c♯², d², e² (two pipes), f♯², g², a², b², c♯³, d³ (Hu 1982:45). Both inhaling and exhaling can make the reeds vibrate, so the instrument's sound can be sustained continuously. Example 3.6 is a *sheng* part for the opening of "Xingjie." Although the *sheng* plays more than one pitch at a time, producing a type of "harmony," its part is better thought of as a melody (corresponding to the lowest note in each "chord" in this example) to which additional notes (a fifth, a fifth and an octave, or a unison and a fifth) are added. The additional notes follow stereotypical patterns for each scale degree.

STRINGED INSTRUMENTS

Bowed, plucked, and struck strings are all part of the *Jiangnan sizhu* ensemble. Despite the name "silk and bamboo," steel strings have become

FIGURE 3.3 *Sheng* and *yangqin* played by Hou Shiquan *(left)* and Zhou Hui in the Zhongguo Music Club

Adapted from Gan (1985:420)

EXAMPLE 3.6 "Xingjie" *(sheng)*

standard for the leading *erhu*, the *pipa* is now played with steel strings or nylon wound around a steel core, and the *yangqin* has had metal strings (originally made of bronze, now usually steel) since its inception. Silk strings were widely used for the *erhu* and *pipa* until at least the late 1940s.[5]

Erhu

The *erhu* is a two-stringed bowed lute or "fiddle" (figures 3.2, 3.4, 3.6, and 3.7). Like most such lutes in China, the bowhair passes between the two strings, and the bow is removed from the instrument only when changing the strings or the bow. Two *erhu* are commonly played in *Jiangnan sizhu*, one, the leading *erhu*, tuned to d¹ and a¹ and the other to either b and f♯¹ or a and e¹. The latter is referred to as *fanhu*, "counter" or "cross" *(er)hu*, a term describing a musical function rather than an instrument type and analogous to "cross-tuning" for guitar or "cross-harp" harmonica playing. The only difference between the two instruments is that the strings are thicker for the *fanhu.* The musician playing this instrument is said to "play *fan.*"

FIGURE 3.4 *Yangqin* and *erhu* played by Zhang Zhengming *(left)* and Chen Yonglu in Zhang's home

Steel strings are most commonly used, but the lower-pitched inner string or both strings may be of silk, especially on the *fanhu.* A range of a major ninth (that is, the notes under the fingers in first position) is characteristic of *Jiangnan sizhu erhu* playing. In certain pieces or passages, the range may be extended to a perfect twelfth by moving to second position. The resonator (body) may be cylindrical, hexagonal, or octagonal. The top of the neck is usually undecorated; the dragon or bat heads that often adorn *erhu* from the Canton area are rarely seen in Shanghai. Most *Jiangnan sizhu* musicians play with a rigid wrist on the right (bowing) arm. Either the fingertips or the pads of the first, second, or third joint of the left fingers stop the strings. Some players use the tips of some fingers and the pads of others (most commonly the pads of the ring or ring and middle fingers), some play entirely with the fingertips, and others play entirely with the pads. The portion of the finger that stops the string affects the timbre, and the contrast between playing with the pads and tips can be used for different effects.[6] The fingertips are widely believed to be more nimble (solo performers also say that it is more "scientific" to play with the fingertips; this type of statement is common among those who admire Western art music, in this case the vast repertory and prodigious technique associated with the violin), and some players move from the pads to the tips of the fingers when the tempo of a piece accelerates.

In *Jiangnan sizhu* the *erhu* is generally played in a less florid manner than the *dizi* and is by convention usually confined to a small range, but many types of subtle techniques are employed to create variety and interest in the *erhu* part. *Langyin,* "wave note," is a special bowing technique for long sustained notes. It is always on a "pulling" bow stroke (to the right), and the right hand is slowly moved up and down, producing a slow undulating effect. *Daiyin,* "leading note," also called *dianzhi huayin* "padded finger sliding note," is a glissando that usually spans the interval of a minor third (example 3.7a). It begins with one of the notes stopped by the little finger in first position (a^1 or e^2); as the left wrist is tilted upward, the ring and middle fingers take over the stopping of the string, and the glissando ends with the middle finger stopping the string at a pitch a minor third lower than the original. The sound should be continuous, with the successive changes of left-hand fingering inaudible. *Shanghuayin,* "ascending sliding note," is a rapid and narrow ascending glissando preceding a note, starting from an indefinite pitch (example 3.7b). *Huihuayin,* "returning sliding note," as the name implies, is a glissando moving away from a note and then returning to it (example 3.7c). The movement is always to a note lower than the starting pitch; the execution is relatively slow, and the movement is usually less than a semitone. *Menyin,* "covered note" (example 3.7d), is similar to a *huihuayin* but different in the execution and resulting sound. In a *huihuayin* a finger of the left hand moves up and down along the string; in a *menyin* the change is in the pressure of the left hand as it pushes the string toward the neck. A quick release and subsequent increase in pressure produces a dip in pitch followed by a return to the original pitch, with the resultant sound perceived as a pulse subdividing a sustained note (much like the *dayin* on the *dizi*).

Two other techniques are applied only to particular notes. *Touyin,* "appearing note," begins with the bowing of the open string followed quickly by stopping the string with the index finger to produce the note

EXAMPLE 3.7 *Erhu* ornaments

a whole tone higher (example 3.7e). The result is not a glissando but an effect with a strong attack somewhat akin to a "hammer-on" on guitar, where a finger of the left hand articulates a note by striking a string against the fingerboard. *Zuoceyin*, "left side note," is played when there is a downward leap of an octave from e^2 to e^1 (example 3.7f). The first note is played with the little finger on the outer string, while the second is played by the index finger on the inner string and is preceded by a rapid glissando starting slightly above the ending pitch and emphasized by a twisting of the wrist toward the player's left. Finally, short and, occasionally, long trills are part of the *erhu*'s idiomatic vocabulary (figure 3.7g and h) and are played by quickly stopping and releasing a string one or more times at the location producing the note a step above a melody note (which can be either an open string or a stopped string).

These techniques are illustrated in the examples below. Example 3.8, the opening of "Zhonghua Liuban," includes *daiyin* (measure 1), *huihuayin* (measure 4), and a short trill (measure 2). Example 3.9, the opening of "Xingjie," employs *shanghuayin* (first note of measure 1), *menyin* (second note of measure 1), *touyin* (last note of the example), *zuoceyin* (the e^1 in measure 2), and a long trill (measures 2 and 3). Example 3.10, from the fast section of "Xingjie," shows the continuous sixteenth notes that typify fast passages (starting in measure 3); as can be seen in this example, short trills are the only ornaments still frequently included when the tempo accelerates. Example 3.11 is a *fanhu* part for the opening of "Zhonghua Liuban." The range is lower than that of the standard *erhu* part, and the playing style is much less ornamented.

Pipa

The *pipa* is a plucked lute with four strings, a pear-shaped body with a slightly rounded back, and a flat wooden face (figure 3.1). There are four

Adapted from Zhou Hao (unpublished)

EXAMPLE 3.8 "Zhonghua Liuban" *(erhu)*

Adapted from Renmin (1983:4)

EXAMPLE 3.9 "Xingjie" *(erhu)*

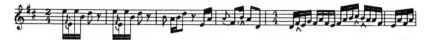

Adapted from Renmin (1983:4)

EXAMPLE 3.10 "Xingjie" *Kuaiban (erhu)*

Adapted from Zhou Hao (unpublished)

EXAMPLE 3.11 "Zhonghua Liuban" *(fanhu)*

frets on the neck of the instrument and twelve more on the body. The standard tuning is A, d, e, and a, although G, c, d, and g is occasionally used, in which case the other stringed instruments are also tuned down a whole tone and the *xiao* and *dizi* play in the key of C instead of D. Strings made of wound steel or nylon wound around a steel core are most commonly used today. The instrument is plucked with natural or artificial fingernails; most players today use the latter, made of plastic and attached with masking tape. All five fingers of the right hand are used for tremolo and other special techniques, but the thumb and index finger do most of the plucking for single-line melodies. In *Jiangnan sizhu*, as well as in the modern solo *pipa* tradition, the instrument is often described as being held vertically. In fact, it is usually held at somewhat of an angle, but the manner of holding and playing the instrument is clearly distinguished from the near-horizontal position familiar from numerous Tang Dynasty paintings and still preserved in *nanguan (nanyin)* as played in Fujian and Taiwan.

In *Jiangnan sizhu*, the *pipa* is played almost exclusively in the middle and upper registers. Although open strings are sometimes played for punctuating the melody, the lower-pitched fretted notes (on the neck) are almost never played. The *pipa* is traditionally one of the most virtuosic of Chinese instruments, and the solo repertory for the instrument features a broad array of techniques and special effects. However, in the *Jiangnan sizhu* ensemble, only a few of these techniques are employed.[7] The full *lunzhi* (rolling fingers), a tremolo using all five fingers to produce a sustained sound, is seldom played except on the sustained notes that begin and end some pieces. However, a half-*lunzhi* (example 3.12a), consisting of four rolled notes leading to a melodic note, is quite common. These four rolled notes are more or less evenly divided over the duration indicated in the notation, but they may be delayed,

provided that the melodic note falls on the correct beat. Another technique is *tui*, "push," where the string is rapidly pushed along a fret toward
the player and then returned to its original position (example 3.12b).
The result is similar to a slide up to an upper-neighbor grace note and
back again, but the slide is usually less than a whole step, and since it is
executed rapidly the effect is more of an accent than a melodic elaboration. Harmonics are employed (indicated by a circle above or below a
note), as are simultaneities (usually octaves or unisons) where an open
string and stopped note are played together. *Sao*, "sweep," is a rapid strum
across the lower three open strings leading to a fretted note on the top
string (example 3.12c; the lower three notes sound an octave lower than
written). It is used for rhythmic emphasis and functions as a percussive ac-
centuating device more than as an arpeggio. Another technique has, to
my knowledge, no special name but is a short grace note a step below
a melody note. The lower note is plucked on the beat, and a finger of
the left hand immediately presses the string against the fret producing
the higher note (example 3.12d). This left-hand technique is identical to
the *touyin* for the *erhu*, except that the *erhu* technique is played with the
index finger while the *pipa* technique may be played with any finger.

EXAMPLE 3.12 *Pipa* ornaments

Example 3.13, the opening of "Zhonghua Liuban," begins with a full
lunzhi and includes harmonics (measures 2 and 8) and *tui* (measures 2
and 5). Example 3.14, the opening of "Xingjie," is in a somewhat different style, with the half *lunzhi* being the favored ornamental technique.
Example 3.15, from the fast section of "Xingjie," illustrates the use of *sao*
(measures 3 and 4). The long streams of sixteenth notes are different
from those played on the *dizi* and *erhu* in that a single note is often
plucked three or four times in succession. In some cases, several measures of a fast passage may consist entirely of a series of notes played four
times each.

Adapted from Jin Zuli (unpublished)

EXAMPLE 3.13 "Zhonghua Liuban" *(pipa)*

Adapted from Zhang Zupei (unpublished)

EXAMPLE 3.14 "Xingjie" *(pipa)*

Adapted from Zhang Zupei (unpublished)

EXAMPLE 3.15 "Xingjie" *Kuaiban (pipa)*

Sanxian

The *sanxian* played in *Jiangnan sizhu* is the small or "southern" form of the instrument (figures 3.5 and 3.6). The body, covered on both sides with snakeskin, is made of wood in the shape of a rectangle with rounded corners. The neck, also of wood, is relatively long and unfretted. The three strings (silk or nylon) are tuned to d, a, and d[1], and the instrument is plucked with natural or artificial fingernails or with a plectrum. The *sanxian* is important rhythmically, and its part tends to be less florid than that of the *pipa*. Open strings are often played for rhythmic emphasis, with the result being that many wide intervals are characteristic of *sanxian* melodies. A tremolo is often used on sustained notes; although notated here with the same symbol as that used for the *pipa lunzhi*, it is produced by rapid plucking alternating the thumb and index finger, rather than by a five-finger roll. Harmonics are played, but other ornamentation is used sparingly. Example 3.16 is a *sanxian* part for the opening of "Zhonghua Liuban."

Qinqin

The *qinqin* is a fretted, plucked lute (figure 3.6). The instrument played in *Jiangnan sizhu* has a plum-blossom-shaped body (like a circle with petal-shaped edges) with a flat wooden front and back. Although some instruments have three tuning pegs, only two strings (of silk or nylon) are usually used, tuned to d and a. The optional third string is tuned to a unison with the lower string (d). The *qinqin* is dynamically the softest instrument in the ensemble, and its part is considered to be a subordinate one. The style is closest to that of the *sanxian*, with frequent use of tremolo

FIGURE 3.5 *Sanxian (left)* and *xiao* played by Taoists at the Baiyun'guan Temple

Adapted from Gan (1985:97)

EXAMPLE 3.16 "Zhonghua Liuban" *(sanxian)*

and wide leaps (often the result of playing open strings to punctuate the melody). Example 3.17 is a *qinqin* part for the opening of "Zhonghua Liuban."

Yangqin

The *yangqin* is a struck or hammered zither, usually trapezoidal (figures 3.3 and 3.4). Other names for the instrument include *daqin* and *qiaoqin*, both meaning "struck (string) instrument," and *tongsiqin*, "bronze silk (string) instrument." The *yangqin* used in *Jiangnan sizhu* usually has rounded corners but lacks the curving cutaways in the sides found in the *hudie* ("butterfly") *yangqin* (illustrated in Mackerras 1980:275). The strings are of bronze and struck with two flexible bamboo beaters. The

FIGURE 3.6 *Qinqin, erhu,* and *sanxian* played by *(left to right)* Xu Xingfa and two unidentified musicians in the Mid-Lake Pavilion

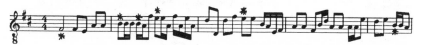

Transcription of performance of Chuan Jiafu (field recording, March 11, 1985)

EXAMPLE 3.17 "Zhonghua Liuban" *(qinqin)*

instrument most commonly played in *Jiangnan sizhu* has two bridges with eight (occasionally seven) courses of strings passing over each bridge. In the lower octave, each course is a single string; for the higher pitches, two or three strings are used. The total range is two octaves and a fifth, from d to a². The instrument is tuned diatonically, but the top two courses of strings are usually both tuned to a², so that there is no g² in the upper register. Occasionally, larger *yangqin* with a wider range are played, but only two of the Shanghai *Jiangnan sizhu* clubs currently use such instruments. *Jiangnan sizhu yangqin* players favor very flexible beaters made from bamboo. The portion of the beater that strikes the string may be covered with leather or felt, which muffles the sound slightly, resulting in a lower volume and less bright timbre. A player may select padded or unpadded beaters for different pieces or for different ensemble sizes.

The *yangqin* is a comparatively recent addition to the *Jiangnan sizhu* ensemble; it was popularized by Ren Huichu in the early days of the

Wenming Yashe (Literary Brightness Elegant Ensemble), formed in 1911. Ren, who owned a music store, later became involved in the construction of *yangqin* designed for use in the *Jiangnan sizhu* ensemble. Several of these instruments, built around 1925, still survive and are prized for their timbre, ease of tuning, and capability of staying in tune (Zhou Hui, personal communication). Today, the best *yangqin* being produced are invariably larger instruments intended for soloists or performers in Modern Chinese Orchestras. Small instruments are still manufactured, but they are intended primarily for beginners or tourists and are looked upon by serious musicians as little more than toys.

The *yangqin* is played at an even speed and tempo, with few pauses between musical phrases. The playing of notes one or two octaves apart, either simultaneously or sequentially (usually, but not always, with the higher note played first), is an important idiomatic technique, and certain notes of a melody may be displaced an octave. As with the *pipa* in *Jiangnan sizhu*, long tremolos are infrequent, but a special kind of short tremolo, *dantanlun*, "single plucked roll" (example 3.18a), is very characteristic of *Jiangnan sizhu yangqin* playing. In this technique, the player strikes a beater against the string only once; but when the force and angle are correct, the flexibility of the beater causes it to bounce on the string, resulting in about three repetitions of the note. Rarely, this technique may be applied simultaneously to two notes, usually an octave apart, in which case it is known as *shuangtanlun*, "double plucked roll" (example 3.18b). At the very beginning and end of a piece, a rapid alteration between two notes an octave apart is often played. This technique, which has no special name that I am aware of, is shown in example 3.18c.

EXAMPLE 3.18 *Yangqin* ornaments

Example 3.19, the opening of "Zhonghua Liuban," shows the use of octaves to accentuate strong beats (the beginning of measures 2, 3, and 4), occasional octave displacement in the melody (the c♯¹ in measure 2), and the frequent addition of *dantanlun* throughout the excerpt. Example 3.20, the opening of "Xingjie," also illustrates a common method for sustaining a note, with the lower octave followed by several repetitions of the upper octave (the b's in measures 2 and 3). Example 3.21, from the fast portion of "Xingjie," is essentially an elaboration of a melody moving in eighth notes. However, variety is created by the interspersing of unison and octave repetitions of a note and by the occasional

Adapted from Zhou Hui (unpublished)

EXAMPLE 3.19 "Zhonghua Liuban" *(yangqin)*

Adapted from Yang (1958:27)

EXAMPLE 3.20 "Xingjie" *(yangqin)*

Adapted from Yang (1958:27)

EXAMPLE 3.21 "Xingjie" *Kuaiban (yangqin)*

shifts to sixteenth-note melodic motion (the end of measure 2). The placing of lower-octave notes on the off-beat occuring throughout this last example is characteristic of the *Jiangnan sizhu* style of *yangqin* playing, particularly in fast passages.

PERCUSSION

The percussion is played by a single musician holding a clapper in the left hand and a drumstick in the right. The instrument played with the right hand may be either a drum or a woodblock. The percussionist's role is referred to as *guban,* "drum and clapper," whether or not the drum is played.

Ban

The *ban* is a wooden clapper consisting of two slabs of wood attached together loosely by a cord at one end (figure 3.7). Chinese musicologists usually refer to this instrument as the *paiban,* "beat clapper." One slab is twice the thickness of the other and is actually formed from two pieces of wood permanently tied tightly together. The two parts of the clapper have flat surfaces on one side, which are struck together, while the outer sides may be contoured.

FIGURE 3.7 *Guban* (drum and clapper) and *ruan* played by Yin Xiaoxiang (*foreground*) and unidentified musician in the Zhongguo Music Club

The single slab of the clapper is held in the palm of the left hand. The thumb separates the two slabs, and the heavier double slab is allowed to hang down freely. The playing technique is a smooth two-part wrist movement: a clockwise twist moves the single slab upward to the player's left, and a counterclockwise return motion strikes it against the freely hanging double slab. Thus, unlike most idiophones comprised of two similar or identical pieces (such as castanets, claves, or concussion bells), the player does not actually strike the two parts together; rather, one moving part is struck against the other, which is held relatively stationary by the force of gravity.

Biqi Gu

The name *biqi gu* means "water chestnut drum"—the color and shape resemble a water chestnut with both ends sliced off (figures 3.7 and 3.8). This instrument is identical to that played in *Kunqu* and *shifan* music, where it is known as the *diangu*, "dot drum." A description of the latter states: "Also called *huaigu*. A thick wood frame, raised in the middle, ta-

FIGURE 3.8 *Biqi Gu* and *erhu* played by Chen Yongnian *(left)* and unidentified musician in the Mid-Lake Pavilion

pering down on the sides, covered on both faces with cow skin. The drumstick [like a dowel] is of wood or bamboo" (Miao Tianrui, Ji, and Guo 1984:79). A larger drum of the same design, the *shugu* (not played in *Jiangnan sizhu*), is "about 30 cm in diameter and has a narrow wooden shell (about 7 cm in height) covered on both sides with oxhide tacked around the perimeter"; the *diangu* is "about two-thirds" as large (Thrasher 1984b:379). The frame is not hollow, but is pierced by a hole about two inches in diameter perpendicular to the drum heads. Because of this design, as with the single-headed drum used in Peking opera, only the center portion of the skin serves as a vibrating membrane, so the pitch of the instrument is rather high. The drumstick is usually held so that both the vibrating portion of membrane and the rim of the drum (where wood is directly beneath the skin) are struck simultaneously. The drum is placed flat on a table or tilted slightly away from the player by placing a metal ring or other hard object under the edge of the drum closest to him.

Bangzi

The *bangzi* is a rectangular wood block, partially hollowed out with a horizontal slit. The instrument is equivalent to the large wood block played in Cantonese opera and Cantonese Music and is sometimes identified as *Guangdong bangzi* (Cantonese *bangzi*). It is placed flat on a table and, like the *biqi gu*, is played with a single thin stick of wood or bamboo.

Although the percussion part in *Jiangnan sizhu* is not technically demanding, the percussionist often has the primary responsibility for controlling the tempo of a piece. For this reason, the *guban* player is usually an experienced performer, since he must have a feel not only for the appropriate tempo for each section of a piece but also for the transitions between sections and changes in tempo within a section. In general, the clapper is played on the strong beat and the drum serves to subdivide the beat into two, four, or eight pulses. Example 3.22a shows the most common pattern used for "Zhonghua Liuban" and the slow portions of "Xingjie." In the portion of "Xingjie" played at medium tempo, the pattern in Example 3.22b is often played. In the fast third cycle of "Zhonghua Liuban," the drum may play only between every other clapper stroke (example 3.22c). In the fast portion of "Xingjie," the drum is commonly played with a steady pulse both on and between the clapper beats (example 3.22d).

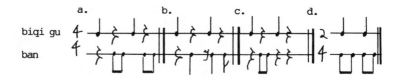

EXAMPLE 3.22 Percussion patterns

Adapted from Shanghai (1960:6)

EXAMPLE 3.23 "Xingjie" (*dizi* and percussion)

At least one scholar of *Jiangnan sizhu*, Xu Qingyan (Shanghai Qun-zhong 1960:4), believes that in the past the percussion part in *Jiangnan sizhu* was much less regular and simplistic than it is today and showed more traces of the music's rhythmically complex ancestor, *shifan* music. Example 3.23 is an excerpt from his arrangement of "Xingjie." The drum line is quite varied and even follows the rhythm of the *dizi* melody at the beginning of the second and third measures.

FOUR

Repertory

66 "The repertory of *Jiangnan sizhu*" is a concept that may be understood in several ways. In the narrowest sense, the repertory is limited to the Eight Great Pieces, while in the broadest sense it includes all pieces played by *Jiangnan sizhu* ensembles. Both of these definitions are problematical: the concept of the Eight Great Pieces is a somewhat arbitrary grouping of recent historical origin (see chapter 1), while the repertory frequently played by *Jiangnan sizhu* ensembles includes pieces that are indisputably from other parts of China. Most definitions lie between these extremes, and many musicians and scholars have their personal lists of pieces they consider to be "authentic" *Jiangnan sizhu*.

"Jiangnan style" is a term often invoked in discussions of the repertory. Although musical style is an elusive concept,[1] it is clearly central to the nature of the music and is a parameter instinctively used by musicians for evaluating new or reconstructed repertory. Chen Yingshi's definition of the music is typical: "*Jiangnan sizhu* is a musical genre in which silk stringed and bamboo wind instruments are of primary importance, and which is played in the musical style of the Jiangnan area" (1985:33). Chen's definition allows inclusion not only of new compositions but also absorption of pieces from elsewhere in China (if they take on the Jiangnan style). Since identification of a regional style is inevitably somewhat subjective, it also leaves room for differing opinions concerning the specific pieces that belong to the repertory.

Although I accept Chen's flexible definition in spirit, here I will emphasize the Eight Great Pieces, since they are inarguably central to the tradition and as such are the logical place to begin discussion and analysis of musical structure and style. I will refer to the other pieces played by *Jiangnan sizhu* ensembles as "Additional Repertory," a term of my own referring to all the pieces outside of the Eight Great Pieces played by Shanghai *Jiangnan sizhu* clubs during the period of my fieldwork. I make no assumptions concerning the "correct" size of the repertory or the appropriateness of the inclusion or exclusion of pieces in the Additional Repertory, but I will present some of the prevalent opinions of musicians and scholars concerning the relationship of these pieces to *Jiangnan sizhu*.

REPERTORY PLAYED BY SHANGHAI *JIANGNAN SIZHU* MUSIC CLUBS

The numbers of performances of various pieces played by Shanghai music clubs as I documented them on 108 occasions are listed in table 4.1. While these numbers are not intended to be a complete tabulation of performances attended during my stay in Shanghai, they do reveal much about what the *Jiangnan sizhu* clubs actually play.[2] In the table, the Eight Great Pieces are indicated with asterisks. For each piece, the total number of performances and the number of different groups that performed it are given.[3] In this chapter, parenthetical numbers following the title of a piece and its translation refer to the frequency rankings shown in the left-hand column of table 4.1. It can be seen that the Eight Great Pieces (particularly the first four) represent a very high percentage of *Jiangnan sizhu* clubs' musical activity, although one ("Man Sanliu") is far less frequently played than the other seven. Not surprisingly, the most frequently played repertory also tends to be widely known. However, among the relatively less frequently played repertory, pieces that are played occasionally by four or more different clubs (15, 16, 17, 19) can be distinguished from those played comparatively often by only one or two clubs (12, 13, 14, 18).

THE EIGHT GREAT PIECES

All of the Eight Great Pieces are contained in some form in one or more of three collections of musical notation from the 1920s to 1930s (Wu Yuan 1920; Zheng Jinwen 1924; Guofeng 1939). In the following discussion, these three sources will be referred to collectively as "early *Jiangnan sizhu* notation." Curiously, none of the three collections includes the words *"Jiangnan"* or *"sizhu"* in their titles. The first two identify this repertory as *putong qu*, "ordinary" or "common" tunes, while the Guofeng collection is labeled as *xiandai liuxing Zhongguo yinyue*, "modern popular Chinese music." In all of these collections, the notation is of melodies in a somewhat skeletal form. As performed today, these pieces are often greatly expanded versions of short tunes. Some of the pieces contained in the early notation are clearly expanded versions, but

TABLE 4.1
Repertory Played by Shanghai *Jiangnan Sizhu* Music Clubs

COMPOSITION	TOTAL	CLUBS
* 1. Zhonghua Liuban	262	11
* 2. Sanliu	119	11
* 3. Xingjie	115	10
* 4. Huanle Ge	104	10
* 5. Yunqing	55	9
* 6. Sihe Ruyi	50	8
7. Nichang Qu	42	9
* 8. Man Liuban	20	7
9. Pinghu Qiuyue	19	5
10. Chunjiang Hua Yueye	16	7
11. Yangba Qu	15	4
12. Huaigu	11	2
13. Hangong Qiuyue	9	2
14. Xuhua Luo	9	1
15. Zhegu Fei	9	4
* 16. Man Sanliu	8	4
17. Zouma	8	4
18. Piying Diao	7	1
19. Lianhuankou	5	4
20. Zizhu Diao	5	2
21. Qinglian Yuefu	4	1
22. Hangong Qiuye (Cantonese)	3	3
23. Suyang Qiao	3	1
24. Xunyang Yeyue	3	1
25. Dao Chun Lai	2	2
26. Hantian Lei	2	2
27. Kuailede Nongcun	2	2
28. Pu'an Zhou	2	1
29. Xiaotao Hong	2	1
30. Yu Da Bajiao	2	1
31. Dengyue Jiaohui	1	1
32. Jiaoshi Mingqin	1	1
33. Kongque Kaipin	1	1
34. Pipa Guqu	1	1
35. Yidian Jin	1	1
36. Yinhe Hui	1	1
37. Yu Furong	1	1
38. Yu Ge	1	1
39. Zhaojun Yuan	1	1

* The Eight Great Pieces are marked with asterisks.

indications of meter and/or tempo are inconsistent, and it is impossible to know what degree of embellishment in performance was assumed by the compilers of these collections. Some of these pieces are known by more than one title; some alternate titles are interchangeable alternative names, but others reflect variant treatments, particularly with regard to tempo or the degree of expansion.

The titles of some *Jiangnan sizhu* pieces are not easily translated. Unlike much Chinese instrumental music (which tends to have programmatic titles and subtitles), many of the titles are abstract, referring to technical aspects of a piece's origins, form, meter, or tempo. The word *"ban"* is particularly problematic. When *ban* follows a numeral in the title of a piece, it indicates the number of metrical units in a phrase or in the entire piece; in this context, *ban* may be translated as "beat," but in some ways its meaning is closer to "measure." When *ban* follows an indication of speed, it represents a concept that encompasses both tempo and meter. *Hua*, literally "flower," implies the practice of "adding flowers" and is best translated as "ornamented."[4] *Sihe* means "four together"; it is a structural description of a piece made up of four tunes, but it is also used more freely to indicate a multisection piece in which the number of sections may or may not actually be four. Finally, some titles should be understood as providing technical information in an abbreviated form. For example, "Zhongban" is the colloquial name for "Zhonghua Liuban," which in itself implies "Zhongban Hua Lao Liuban" (Ornamented old six beats in medium tempo).

"Zhonghua Liuban" (Medium ornamented six beats) (1) is derived from a short instrumental tune usually known as either "Lao Liuban" (Old six beats) or "Lao Baban" (Old eight beats). The earliest notated version of this tune is the 1814 collection of string ensemble notation *Xiansuo Beikao* [A reference appendix for strings] compiled by Rong Zhai (edited and transnotated in Yang Yinliu and Cao 1979).[5] This includes a piece entitled "Shiliuban" (Sixteen beats), which is a set of variations on "Lao Baban." Another important early written source for the tune is found in Li Fangyuan's 1895 *pipa* collection *Nanbeipai Shisan Datao Pipa Xinpu* [New notation for thirteen northern and southern school *pipa* suites], where it is entitled "Yushun Xunfengcao" (Fragrant winds of [the emperors] Yu and Shun), with the comment that the "popular" title is "Lao Baban." "Zhonghua Liuban" is still sometimes referred to as "Xunfeng Qu" (Fragrant wind tune), but it is generally assumed that this title is the creation of Li Fangyuan and that "Baban" is the more traditional name. Neither of these source tunes is identical structurally to the version of "Lao Liuban" on which "Zhonghua Liuban" is based, but "Shiliuban" is closer to it than is the Li Fangyuan version.

The intricacies of the "Liuban"/"Baban" complex, the pieces derived from them, and the meanings of the numerals "six" and "eight" are subjects of controversy among both performers and scholars. Some of these problems will be examined in the following chapter on formal structure; here it is sufficient to note that early *Jiangnan sizhu* notation includes several versions of "Liuban," including "Lao Liuban," "Liuban," "Kuai Liuban" (Fast six beats), "Hua Liuban" (Ornamented six beats), "Huahua Liuban" (Double ornamented six beats), and "Sanhualiu" (Three times ornamented six). Since most of this notation is rather skeletal in nature, it is difficult to say exactly when the version now known as "Zhonghua Liuban" became popular, but "Huahua Liuban" from the Guofeng collection most closely resembles it. "Man Liuban" (Slow six beats) (8) is a further expanded and longer piece based on "Liuban"/"Baban." Pre-1949 collections do not include this title, but the Guofeng "Sanhualiu" is rather similar to it.

"Sanliu" (Three six) (2) can also be traced to the Li Fangyuan collection. The relevant piece in that collection is named "Meihua Sannong" (Three playings of plum blossoms) and, as with "Xunfeng Cao," this more poetic title is thought to be an invention of Li's. This piece is unrelated to the well-known *qin* piece of the same name. The three early collections of *Jiangnan sizhu* notation include both of these titles as well as "Hua Sanliu" (Ornamented three six), "Sanliuban" (Three six beats), and "Yuanban Sanliu" (Original *ban* three six). All of these are structurally identical to the present-day "Sanliu," but structurally different from Li Fangyuan's version. "Man Sanliu" (Slow three six) (16) is an expansion of "Sanliu" that includes an additional section. This additional section is not found in any early *Jiangnan sizhu* notation, but it is very close to a section in Li Fangyuan's "Meihua Sannong," which suggests that it may preserve a vestige of an earlier version of the piece.

"Xingjie" (Street procession) (3) is also known as "Xingjie Sihe" (Street procession, four together). The longer title is used in the Wu and Guofeng collections, with the latter containing three different versions of the piece. "Sihe Ruyi" (Four together, as you please) (6) is included in Wu, while the other collections contain the alternate titles "Sihe Ban" (Four together beats), "Yuanban Sihe" (Original *ban* sihe), and "Huaban Sihe" (Ornamented *ban* sihe). "Xingjie" and "Sihe Ruyi" share sections based on the same short tunes; although they probably date from an earlier period, I have not located any pre-1920 collection containing these tunes.

Only one notated example among the early *Jiangnan sizhu* collections exists for each of the other two of the Eight Great Pieces. "Huanle Ge" (Song of joy) (4) is contained in Guofeng. The piece is sometimes said to be derived from a folk song, but I have not located any other early notation for "Huanle Ge." "Yunqing" (Cloud celebration) (5) is found in Wu. The piece is derived from a tune of the same name that is contained in the string, wind, and percussion piece "Luogu Sihe" (Gongs and drums, four together); although widely assumed to originate from a relatively early date, the only published notation available for "Luogu Sihe" is that contained in Shanghai Qunzhong (1960).

Figure 4.1 lists all of the variants (or variant titles) for the Eight Great Pieces as found in the early collections of musical notation discussed above.

ADDITIONAL REPERTORY

All pieces except the Eight Great Pieces played by *Jiangnan sizhu* music clubs are included under this heading. Most were originally instrumental solos, instrumental pieces used in conjunction with vocal genres, or *sizhu* traditions from specific parts of Jiangnan or from other regions of China; a few were recently composed for *Jiangnan sizhu* ensemble. The Additional Repertory can be grouped into five categories.

Ensemble Music from the Jiangnan Area

The most popular of these pieces is "Nichang Qu" (Rainbow clothing tune) (7). It is considered to be from Hangzhou and may have been introduced to Shanghai by Wang Xunzhi. The title is mentioned in a Tang Dynasty poem, but the date of origin of the piece played today is unknown. There is a *pipa* solo of the same title in Li Fangyuan's collection that does not seem to be musically related to the *Jiangnan sizhu* piece. No early notation for the *sizhu* version has been located. The piece is invariably played in what might be called "soft style"—that is, featuring the *xiao* instead of the *dizi* and excluding percussion instruments.[6] The piece is sometimes known as "Xiao Yue Er Gao" (Small the moon is high) or simply "Yue Er Gao" (The moon is high), but it is musically unrelated to the well-known *pipa* piece "Yue Er Gao."

"Yangba Qu" (Yang Eight Tune) (11) is also known as "Dao Baban" (Inverted eight beats) and "Fan Wang Gong" (*Fan* obliterates *gong*). A portion of the piece is based on "Lao Baban," but with a modal change in which the fourth scale degree replaces the third; the two alternate titles refer to this treatment, which is unusual in *Jiangnan sizhu* (*gong* and *fan* are traditional names for the third and fourth scale degrees). Although sometimes referred to as a *pipa* piece, the only notation I have located (Sun 1977) identifies it as *Jiangnan sizhu*. The piece is played in the soft style.

FIGURE 4.1

Early notational sources

	LIUBAN	SANLIU	XINGJIE	SIHE	OTHER
Rong 1814	Shiliuban				
Li 1895	Xunfeng Cao	Meihua Sannong			
Hu 1920	Lao Liuban Kuai Liuban Hua Liuban Huahua Liuban	Meihua Sannong Hua Sanliu	Xingjie Sihe Xingjie Sanliu	Sihe Ruyi	Yunqing
Zheng 1924	Liuban	Sanliuban		Siheban	
Guofeng 1939	Lao Liuban Kuai Liuban Hua Liuban Zhongban Hualiu Huahua Liuban Sanhua Liu	Sanliu Yuanban Sanliu Meihua Sanliu	Xingjie Sihe (3 versions)	Yuanban Sihe Huaban Sihe	Huanle Ge Liuban

"Xuhua Luo" (Catkin flowers falling) (14) is an expansion of "Lao Liuban," played in the soft style. The version played in Shanghai is based on the notation of *erhu* master Chen Yonglu and features his instrument prominently (he performs with the Tianshan Music Club). "Piying Diao" (Shadow theater [literally "leather shadow"] melody) (18) is music from the Shanghai shadow puppet theater. It is unique among the repertory played in *Jiangnan sizhu* music clubs in that gongs and cymbals are added to the *sizhu* ensemble. "Suyang Qiao" (Su [zhou]-Yang [zhou] bridge) (23) is a piece that combines the versions of "Qiao" ("Sihe Ruyi") from the two cities named in its title. It does not contain the solo sections that distinguish the Shanghai version (discussed in chapter 2), but it does include antiphonal sections in which winds and strings alternate. All three of these pieces (14, 18, 23) are currently played only by the Tianshan Music Club in Shanghai. No published notation has been located for any of them; although Gan (1985) does contain Suzhou and Yangzhou versions of "Qiao," they are quite different from the version played by the Tianshan group.

"Zizhu Diao" (Purple bamboo melody) (20) is adapted from *Huju* opera. No early notation for this piece has been located, but it is often included in more recent collections, such as Sun (1977). "Dengyue Jiao-hui" (Moon and lanterns mutually shining) (31)—the title refers to the Lantern Festival, in which paper lanterns are displayed beneath a full moon—is from the Hangzhou area, probably brought to Shanghai by Wang Xunzhi, and is played in the soft style. Notation for the piece is not included in any *sizhu* collections I have seen, but it is often included in collections for *zheng* solo. The piece is musically unrelated to the *pipa* solo of the same name.

Pipa Pieces

These pieces are collectively known as *guqu*, "old pieces," or *pipa taoqu*, "*pipa* suites."[7] In their original form, these may not be associated with any particular region, but in some cases they have become associated with *Jiangnan sizhu*, as they are often played in ensemble settings by *Jiangnan sizhu* musicians. All these pieces are played in the soft style; in performance, they are distinguished by their relatively low dynamic level, the prominence of the *pipa*, the use of *xiao* rather than *dizi* as the leading wind instrument, and the absence of percussion instruments.[8]

I heard five of these pieces played by Shanghai *Jiangnan sizhu* music clubs: "Hangong Qiuyue" (Han palace and autumn moon) (13), "Qing-lian Yuefu" (Green lotus ballad) (21), "Pu'an Zhou" (Buddhist chant [23]; not related to the *qin* piece of the same name), and "Xunyang Yeyue" (Xunyang [river], evening and moon) (24). These pieces are included in various collections of *pipa* notation, but the versions closest to those played by Shanghai music clubs can be found in Li Guangzu's compilation (1982) of the versions played by his father, the late Li Ting-song. The elder Li was a prominent exponent of the Pudong school of *pipa* playing and an important figure in Shanghai *Jiangnan sizhu* circles, and he often played with some of the musicians who perform these pieces today.

"Chunjiang Hua Yueye" (Spring, river, flowers, moon, and evening) (10) is derived from "Xunyang Yeyue." The original piece was included in the Li Fangyuan collection and many subsequent compilations. It was adapted for ensemble by members of the Datong Music Club in 1925, and the adapted version has become better known—both as a solo and ensemble piece—than the original. In "Chunjiang Hua Yueye," most of the musical material of "Xunyang Yeyue" is preserved, but some sections are expanded or contracted, the subtitles are changed, and one section is played at an accelerated tempo. "Chunjiang Hua Yueye" and "Xunyang Yeyue" are often thought of as interchangeable alternate titles for the same piece; as played by *Jiangnan sizhu* musicians, however, they are quite distinct. The relationship between the two pieces is easily heard, but they are different enough that knowing one would not be sufficient to enable a performer to play the other without learning it as a separate piece. At present, only one *Jiangnan sizhu* music club in Shanghai, the Hezhong club, plays "Xunyang Yeyue," and the members stress the fact that they are the only group that has preserved this predecessor of "Chunjiang Hua Yueye."[9]

Non-Jiangnan Repertory

Two of these pieces have become assimilated by *Jiangnan sizhu* musicians to the extent that they are now widely considered to be in the Jiangnan style. "Huaigu" (Cherishing the past) (12) is often said to have been transmitted to Shanghai from Fujian province. However, it was originally part of the repertory of the Kejia (Hakka) people from north-central China and is still well-known as a Kejia *zheng* piece. "Zhegu Fei" (Partridges flying) (15) is from Hunan province and has been widely played as a *dizi* or *xiao* solo. I have not located early notation for either of these pieces, but "Zhegu Fei" was already widely known in Shanghai in the 1930s (Qin Pengzhang, personal communication).

A much larger number of non-Jiangnan pieces are still identified as belonging to their original repertories. Although some are frequently played in *Jiangnan sizhu* music clubs, they are not viewed as having acquired a Jiangnan style. All pieces in this subgroup were originally from Guang-dong province. Of these, "Yidian Jin" (One drop of gold) (35) is from the

sizhu music of the Chaozhou people (*Chaozhou xianshi*). The others are all
Cantonese Music: "Pinghu Qiuyue" (Calm lake and autumn moon) (9),
"Zouma" (Running horses) (17), "Lianhuankou" (Interlocking chain)
(19), "Hangong Qiuyue" (Han palace and autumn moon [22]; derived
from the *pipa* piece of the same name, but distinctly different from it),
"Dao Chun Lai" (The coming of spring) (25), "Hantian Lei" (Thunder on
a dry day) (26), "Xiaotao Hong" (Small red peach) (29), "Yu Da Bajiao"
(Rain striking the bananas) (30), "Jiaoshi Mingqin" (Sounding the *qin* on
a rock [among the] bananas) (32), "Kongque Kaiping" (The peacock
spreads its tail) (33), "Yinhe Hui" (Meeting at the silver river [Milky Way])
(36), and "Zhaojun Yuan" (Zhaojun's resentment) (39). In Shanghai *sizhu*
clubs, these pieces are always played in the soft style (although *dizi* and
percussion are often present in the "indigenous" Chaozhou and Cantonese traditions of performing this repertory). Many collections of notation
for Cantonese Music have appeared since the early part of this century.
Discussion of the background of most of these pieces can be found in
Witzleben (1983a:53–60).

New Compositions

Only one piece from this category, "Kuailede Nongcun" (Happy villages)
(27), probably dating from the 1950s, is listed in table 4.1.[10] I have not
located notation for this piece in any of the collections of *Jiangnan sizhu*
or *dizi* music to which I have had access and cannot ascertain if published
notation for it exists. At the *Jiangnan sizhu* festival in 1985, five new compositions were played by Modern Chinese Orchestras and children's
groups: "Chun Man Pujiang" (Spring fills the Pu River), "Chun Zao"
(Spring morning), "Chunfeng Chui Jiangnan" (The spring wind blows
in Jiangnan), "Chunhui Qu" (Spring brightness tune), and "Hao Jiangnan" (Jiangnan is good). Another new piece, "Jiangnan zhi Chun"
(Spring in Jiangnan), was played by the Jiangnan music club. In addition, new arrangements of "Zhonghua Liuban," "Sanliu," "Xingjie," and
"Nichang Qu," and the string, wind, and percussion piece "Luogu Sihe"
and an instrumental arrangement of the folk song "Moli Hua" (Jasmine
flower) were performed at this event.

Pieces of Unknown Origin

I have no information concerning three pieces I heard on one occasion
each: "Pipa Guqu" (Old tune for *pipa*) (34), "Yu Furong" (Jade lotus)
(37), and "Yuge" (Fisherman's song) (38), not the *qin* piece of the same
name. Further research may place them in one of the categories above.[11]

IDENTIFYING *"JIANGNAN SIZHU* REPERTORY"

To decide which pieces are really *Jiangnan sizhu* and which are merely played in conjunction with *Jiangnan sizhu,* one determinant may be the closeness or duration of a piece's association with the Jiangnan area. Another is the ensemble style: some scholars and musicians believe that the Eight Great Pieces feature a heterophonic texture, while those in the Additional Repertory tend toward unison. However, the greater divergence among the melodic lines heard in the Eight Great Pieces may stem from greater familiarity—the better a player knows a piece, the more likely he is to experiment and elaborate the melody—rather than from an inherent difference between these pieces and those in the Additional Repertory.

Among the various types of Additional Repertory, the pieces discussed above as "ensemble music from the Jiangnan area" are, predictably, most likely to be called *Jiangnan sizhu:* they are strongly associated with the Jiangnan region, and some are even derived from the same "mother tunes" as the Eight Great Pieces. Some of the *guqu* are among the most popular of the Additional Repertory but are often viewed as being somewhat different from *Jiangnan sizhu* because of the instrumentation, the relative importance of the *pipa,* and the fact that they are not specifically from the Jiangnan area. Some musicians think of these pieces as being "classical," while the Eight Great Pieces are closer to "folk," and it is clearly true that at least the *pipa* part in *guqu* is much more "fixed" than in the Eight Great Pieces. "Zhegu Fei" and "Huaigu" are originally from other parts of China, and while some musicians believe that they are still somewhat "foreign," others feel that they have acquired the Jiangnan flavor. "Zhegu Fei," despite its Hunan origin, has become famous as a *dizi* solo, and is widely considered to be one of the most representative examples of the Jiangnan style of *dizi* playing. The pieces from Guangdong are clearly labeled as belonging to other genres, and although some of them are quite popular, they are always identified as being "Cantonese Music" or "Chaozhou Music." As for recent compositions, none are regularly played by any of the *Jiangnan sizhu* music clubs. However, some of the pieces from the Cantonese repertory (19, 32, 36) are compositions by Lü Wencheng from the early part of this century, and, in a sense, these are "new compositions" when compared with more traditional repertory. This serves to illustrate that the categories used here are not sharply delineated and that a single piece can have attributes that allow it to be ascribed to more than one category.

REPERTORY & IDENTITY

The Eight Great Pieces are the heart of the *Jiangnan sizhu* repertory, and any musician who claims or desires to be an expert in the tradition must know them all. However, most music clubs have at least one or two pieces from the Additional Repertory that they play frequently. Members of a music club often take pride in having mastered certain pieces that other clubs do not play or, in their opinion, do not play correctly; thus, the choice of Additional Repertory is a primary determinant of the musical identity of a particular club or individual. One music club, Tianshan, devotes more than half of its time to playing Additional Repertory; other groups play only a few of these pieces—or none at all—in a session. Whether or not these pieces are actually called *Jiangnan sizhu* by the musicians (some players make a point of the fact that they can play not only *Jiangnan sizhu* but other genres as well), they serve as an indicator of a club's specialties and/or musical orientation.

A musician's development as a *Jiangnan sizhu* expert can be measured in two ways. For the Eight Great Pieces, a hierarchy of difficulty based on length, tempo, and ease of memorization is commonly acknowledged. For this repertory, progress in learning the music can be mapped, at least in part, by which pieces a player has mastered. For the Additional Repertory, progress is of a more personalized kind: by choosing which of the more obscure pieces to apply himself to, a musician makes both an aesthetic decision and a choice of which club or individuals he wishes to associate with most closely. Through these decisions, he moves toward establishing his identity as an individual within the world of *Jiangnan sizhu*.

The interplay of individuality and commonality can be seen as a key to the interpersonal dynamics of this ensemble tradition (and perhaps others). In the repertory of *Jiangnan sizhu*, widely known pieces are juxtaposed with those known only to a select few. A *Jiangnan sizhu* musician shares a common tradition with a large number of other players with whom he interacts musically and socially on a regular basis. He also may share a more specialized subtradition with a smaller group, with whom he interacts at a more intimate level of communication. In other words, through participation in a *Jiangnan sizhu* music club an individual belongs both to a small community in Shanghai society (those who know and play the music) and to a more exclusive one (the music club). Still more exclusive communities may also be established: musicians within a club who know specific pieces, who meet in certain players' homes, or who share historical associations through a teacher or former group. The cultivation of a certain repertory serves to assert several levels of exclusiveness without negating the sense of inclusiveness within the *Jiangnan sizhu* community at large.

FIVE

Form

Chinese scholars often refer to several "systems" (*xitong*) among the Eight Great Pieces.[1] Seven are said to belong to the "Liuban" system, "Sanliu" system, or "Sihe" system; "Huanle Ge" is an independent piece. Pieces within a system share common musical material and/or origins; interrelationships also exist among pieces in different systems.

ORGANIZATIONAL PRINCIPLES

Most of the Eight Great Pieces are developed from one or more smaller musical units known as *qupai*. In previous chapters, I have used the word "tune" for these units, but *qupai* (literally "titled tune" or "titled song") does not have an exact English counterpart. The word *qupai* is most commonly encountered in writings on *Kunqu* opera. *Qupai* in *Kunqu* are distinct melodic units with titles which may be set to a variety of texts. While the skeleton melody is relatively fixed, a *qupai* will be realized differently for different texts, operas, and roles, and individual singers' interpretations also vary, even in performances of the same scene. Some of the *qupai* used in *Jiangnan sizhu* may have been derived from *Kunqu qupai*, but they are more often referred to as "instrumental" (*qiyue*) *qupai*. If we understand a "piece" to be a self-contained musical unit that is performed as an entity and a "tune" to be a smaller archetypal musical unit that is the source of various pieces or portions of pieces, *qupai* usually function as tunes in *Jiangnan sizhu*. In this function, a *qupai* can also be thought of as a "theme" (as in "theme and variations"). However, in other contexts, the original *qupai* is not merely a theoretical musical source but is performed alone in a form close to its archetype. Thus, an instrumental *qupai* may be a piece in its own right, the source of a section of a piece, or the source of another complete piece.

Over the course of time, an instrumental *qupai* may be transformed into many different pieces, some of which have little apparent relationship to each other or to the original *qupai*. In many cases, these transformations or metamorphoses of musical material are the result of melodic variation or modal shift, but in *Jiangnan sizhu*, they usually involve some type of what may be called "expansion." When expanded, the original melody is slowed in tempo and, as the original notes become farther apart temporally, other notes are interpolated. The result is a new piece that may have sixteen or more notes corresponding to each note in the original *qupai*.

Chinese scholars call this process *fangman jiahua*, "making slow and adding flowers," but many *Jiangnan sizhu* musicians simply refer to it as *kuochong*, literally "expansion." Expansion may be metrically strict (in which each beat of the original *qupai* corresponds to a given metrical unit in the new piece) or free (in which the correspondence is not consistent and/or some phrases are deleted or interpolated). In some cases, expansion may be metrically strict but melodically free.[2]

An instrumental *qupai* on which expanded pieces are based is sometimes referred to as the "mother tune" *(muqu)*, with the implication that all the pieces derived from it are offspring. This term will be adopted here for the purposes of analysis with the understanding that the source "tune" may also sometimes be performed as a self-sufficient "piece." The concept of a mother tune used as the source for a variety of pieces is in some ways similar to the *cantus firmus* in Western music. However, the resemblance is only superficial: in the Chinese case, the new pieces usually evolve through aural transmission rather than being consciously designed by an individual composer, and the original tune is not actually played along with the expanded or elaborated version. A somewhat closer analogy is found in the Javanese concept of *irama* and the Thai concept of *thăw*:

> In essence, both *thăw* and *irama* represent a process of expansion and/or contraction allowing a single piece to assume different lengths, instrumentation, different styles and degrees of improvisation, and consequently, different meanings and ethos. . . . So different in sound are the different expansions and contractions of the same piece that the Thais make a contest of guessing the piece, while the Javanese ascribe contrasting moods and differing degrees of refinement to the different expansions and contractions. In both *thăw* and *irama*, one begins with a cycle of *x* number of beats (always divisible by two), and then the cycle either expands by doubling or contracts by halving. (Becker 1980:454)

In both China and Java, a single piece may contain cycles of the germinal musical unit played sequentially with different degrees of expansion, and the level of semi-improvisational input is high. However, in Javanese *gamelan*, the underlying skeletal melody known as the *balungan* is still heard on certain instruments in the expanded treatments. Even when the skeletal melody itself is played in an expanded form (as in *irama* 3 and 4), the surface level of the music involves instruments playing eight or sixteen notes for each note of the theme. In *Jiangnan sizhu*, all instruments play at close to the same melodic density (number of notes per unit of time). In an expanded treatment of the mother tune, the original melody is heard only in the minds of musicians and knowledgeable listeners.

Cipher notation will be used for the analysis in this chapter (a brief introduction to the notation can be found in appendix B). Although no type of notation is without drawbacks, this system makes correlations and discrepancies in the structural tones of multiple examples readily apparent: in this analysis, pitch-class equivalents are more significant than similarities in register or melodic curve. In addition, since *Jiangnan sizhu* is among the most pentatonic of Chinese musics, particularly with regard to the tones of the skeletal melodies, the fourth and seventh scale degrees function much like non-scalar tones or "accidentals"; in cipher notation, their occurrence is immediately apparent. Passages in which the seventh scale degree is prominent usually represent a type of temporary shift in tonal materials known as *jiezi*, "borrowed note," where one scale degree is substituted for another.[3] In the examples of *jiezi* which occur in *Jiangnan sizhu*, the first scale degree is replaced by the seventh or, more rarely, the third degree by the fourth.[4]

THE "LIUBAN" SYSTEM

"Zhonghua Liuban" and "Man Liuban" are both derived from the mother tune "Lao Liuban" (Old six beats). Although there are many variants of this tune, some of which are named "Lao Baban" (Old eight beats), the *Jiangnan sizhu* pieces in the "Liuban" system are derived from a variant that is sixty metrical units in length, and the most convincing explanation for the title is that the "six" is a contraction of this "sixty" (Shen Fengquan, personal communication).[5] Example 5.1 gives this variant of "Lao Liuban" as it is found in the Guofeng collection of *Jiangnan sizhu* notation (1939:31) along with two earlier notated sources (Rong Zhai's "Shiliuban" and Li Fangyuan's "Xunfeng Cao"). It can be seen that all three share most of the same material but that "Xunfeng Cao" lacks a section in the middle while "Shiliuban" has a different ending.

Example 5.2 illustrates how "Lao Liuban" is related to "Zhonghua Liuban" and "Man Liuban" through the process of expansion. The three

a) 3 3 6 2 |1   5 6 |1   6 1|1 3 2 |3 3 6 2 |1   5 6 |1   3 2 |1 6 5 |

b) 3 3 6 2 |1   5 6 |1   6 1|1 3 1 |3 3 6 2 |1   5 6 |1   3 2 |1 6 5 |

c) 3 3|6 2 |1 | 5 6 |1 | 3 2 |1 3|2 |3 3 |6 2 |1 | 5 6 |1 |3 2 |1 6|5 |

a) 5 5 3 3|5 5 2 | 3 2 1 1|6 1 2| 3 2 2 3|5   5 6|i   6 i|i 6 5 |

b) 5 5 3 3|5 3 2 | 2 3 2 1|6 1 2| 3 2 2 3|5   5 6|i   6 i|i 6 5 |

c) 5 5|3 3|5 5|2 | 3 2|1 6|6 1|2 | 3 2|2 3|5 | 5 6|i | 6 i|i 6|5 |

a) 5 6 5 3|2   2 3|5   5 6|5 3 2 | 2 5 5 2|3 2 1 | 6 1 5 6|1 3 2 |

b) 5 6 5 3|2   2 3|5   5 6|5 3 2 | 2 5 5 2|3 2 1 | 6 1 5 6|1 3 2 |

c) 5 6|6 3|2 3|5 |

a) 2 5 5 2|3 2 1 | 3 3 6 2|1   5 6|1   3 2|1 6 5 ||

b) 2 5 5 2|3 2 1 | 6 1 1 2|3 6 5 3|2   6 5|3 2 1 |

c) 2 5|5 2|3 2|1 | 3 3|6 2|1 |5 6|1 |3 2|1 6|5 ||

b) 7 6 5 6|1 3 2| 2 5 5 2|3 2 1 ||

Sources: a) Guofeng (1939:31); b) Yang and Cao (1979:7); c) Li (1895)

EXAMPLE 5.1 a) "Lao Liuban," b) "Shiliuban," and c) "Xunfeng Cao"

excerpts represent the first phrase of "Lao Liuban" (skeleton melody, as in example 5.1a) and the corresponding phrases of "Zhonghua Liuban," and "Man Liuban" (both prescriptive *dizi* notation). In general, expansion is conceived of as being in a ratio of two, four, eight, or sixteen notes to one in the mother tune, although, as can be seen here, the actual melodies played on any instrument rarely maintain a constant density. At the conceptual level, "Zhonghua Liuban" and "Man Liuban" can be thought of as threefold (8/1) and fourfold (16/1) expansions, respectively, of the mother tune. That is, although the melodies of the expanded pieces do not move at a constant density, for much of their melodic motion eight notes in "Zhonghua Liuban" and sixteen notes in

a) 3 _____ 3   6 _____ 2 |1

b) 3 - | 3 -2 5 - 3 | 6 - | 2̣ 5 5 32 | i i

c) 3 - 35 2 | 3-5 6i 5624 3653 | 6 56i7 6i57 656i | 223 54 356i 5235 | i -i

a)   5 _____ 6 |

b) 0 3 5 | 2 3 2 7 6 -i 2 3 | 5 -6 3 2 | 5 3 0 2̇3 |

c) i6i2 32̇53 | 2356 32̇i5 6i23 2i6i | 5 -i 3235 6i36 | 5 356i 5632 6532 |

a) 1   6 _____ 1 |

b) i2 i 7 6 6 2 | i7 6 i 2 2i | 32 35 6 2 i 3 | 5-6 i 7 6 -2 3 5 |

c) ii i2i7 656i 2i62̣ | i 656i 25 2i | 3-2 35 6i2̇3 i76i | 5-6 i32̇i 6765 3432 |

a) 1   3   2 |

b) 1 1 0 i 2̇ | 6 7 6 5 1 7 6 1 | 2 35 1 5 6 1 | 2 6i 5i 65 |

c) i-2̇ 65 i2̇35 2̇i65 | 3235 62̇i2̇ 56i7 6235 | 2 -2 3432 1231 | 2 23 5-4 2354 |

Sources: a) Guofeng (1939:31); b) Gan (1985:93); c) Shanghai (1960:47)

EXAMPLE 5.2 a) "Lao Liuban," b) "Zhonghua Liuban," c) "Man Liuban"

"Man Liuban" (as notated here, these are sixteenth notes) correspond to each note (eighth note pulse) in "Lao Liuban."

"Zhonghua Liuban" is most often played with an incomplete repeat: the first and last eight metrical units are played only once, while the intervening forty-four metrical units may be repeated. A third repetition or "cycle" may also be played; the third cycle is invariably played at an accelerated tempo with a corresponding decrease in melodic density per beat unit. Although referred to simply as the "third time" (*di san bian*) of "Zhonghua Liuban," it is actually a melodically distinct less-expanded (or more contracted) derivative of "Zhonghua Liuban," very similar to the version known as "Kuaihua Liu" (Fast ornamented six). Written and oral sources refer to the playing of "Man Liuban," "Zhonghua Liuban," "Kuaihua Liu," "Kuai Liuban" (Fast six beats), and "Lao Liuban" in an uninterrupted sequence known collectively as "Wudai Tongtang" (Five generations in the same hall). Although I have never heard a performance or recording of this treatment (informants state that it is too long), on two occasions I did hear "Man Liuban," "Zhonghua Liuban," and the accelerated third cycle of "Zhonghua Liuban" linked together in a similar manner. All of these treatments illustrate the principle of sequential cyclical repetition of derivations from a mother tune, progressing from expanded to compact.

As the titles illustrate, this progression is also conceived of as moving from slow to fast. However, the absolute melodic density may actually stay relatively constant; what does accelerate is the tempo of the occurrence of *ban*, which here refers to what might be called "strong beats" or, more precisely, the beats (whether or not they are marked or emphasized in a performance) corresponding to the beginning of a metrical unit. As mentioned previously, all of these "Lao Liuban" derivatives have sixty metrical units; in a compact form, these units correspond to beats or pulses. In "Lao Liuban" there are two of these beats per measure (as notated in example 5.1 and 5.2). In an expanded form, secondary beats may be added to subdivide the metrical units. These secondary beats are called *yan*, "eyes." The combination of *ban* and *yan* in a piece results in a metrical pattern called *banyan*, which is analogous to a time signature. An expanded version of a piece may be described as "one *ban*, one *yan*," and a much more expanded version as "one *ban*, seven *yan*." In traditional *gongchepu* notation, this distribution of beats is indicated by symbols next to the notes. In cipher or staff notation, it is represented by the placement of barlines and choice of note values.

In theory, a *ban* pulse in *Jiangnan sizhu* is marked by a stroke of the clapper and a *yan* pulse by the stroke of the drum or woodblock. However, the music is often played without percussion; in this case, the acceleration of the occurrence of *ban* pulses is not manifested in the music itself but is sensed by the experienced performer and knowledgeable listener. Even when percussion is used, it tends to perform a time-keeping function rather than serving as a strict indicator of the *banyan* pattern. Thus, discrepancies in the *banyan* structure are found among various performances and notated versions of a given piece. "Zhonghua Liuban," for example, may be found in various collections with time signatures of 2/4, 4/4 and 8/4, and the percussion pattern played may be either "one *ban*, one *yan*" or "one *ban*, three *yan*."

"HUANLE GE"

"Huanle Ge," like the "Liuban" pieces, uses the principle of expansion. Unlike those pieces, however, the expanded versions of the mother tune have not acquired independence as separate pieces. Rather, the complete piece consists of two or three cycles of a single musical unit, moving from expanded to compact. Early notation (Guofeng 1939) gives only the mother tune, which corresponds to the final cycle; modern notation also includes the expanded version. The form of the piece can be outlined as A₂ A₁ A. Example 5.3 gives the slow, expanded version (A₂) and the mother tune (A) for the first portion of "Huanle Ge." The optional middle section (A₁) is rarely, if ever, notated; in contemporary practice, it is an accelerated repeat of the first section rather than a section with a distinct melodic identity of its own.

Sources: a) Lu (1982:76); b) Guofeng (1939:39)

EXAMPLE 5.3 "Huanle Ge": a) expanded melody and b) mother tune

The principle of expansion is fundamentally a simple one. From examining musical notation, the relationships between compact and expanded forms of the pieces discussed above are easily seen, and "making slow and adding flowers" is widely taught in the conservatory setting as an easily grasped indigenous compositional device. It would be a mistake, however, to view the process as a mechanical one. "Zhonghua Liuban," "Man Liuban," and the slow section of "Huanle Ge" have acquired distinct melodic identities that a performer must learn as if they were individual pieces. Merely applying principles of expansion to the corresponding mother tunes could result in a myriad of results bearing little resemblance to the expanded versions actually played in *Jiangnan sizhu*. In particular, it can be observed that not all of the notes in the skeletal melody are preserved in the expanded version: in "Huanle Ge," for example, many of the notes corresponding to the second beat of each measure of the expanded version differ from those in the original. Because of their complex melodic identity, pieces or sections of pieces which are greatly expanded are considered to be difficult to learn. "Lao Liuban" can be memorized in a few minutes, but many hours are required to memorize "Zhonghua Liuban," and many performers who have played the latter piece for years still cannot perform it without notation.

THE "SANLIU" SYSTEM

"Sanliu" is an example of what Chinese scholars call the "circulating" formal structure (*xunhuan qu*), which can be thought of as a kind of "inverted rondo." As in the rondo form, a recurring "refrain" alternates with contrasting "interludes"; in the Chinese form, the piece begins with an interlude rather than with the refrain. The refrain is known as the *hetou* (literally "together head"; in this context, "head" is probably a meaningless suffix), and this name often appears in musical notation for "Sanliu" as a directive to repeat the refrain. In "Sanliu," relationships also exist among some of the interlude sections, so the overall structure has been described as a "circulating form with elements of theme and variations" (Li Minxiong 1982:318). The piece is in eleven sections, the first ten roughly equal in length, the last a shorter coda. The formal structure can be outlined as A B C B C_1 B D B C_2 B E, where the B sections are verbatim repeats of the *hetou* and the C sections variants of each other. "Man Sanliu," as mentioned in the previous chapter, is a strict expansion of "Sanliu," but with the addition of a short passage called the *yaopian* between the first A and B sections.[6] The earliest notated source to which these two pieces are related is "Meihua Sannong," found in the Li Fangyuan 1895 collection. This relationship, widely acknowledged in writings on *Jiangnan sizhu* but not fully explicated in print, is an interesting one and is deserving of some elaboration here.

Figure 5.1 outlines the formal structures of "Sanliu," "Man Sanliu,"

FIGURE 5.1
"Sanliu," "Man Sanliu," and "Meihua Sannong"

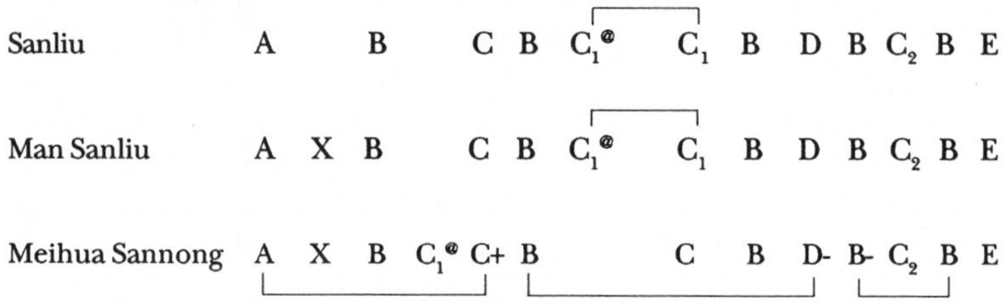

and "Meihua Sannong." The section labeled "X" in this outline has no corresponding section in "Sanliu," but it is similar to the *yaopian* section found in "Man Sanliu." The section labeled "C+" in "Meihua Sannong" includes ten measures with no counterpart in "Sanliu." The last five measures in "Sanliu's" D and the first eight in the following B are not found in "Meihua Sannong," and the corresponding sections are therefore labeled as "D-" and "B-." Finally, a brief passage played at the beginning of C_1 ($C_1^@$) in "Sanliu" is moved to the beginning of the first C in "Meihua Sannong." This passage is included as part of the C_1 section in notation for "Sanliu" (indicated by the bracket linking $C_1^@$ and C_1 in figure 5.1), but its different placement in the two pieces indicates that it could also be considered as a separate section in its own right.[7] In summary, the overall formal scheme of the two pieces is similar, but "Sanliu" is somewhat more regular, while "Meihua Sannong" includes a shortened variant (B–) of the *hetou* (which is never varied in "Sanliu").[8] The original notation for "Meihua Sannong" is arranged in four sections (the last functioning as a short coda) with subtitles, which are indicated by horizontal brackets in figure 5.1. Most notations for "Sanliu" indicate verbatim repeat of the B section; although individual sections are not given subtitles in most contemporary notation, the periodic indications to repeat the *hetou* effectively mark the eleven sections of the piece.

THE "SIHE" SYSTEM

Two sections of "Sihe Ruyi" and "Xingjie" are derived from the same two *qupai*. In addition, both of these pieces, along with "Yunqing," share melodic material with the string-wind-percussion piece "Luogu Sihe." Therefore, all four of these pieces are often referred to by scholars as belonging to the "Sihe" system.

"Luogu Sihe" is a *taoqu; tao,* among its several meanings, is a measure word indicating a set of something. In a musical context, a *taoqu* can be thought of as a "suite," composed of any number of different sections, derived from the same or different *qupai,* usually with individual subtitles, and often contrasting in tempo or instrumentation. "Huanle Ge" is a relatively simple *taoqu* in which the sections are all based on the same tune, as is the archaic "Liuban"-derived "Wudai Tongtang." "Sanliu" also has elements of a *taoqu,* although its sections are relatively brief and lack metrical contrast and (other than the coda and the indication *hetou*) individual subtitles. The published notation for "Luogu Sihe" (Shanghai Qunzhong 1960) is in eleven sections, all except one having one or more subtitles. Five of the sections are for percussion only, while the remainder are for melodic instruments and percussion.

The seventh and eighth sections are the two *qupai* also found in the "Sihe Ruyi" and "Xingjie." These two pieces are also examples of *taoqu*, "Sihe Ruyi" having four main sections and "Xingjie" three. The three sections of "Xingjie" are related to the second, third, and fourth sections of "Sihe Ruyi."

The opening of "Xingjie" and the second section of "Sihe Ruyi" both bear the title "Xiao Baimen" (Small worshiping at the gate), which is often considered to be an alternate title for "Xiao Kaimen" (Small opening the gate). "Xiao Kaimen" is one of the most popular *qupai* titles in China and is found in the repertory of a wide variety of musical genres. In addition, variant titles are common, including "Da Kaimen" (Large opening the gate) and other titles that refer to the tonal center or mode ("Wuzi Kaimen," "Chezi Kaimen," etc.). Unlike "Lao Liuban," the titles "Kaimen" and "Baimen" are applied to many different tunes that appear to be melodically unrelated; even notated skeletal tunes specifically named "Xiao Kaimen" often appear to bear only the most tenuous relationship to each other. According to Li Minxiong, all the variants of "Kaimen" or "Baimen" that he has examined can be analyzed as related melodically, but others believe that "Kaimen" is a "floating title" that has been applied to a variety of unrelated melodies. This subject is a complex one, and it remains to be resolved whether all tunes named "Kaimen"— or said to be derived from it—are related to each other, whether all

```
a)  6    5    3    5   |6    i    6    5    235i 6532 1232 121

b)  6    i    5    3   |6    5    6    i  | 356i 6532 1    -  |

c)  6i23 1653 6   - 53| 6i23 1653 6   - 12| 356i 5235 1 -2 1  |


a)  6 5  3235| 6   2-1 6161 2123| 6 i3 23i6 55 532| 1-2 121

b)  6 2  i 7 | 6   - 5| 6i53       6 0  0 3| 5356    i -7 |

c)  6i23 1653 6   - 5| 6 -5        6 -i      5 -6    i327 |


a)  6    5    3    2 3| 5 53 235  0  i2 6165| 3532 1612 3 -1 6 5|

b)  6 -i 5645| 3        | 5 -6 i7| 6 -i 5 4  |3 5 2 5| 3 -2     |

c)  6i23 2i65 3   - 23| 5 -6 i327 6 -i 5 2  |3 5 2612  3    -  |
```

Sources: a) Li Minxiong (unpublished); b) Lu (1982:66); c) Shanghai (1960:5)

EXAMPLE 5.4 "Xiao Baimen"/"Xiao Kaimen": a) "Shuang He Feng," b) "Sihe Ruyi," and c) "Xingjie"

"Baimen" tunes and derivatives are related to each other, and whether all or some in each group are related to any or all in the other group.

"Xiao Baimen" is a far less common title than "Xiao Kaimen," and it is best known as found in the "Sihe" system of *Jiangnan sizhu*. It is impossible to say just how "Baimen" fits into the "Kaimen"/"Baimen" complex, but it is clear that at least one piece said to be specifically based on "Xiao Kaimen" is clearly related to "Xiao Baimen": the *dizi* piece from Shandong province entitled "Shuang He Feng" (A pair of phoenixes). Example 5.4 compares a portion of this piece with the corresponding portions of "Xiao Baimen" as found in notation for "Sihe Ruyi" and "Xingjie."

Similarities among the three examples are clearly present, but they are much less straightforward metrically than those in the "Liuban" pieces and may change from one measure to the next. All of these examples are of anonymous authorship and have evolved through a process in which aural transmission plays a major role. Such irregular stretching and contracting of musical passages may be the result of accident, conscious innovation, or a combination of factors. At times the alignment of the musical notation in this example may appear contrived, suggesting excessive manipulation for the purposes of establishing relationships among the three pieces. However, Chinese musicologists often acknowledge even more obscure relationships.[9] All of the melodies in example 5.4 are prescriptive performance notation for *dizi*, and all have undergone the process of expansion. Since there is no standard mother tune for "Kaimen," it is impossible to say which of these examples corresponds most closely to the "original." However, it is clear from these examples that, unlike "Zhonghua Liuban," "Man Liuban," "Huanle Ge," and "Man Sanliu," the expansion process found here is far from being metrically strict.

The second *qupai* contained in "Luogu Sihe" that is also shared by "Xingjie" and "Sihe Ruyi" is called "Yu Elang" (Jade moth). This is the second section of "Xingjie" and the third section of "Sihe Ruyi." Unlike "Liuban" or "Kaimen" it is not a widely known *qupai;* although a musically unrelated old Chinese folk song bears the same title, the only non-*Jiangnan sizhu* example I have found in which "Yu Elang" appears as the name of an instrumental *qupai* is in Taoist music from Shanghai. Example 5.5 compares the skeletal melodies of "Yu Elang" as found in "Sihe Ruyi," "Luogo Sihe," and "Xingjie." All three examples correspond closely in the middle portion. "Sihe Ruyi" and "Luogo Sihe" share an opening passage which, after the first few measures, is quite similar, and they appear to represent a more complete version of "Yu Elang" than that found in "Xingjie." The conclusion of the "Sihe Ruyi" version, which is not contained in the other two pieces, will be discussed later.

The third section of "Xingjie" and the fourth section of "Sihe Ruyi" are also loosely related. Many passages in these sections of the two pieces are similar, but others differ, and each has interpolated passages not found in the other. However, there are enough corresponding passages

a) 32 1653| 2   1653|2 1 5| 62i6 55| 06 5356| i2 6i65| 43 52| 3532 i i| 02

b)   6 12 5356| 121   0|112 36543| 22 0| 5 56 17| 6 5   43| 52 3532| 161 0 |

c)

a) 7276| 5356 i i| 02 33| 1653 2 |1653 2| 5453 2 | i5 62i6| 535   5453|2

b) 7 76 5356| 161 0 | 332 |1235 2-3|1235 2| 5643 2-3|15 6216| 535 0| 1235 2 |
                                                      |15 6216| 565 0| 3 5 32 |

c)   33 1 3| 2   1653|2 5653|2   15| 62i6 5-6| 5 5653 353|

a) 5453| 2   55| 2 5 5321| 61 6| 77 6| 3 5   6| 77 6 | 36   53| 2 02| 02 03| 2

b) 5643 2 .|| 35 3532| 1 1 61| 6 77| 6 3 5 ||: 6 77| 6-5 35:|| 53 2| 02 02| 13 2|
    1235 232 ·||

c) 5653 25   3 5 3 | 5 1 61| 6 77| 6 3235| 6 77| 6   36 | 53 2| 32 02| 03 2 |

a) 33| 31 2| 53 31| 2 35| 3532 11| 6 1   6 | 113 212| 2532 55| 0i 6i65| 356i 6532 |

b) 35 31| 2 53| 51 2| 35 3532| 11 6512 6 ||

c) 33 31| 2 53| 31 2| 35 3 2 |11 6 1   6 ||

a) i 1653| 2 7276| 5356 i2| i5 67| 6 ||

Sources: a) Guofeng (1939:18); b) Shanghai (1960:5); c) Guofeng (1939:13)

EXAMPLE 5.5 "Yu Elang": a) "Sihe Ruyi," b) "Luogu Sihe," c) "Xingjie"

(shown in example 5.6) to suggest that this section of both pieces evolved from a common ancestor. Dissimilar passages are not shown in this example; the numbers in parentheses (such as "29 mm.") indicate the number of measures omitted.

In "Sihe Ruyi," this section is subtitled "Tou Mai." (*Tou* means "head," here implying "first.") *Mai* means "to sell," but in this context it suggests "to show off" (as in the expression *mai guai*, meaning "to show off one's talent"), referring to the solo passages played by each instrument in turn.[10] Later in the section, subtitles indicate the passages called "Second *Mai*" and "Third *Mai*" (noted in example 5.6). These three passages are also

a) (29 mm.) 16 51│66 05│46 52│33 05│(2 mm.) 16 51│67 6 │   06 06│07

b) (9 mm.) 16 51│62 16│33 52│35 6 │   16 51│62 16│(7 mm.) 06 06│07

a) 6│33 52│3 35│3532 11│61 62 │ 16 62 │ 16 16│12 36│32 16│12 35│32 11│61 6│

b) 6│33 52│3 35│3 2 11│61 6 ‖:16 62.‖ 16 16│12 35│32 16│12 35│32 11│61 6│

a) (8 mm.) 61 6│2 1│ 2 1│ 11 02│3 36│53 2 │(3 mm.) 16 51 66│02 16│

b) (18 mm.) 61│6 26│16 26│16‖ 11 02 3 ‖36 53 23│   11 61 6 02 16
                                 :51 02 3:

a) 51 66│04 36│52 33│   04 36│52 33│02 16│51 67│   6 06│

b) 51 66 05│43 52│33 (2 mm.) 05│43 52│33 02 16 51│66 (12 mm.) 6 06

                                                        [2nd "Mai"]
a) 06 07│6 33│52 3│55 35│21 61│6 16│62 1 6│ 12 35│32 11│61 6│(5 mm.)

b) 06 07 6│33 52│3 35│32 11│61 6│16 62│16 16│12 35│32 11│61 6│(6 mm.)

a) 77│6 35│6 77│6 35│6 77│6 36│53 2│02 02│03 2│33 31│2 53│31 2│55 35│

b) 77 6│35 6│77 6│35 6│77 6│36 53│2 02│02 03│2 33│31 2│53 31│2 35│32

a) 21 61│6 2│ 1 2│ 1 (4 mm.) 61 6│16 62│16 62│16 12│35 32│16

b) 11 61 6│02 16│02 16│(6 mm.) 61│6 16│62 16│62 16│12 35│32 1 │

    [3rd "Mai"]
a) (26 mm.) 2│ 1 2 1 11│02 35│ 3 0‖

b) (11 mm.) 26 16│26 16│11 02 3 ‖

Dissimilar passages are omitted, with the number of measures left out indicated in parentheses (mm.).

Sources: a) Guofeng (1939:18); b) Guofeng (1939:13)

EXAMPLE 5.6 a) "Sihe Ruyi" ("Mai") and b) "Xingjie" (third section) sometimes referred to as the first, second, and third *sai*, meaning "to compete." In the first *mai* or *sai* passage, the solos overlap: that is, the second instrument joins the first for the last few measures, then plays the passage by itself, and is in turn joined by the third instrument for the last two measures of its solo. There is no overlapping in the second and third *mai* passages.

In "Xingjie," this section has no subtitle. In practice, three cycles of this section are usually played, moving from expanded to compact (slow, medium, fast). The very end of the section, however, is played only once and functions as a coda. If all three cycles of this section are played, it is approximately twice as long in performance time as the first two sections combined.

In contemporary performance practice, the *mai* section of "Sihe Ruyi" is followed by a fast cycle of the third section of "Xingjie." Thus, in the most common treatments of these pieces, "Sihe Ruyi" contains two sections that are closely related to "Xingjie," followed by another section that is loosely related to "Xingjie," followed by a verbatim borrowing of the end of "Xingjie" (acknowledged in the notation with the directions to "play 'Xingjie Kuaiban'"). Finally, both pieces may add a short section that is inserted a few measures before the end of the coda. This section is known as "Xiao Liuban" (Small six beats), an abbreviated version of "Lao Liuban" that may be played one, two, or three times.

In addition to the sections closely related to "Xingjie," "Sihe Ruyi" also has an additional section at the beginning of the piece. Although this section is often given the subtitle "Sihe Ruyi," it is in fact very closely related to the first two sections of "Sanliu." This can be clearly seen in the comparison of the skeletal melodies given in example 5.7.[11]

This section of "Sihe Ruyi" is played in an expanded form, so it actually closely resembles "Man Sanliu." This fact is widely recognized by performers, who describe the first section of "Sihe Ruyi" as "'Man Sanliu' without the *yaopian*." An additional distinction is that "Sihe Ruyi" opens with a *dizi* cadenza built on the first three notes of the piece. This cadenza is played three times and is called "Fenghuang Sandian Tou" (The phoenix nods its head three times).

Additional relationships also exist between "Sihe Ruyi" and "Sanliu." A comparison of the skeletal melodies for the extension at the end of "Yu Elang" in "Sihe Ruyi" (end of example 5.5) and the *hetou* sections of "Sanliu" (last half of example 5.7b) shows that the two are nearly identical, with the former contracted by two measures. The melodic material in the C section of "Sanliu" is also contained in the "Yu Elang" section of "Sihe Ruyi." This material appears twice more in "Sihe Ruyi," in the second and third *mai* sections. As can be seen in example 5.8, the skeletal melodies from all three of the passages from "Sihe Ruyi" contain

a) 6̇2̣ 1̇1̣|1̇2̣ 6̇2̣|1̇2̣65 35 |3523 561̇|6̇1̣53 2|55 25 |5321 6̣1̣|6 11|3653

b) 6̇2̣ 1̇1̣|1̇2̣ 62|1 2 35 |2 3 5 1̇|6̇1̣53 2|565 323|5321 6̣1̣|6̣ — ‖

a) 11|3653 212|2532 51|5102 35|3523 535 |0̇1̇ 6̇1̣65|356̇1̇ 6532|1̇ 1̇653|
["Hetou"]
b) 11 3   212|2532 51|5102 35|3523 5355|0̇1̇ 6̇1̣65|356̇1̇ 6532|1̇ 1̇653|

a) 2̇ 7̇2̇76|5356 1̇2̇|1̇5 67|6 ‖

b) 2̇ 7̇2̇76|5356 1̇2̇|1̇5 67|6 ‖

Sources: a) Guofeng (1939:2); b) Guofeng (1939:17)

EXAMPLE 5.7 a) "Sihe Ruyi" (first section) and b) "Sanliu" (A and B)

additional melodic material interpolated in the middle, but the beginning of the "Sanliu" section is identical to all three "Sihe Ruyi" excerpts (except for the different arrangement of the bar lines), and the conclusion of the "Sanliu" section is also closely related (in one case identical) to the "Sihe Ruyi" excerpts.

One further similarity between "Sihe Ruyi" and "Sanliu" can also be found. The variant of the C section in "Sanliu," which has been called C₁,

a) 77 6|35 6|77 6|35 6|77 6|36 53|2 02|02 03|2 33|31 2|53 31|2 35|3532 11|6̣1̣ 6|

b) 77|6 35|6 77|6 35|6 77|6 36|53 2|02 02|03 2|33 31|2 53|31 2|55 3 5| 21 6̣1̣|6

c) 77|6 35|6 77|6 35|6 77|6 36|53 2|02 02|03 2|33 31|2 53|31 2|55 3 5| 21 6̣1̣|6

d) 77 6|35 6|77 6|35 6|77 6|36 5 2|3   35|3532 11|6̣1̣ 6‖

Sources: a) Guofeng (1939:18); b) Guofeng (1939:20); c) Guofeng (1939:21); d) Guofeng (1939:2)

EXAMPLE 5.8 "Sihe Ruyi" [a) "Yu Elang," b) second "Mai," and c) third "Mai"] and d) "Sanliu" (C)

has a parallel in the first *mai* section of "Sihe Ruyi" (see example 5.9). A comparison of these excerpts with those in example 5.8 shows the variant nature of the middle portion of this section that both C₁ and the first *mai* share.

a) 77 6| 77 6| 51 5102|3 51|5102 3|36 53|2 55|3 5 21|6̇1 6 |

b) 77 6|35 6|77 6|35 6|51 5102|3 51|5102 3|36 52|3 35|3532 11|6̇1 6 ‖

Sources: a) Guofeng (1939:19); b) Guofeng (1939:2)

EXAMPLE 5.9 a) "Sihe Ruyi" ("Mai") and b) "Sanliu" (C)

In summary, most of the skeletal melodic material in "Sanliu" (sections A, B, C, and C₁) has a counterpart in "Sihe Ruyi." In addition, since the latter portions of "Sihe Ruyi" and "Xingjie" are related, the C and C₁ sections also have their counterparts in the latter piece.

"Yunqing" is not directly related to any of the other Eight Great Pieces. However, it shares melodic material with "Luogu Sihe," so it is indirectly related to "Sihe Ruyi" and "Xingjie" and may be discussed as part of the "Sihe" system. "Luogu Sihe" includes a *qupai* entitled "Yunqing," but only a part of the *Jiangnan sizhu* "Yunqing" is based on this *qupai*. Example 5.10 shows the relationship between the "Luogu Sihe" *qupai* "Yunqing" and the corresponding section of the *Jiangnan sizhu* piece. As performed today, the *Jiangnan sizhu* "Yunqing" includes some repetition and variation of the material shown in example 5.10. The form of this treatment can be outlined as A B- B B B₁. The first B section is abbreviated, omitting the opening passage. The complete B is played twice, followed by a variation played at an accelerated tempo (not shown here, but identical in length to B). The A, B-, and B sections are marked in the example, as is the point in B which corresponds to the beginning of the B- section (indicated as [-]).

In addition, the unsubtitled section of "Luogu Sihe" preceding the *qupai* "Yunqing" corresponds closely to the latter portion of the *Jiangnan sizhu* "Yunqing." This relationship is shown in example 5.11. Thus, all the musical material in the *Jiangnan sizhu* piece "Yunqing" can be traced to "Luogu Sihe," but the ordering of the material is reversed. This resequencing is an example of yet another way in which preexistent musical material can be reshaped in the creation of new repertory. In the modern *Jiangnan sizhu* version of "Yunqing," this section also includes repetition, both complete and incomplete. Immediately after the last repeat of section B (B₁), the last seven measures of example 5.11 are played, followed by two complete playings of the entire section. If we label this unsubtitled section as "C," the complete structure of "Yunqing" can be outlined as A B- B B B₁ C- C C.

a) <u>6 56</u> <u>1 2 1</u> |<u>021</u> 6 | 6   <u>5 4</u> 3 |<u>0 3 0 5</u>|<u>56i7</u> 6 |6
   [A]
b) 6 <u>56</u>|<u>i6̇2̇6̇</u>|i̇ -| <u>i̇2̇</u> <u>65</u>|<u>i̇3̇2̇i̇</u> 65| <u>i̇2̇</u> <u>6765</u> <u>32</u> 3|0 3|0 5   7|6 <u>-5</u>|<u>665</u>|

a) 6   6 |<u>03 5</u> <u>32</u>|<u>5 5</u> <u>3 1</u> |<u>2-3 2</u> <u>-3</u>| <u>767</u> <u>07</u> | 7̇6̇
b) <u>665</u>| <u>6-5</u>| <u>665</u>| <u>6i̇</u> <u>54</u>| 3-2| <u>56</u> <u>35</u>| <u>32</u> <u>1235</u>| 2 -|<u>2̇3̇</u> <u>i̇7̇</u>|6 -|<u>7623̇</u> <u>2̇76̇</u>| <u>7-6</u>|

a) 7̇ |7̇ 7̇ | 0 2̇| 2̇   7 6 |<u>6535</u> 6 |
b) <u>77</u> <u>672̇3̇</u>| <u>7-6̇</u>| <u>7-6̇</u>| <u>7-6̇</u>|<u>767</u>| 0 2|7 <u>76̇</u>|<u>76</u> 7|0 2̇|<u>i̇6</u> <u>57</u>|6 <u>-5</u>|<u>66</u> <u>5</u>|<u>6-5</u>|

a) 6   <u>6 5</u> 6|<u>0 6</u>   <u>0 56</u>|<u>3567</u> <u>5635</u>| 2   <u>23</u>|<u>6 7 6 5</u> <u>32 3</u>|<u>0 3 0 5</u>|<u>5 2</u> <u>3-2</u> |
                                                   [B-]
b) <u>665</u>|<u>6i̇</u> <u>35</u> <u>665</u>| <u>665</u>| <u>665</u> | <u>6 i̇</u>   <u>5 3</u> |<u>21</u> 2 |<u>6i̇</u> <u>5765</u>| <u>32</u> 3|0 3|0 3|0 2|3 <u>21</u>|

a) <u>323</u> <u>0 6</u> |<u>5 3</u> 2 |<u>2 5</u> <u>35 32</u>|7̇6̇ <u>7̇ 7̇</u> 2|<u>7̇ 2</u> <u>76 57</u>|6   <u>76 72̇</u>|6
b) <u>32</u> <u>3</u>|0 <u>6i̇</u>|<u>57</u> <u>65</u>|<u>21</u> <u>35</u>|<u>23</u> <u>56</u>|<u>35</u> <u>32</u>|<u>76</u> 7|0 2̇|0 2̇|<u>i̇2̇</u> <u>57</u>|6 -|<u>76</u> <u>72̇</u>|<u>65</u> 6 |

a) <u>76 72̇</u>|6 <u>66</u> <u>7 5</u> <u>6-5</u>|<u>35</u> <u>35</u>|<u>65</u> <u>656</u>|<u>02̇</u> <u>2̇5</u>|6 <u>53</u>|<u>51</u> <u>232</u>|<u>06</u> <u>06</u>| <u>53</u> <u>23</u>|
       [B]
b) <u>76</u> 7 |<u>65</u> 6‖ <u>02̇</u> <u>i̇5</u>| <u>6 5</u> <u>35</u>|<u>35</u> <u>65</u>|<u>656</u> <u>02̇</u>|<u>i̇5</u> 6|<u>53</u> <u>51</u>|2   <u>06</u>|<u>06i̇</u> <u>53</u>|2

a) <u>5 3</u> <u>2123</u>|<u>55</u> <u>55</u>|<u>6765</u> <u>323</u>|<u>03</u> <u>05</u>|<u>52</u> 3 | <u>323</u> <u>067</u>|<u>6535</u> 2|<u>25</u> <u>32</u> |
                         [-]
b) <u>5763</u>|2   <u>55</u>|<u>05</u> <u>6765</u>|<u>323</u> <u>03</u>|<u>03</u> <u>02</u>|<u>321</u> <u>323</u>|<u>06i̇</u> <u>5 3</u>| 2 <u>256</u>|<u>3-2</u>

a) 7̇6̇7̇ <u>7̇2̇</u>|<u>7̇2̇</u> <u>7657</u>|6 <u>7672̇</u>|<u>6-5</u> <u>7672̇</u>|6
b) <u>767</u>|<u>02̇</u> <u>02̇</u>|<u>i̇ 5</u> 6|<u>7 7</u> <u>656</u>|<u>7672̇</u> <u>6-i̇</u>|

[-] indicates the point in B that corresponds to the beginning of the B- section

Sources: a) Shanghai (1960:70); b) Shanghai (1956:20)

EXAMPLE 5.10 "Yunqing": a) "Luogu Sihe" and b) *Jiangnan sizhu* version

a) 6560 0-2 |1276 5617 |6560 0 |0-5 356 |5624 323 |0 0 |0-5 356 | 5624 323 |0 0 |0 0-5 |

b) 0   2̇2̇ |1̇ 6 561̇7̇ |6   0 |55 3 61̇ |5 4   3 |0   5 | 3 61̇ 5645 |32

a) 35 3-532 |1216 5617 |6 6675 |6   6675 |6   6675 |6   1265 |1612 3654 |3432

b) 35 |3   2 1̇21̇6 |561̇7̇ |6 |1̇265 61̇23̇ |1̇265 61̇23̇ |1̇265 61̇23̇ |1̇265 1̇265 |3 5   3 2 |

a) 16 |1612 3 53 |2126 535 |01̇ 6 5 | 36   5-643 |2 5-643 |2 1263 |5 123 |1216 5617 ‖

b) 16 1 2 | 3253 2123 |5 5 01̇ |6765 361̇ |5   -3 2 |57 63 2 |1̇21̇6 5 |1̇3̇   2̇ 6 | 561̇7̇ 6‖

Sources: a) Shanghai (1960:69); b) Shanghai (1956:28)

EXAMPLE 5.11 "Yunqing": a) "Luogu Sihe" (untitled section) and b) *Jiangnan sizhu* version

INTERRELATIONSHIPS AMONG THE EIGHT GREAT PIECES

Figure 5.2 illustrates the interrelationships explicated in this chapter. Pieces within the circle are the Eight Great Pieces, while those outside are other repertory from which they are derived or to which they are related. The dotted line indicates a relatively loose relationship (the latter portions of "Xingjie" and "Sihe Ruyi"). The type and strength of the relationships among the Eight Great Pieces varies: "Sihe Ruyi," for example, is closely related to "Xingjie," directly related to the "Sanliu" system, and indirectly related to "Yunqing" and the "Liuban" system. By extension, all of the Eight Great Pieces except "Huanle Ge" are related to each other, but in some cases the relationships are rather distant, such as that between "Yunqing" and the "Liuban" system, which are linked through two indirect relationships with "Sihe Ruyi." In any case, the concept of four "systems" does not begin to express the complexity and variety of the linkages among pieces in this repertory.

In the diagram, shaded sections are those sometimes omitted in performance. These optional sections are: the middle section of "Huanle Ge"; the second and third cycles of "Zhonghua Liuban"; the first and second cycles of the third section of "Xingjie" and the "Xiao Liuban" section near the end of the piece; and the fast section of "Xingjie" (with or without "Xiao Liuban") at the end of "Sihe Ruyi." Aside from these variables, the formal structures of the Eight Great Pieces are fixed. However, as will be seen in the following two chapters, considerable latitude is found in the melodic realizations of these structures as played on different instruments by different individuals.

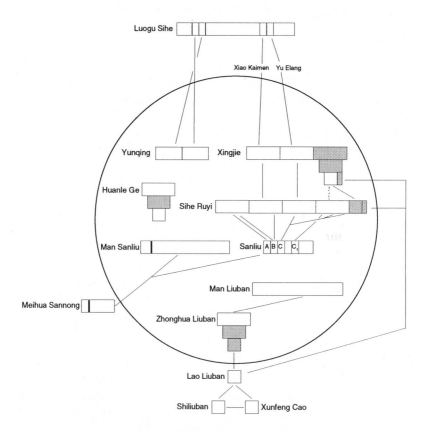

Solid lines indicate related pieces or sections. A dotted line indicates a relatively tenuous relationship. Shaded sections are optional. The Eight Great Pieces are those within the circle. The titles are arranged for economy of space, and no hierarchy is implied. The circle can be thought of as a sphere, with the pieces floating freely inside.

FIGURE 5.2 Interrelationships among the Eight Great Pieces (Graphics by Theodore Kwok)

SIX

Variation

Many *Jiangnan sizhu* musicians believe that each rendition of a piece is unique. Every player of a given instrument plays somewhat differently from other musicians, and his or her own playing will change from one occasion to the next. Musicians within the tradition speak of the practice of *jixing jiahua—jixing* meaning "spontaneous" or "improvised" and *jiahua* meaning "adding flowers"—ornamenting or decorating something, in this case a melody. The aesthetics of performance thus include the making of spontaneous musical choices at a relatively "micro" level. In a broader sense, *Jiangnan sizhu* musicians speak of the differences among players by observing that their styles (*fengge*) are different.

Although the English terms "improvisation," "embellishment," or "style" could conceivably be used to describe these differences, I believe that the phenomenon examined here is best treated as a kind of "variation," in the sense of "changing" or "making different" in some fashion. In Chinese instrumental music, there are several phenomena that could be or have been described as types of variation, including the following:

1. "Thematic variation" in which a melody or fragment is developed or transformed within a single piece, as in the treatment of the "C" sections in "Sanliu"
2. "Structurally related variation" in which new pieces or sections of pieces are derived from a preexistent mother tune, as in the "Liuban" system
3. "Formal variation" in which certain sections or cycles of a piece may be either performed or omitted, as in "Zhonghua Liuban" and "Sihe Ruyi"
4. "Modal variation" in which one or more scale degrees are altered throughout a piece or section, as in the "Baban" variant "Yangba Qu"
5. "Simultaneous variation" in which a commonly shared melody is realized in different ways on different instruments in an ensemble, producing a heterophonic texture
6. "Variation in treatment," such as the difference between "loud" and "soft" settings of a piece (some pieces can be played in either the loud or soft style)

89

a) 3   3   6   2 | 1   5   6 |

b) 3 - 3 2 5 3|6 - 6 i 2 - 3 2|i i 6 2 7 6 3|5 5 3 2 5 3 5 |

a) 1   6   1 | 1   3   2 |

b) i 6 2 1 3 2|3-5 6 i 5 i 632|1 1 2 3 6 5-3|2 - 3 2 6 5 4|

a) 3   3   6   2 | 1   5   6 |

b) 3 3 2 3 6 5 3|6 6 i 2 3 2|i i 6 2-i 6 3|5 3 2 5 3 5-6|

a) 1   3   2 | 1   6   5 |

b) i 6-2 1 3 212|3-5 6 i 5 i 632|i i 3 2 i 6 3|5 3 2 5 i 632|

a) 5   5   3   3 | 5   5   2 |

b) 5 5 i 6 2 i65|3 2 1 3 6 535|6 i65 3 6 5 3|2 2 3 2 1-2|

a) 3   2   1   1 | 6   1   2 |

b) 3 - 5-3 2-i 6 2|1 - 1 2 1 3 2 1|6 - - i 6-5 1 3|2 - 3 2 - 1-2|

a) 3   2   2   3 | 5   5   6 |

b) 3 5 3 2 1 2 3|2 6 5 4 3 3 5|6 i 3 2 5 i 6 3|5 5 i 6 3 32|

a) i   6   i | i   6   5 |

b) i 2 3 i 3 2 i|6 6 i 2 3 2|i i 3 2-i 6|5 3 2 5 i 6 3|

EXAMPLE 6.1 a) "Lao Liuban" and b) "Zhonghua Liuban" (skeleton melody)

EXAMPLE 6.1 (continued)

a) 5   6   5   3 | 2   2   3 |

b) 5 5 6 1̇ 3̇ 2̇ 1̇ | 6 1̇ 6 3 6 5 3 | 2 2 3 2-6 5 3 | 2 6 5 4 3 3 5 |

a) 5   3   5 | 5   3   2 |

b) 6-5 3 2 5 1̇ 6 3 | 5 5̇3̇2̇ 1̇ 3̇ 2̇1̇7 | 6 1̇65 3 6 5 3 | 2 2 3 2 5 3 |

a) 2   5   5   2 | 3   2   1 |

b) 2 1 2-3 5 3 5 | 6 1̇ 6 1 6 5 | 3 5̇5̇3̇ 2̇2̇1̇ 6 2 | 1 1 2 1 3 2 1 |

a) 6   1   5   6 | 1   3   2 |

b) 6 6 2̇ 1̇ 2̇1̇765-6 1̇-7 6-5 3 2 | 1 1-2 3 5 3 | 2 2 3 2 5 3 |

a) 2   5   5   2 | 3   2   1 |

b) 2 1 2-3 5 3-5 | 6 1̇-7 6 1̇ 6 5 | 3 5̇5̇3̇ 2-1 6 2 | 1 1 2 1 3 2 5 |

a) 3   3   6   2 | 1   5   6 |

b) 3 3 2̇ 3 6 5 3 | 6 6 1̇ 2̇ 3 2̇ | 1̇ 1̇ 6 2̇-1̇ 6 3 | 5 3 2 5 3 5-6 |

a) 1   3   2 | 1   6   5 |

b) 1̇ 6 2 1 3 2̇1̇2̇ | 3-5 6 1̇ 5 1̇ 6̇3̇2̇ | 1̇ 1̇ 3̇ 2̇ 1̇ 6 3 | 5 - - - |

Sources: a) Guofeng (1939:31); b) author's interpretive transcription

7. "*Liupai* variation" in which a piece appears in different forms as transmitted by different teachers or musical lineages called *liupai* (schools of performance); sometimes, this is also a type of regional variation

8. "Regional variation" in which a piece appears in different forms in different parts of China, as in the Jiangnan and Shandong variants of "Xiao Kaimen"/"Xiao Baimen"

The differences among musicians' renditions of a piece can be referred to as "individual variation." R. Anderson Sutton has used this term in his studies of Javanese *gamelan* music and defines it to include "1) variation within a single performance by one individual, 2) variation between performances by one individual, and 3) variation between performances by different individuals" (1982:246–47). Individual variation, then, is a concept that conveniently encompasses variation both by and among individuals. Examined here are examples from different performers and from one performer playing on different occasions. These examples are excerpts from "Zhonghua Liuban" as played on the *dizi* and *erhu,* the leading melodic instruments in the ensemble.[1]

The first question to ask in examining individual variation in "Zhonghua Liuban" is "What happens?" Aural analysis provides a partial answer, and transcription of multiple renditions provides visual evidence of the piece's surface structure. The next question to ask is "What remains the same and what changes?" From the answers to these questions we can begin to establish the identity of the piece—that is, what must be present for "Zhonghua Liuban" to be "Zhonghua Liuban"—and understand the parameters and type of individual variation accepted within the *Jiangnan sizhu* tradition. A further step in the investigation may also be possible: to establish clusters of individual renditions which share traits or groups of traits at various levels.

At the broadest level, "Zhonghua Liuban" is very rarely linked with any other piece in performance, but one or two additional cycles of the piece—the last played at an accelerated tempo—may be added. The skeletal structure of the piece, with or without the repeats, which occur at predetermined points is always a metrically strict expansion of "Lao Liuban." At a level of greater specificity, when the pattern of strong-beat notes (the first and third quarter notes of each measure) which correspond to those of the mother tune is examined, it is clear that all instruments tend to converge on the same pitch classes (notes and their octave equivalents). Thus, despite the prevailing heterophonic texture of the music, there is a strong tendency toward multi-octave unison on the strong beats.

Most of the pitch classes of the strong-beat notes are identical to those of the mother tune, but there are a significant number of divergences. While "Zhonghua Liuban" is clearly linked to the source melody, its identity has come to include mandatory deviations from the original. In example 6.1 the tones of "Lao Liuban" are aligned with their corresponding tones in "Zhonghua Liuban." The melody given here for "Zhonghua Liuban" is my own suggested outline and is what could be called an "interpretive transcription." That is, it is more skeletal than what is actually realized on any instrument, but it still shows some of the commonly shared melodic motion that helps give the piece its identity. While not every instrument will play these tones, analysis of prescriptive notation and aural analysis of recorded performances suggests that this skeletal melody indicates the most likely choices of tones to be played.

VARIATION AMONG PERFORMERS

The underlying melodic structure of "Zhonghua Liuban," a structure that both links it closely to the mother tune from which it is derived and distinguishes it from all other related pieces, is shown in example 6.1. Example 6.2 shows some of the surface structure of the piece, what is actually performed and heard rather than sensed or understood. This example is a parsed score for a small section of "Zhonghua Liuban" played by four different *dizi* performers: Cai Cide, Dong Kejun, Jin Minggao, and Lu Chunling. All are well-known *Jiangnan sizhu dizi* players, and each is recognized as having developed an individual style.

The section transcribed corresponds to the last two lines on the first page of example 6.1. In the mother tune, this section is both the midpoint of the piece and the point where the melody reaches its highest pitch level, and it can be considered the "high tide" (*gaochao*) or climax of the piece. The performances on which the transcriptions are based consisted of two or three cycles of the piece, and the multiple lines for each player (such as a1, a2, and a3) represent the same section of the piece played two or three times.[2] Cai and Lu play three cycles of the piece, while Dong and Jin each play two.[3]

The third cycle features a considerable increase in tempo and corresponding simplification of the melodic line; for the moment, only the first two lines of each player's performance will be examined. As mentioned previously, the notes on the strong beats (beats one and three of every measure) are consistent among all performers, but less of a consensus exists on the weak beats. Beat four of measure 28, for example, shows

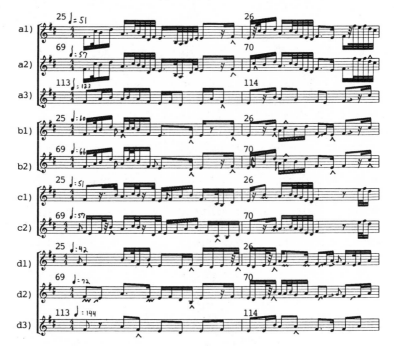

EXAMPLE 6.2 "Zhonghua Liuban" *(dizi)*: performed by a) Cai Cide, b) Dong Kejun, c) Jin Minggao, and d) Lu Chunling

EXAMPLE 6.2 (continued)

Sources of recordings: a) February 4, 1985; b) March 11, 1985; c) February 4, 1985; d) November 18, 1985 (all field recordings)

several different pitch choices. It is obvious that no two variations are identical, but it can be observed that for the first two cycles, each player's renditions are more similar to his other renditions than to those of any other player.

Even in such a brief example, some of the idiosyncratic elements that give a musician's playing an individual "signature" can be observed. Cai, for example, favors a dotted sixteenth note followed by a thirty-second note at the beginning of beats, as on the first three beats of measure 25. Dong favors a rest followed by a sixteenth note with a short trill immediately preceding a strong beat, as at the end of measures 25 and 26. Jin often plays an upper neighbor thirty-second note with a short trill immediately before a beat, as in the c♯'s immediately preceding beat four of measures 30, 31, and 32. His choice of the unusual motive 5–4–2–1 (a-g-e-d) in beat two of measure 26 is the kind of detail that makes a performer immediately recognizable to an expert *Jiangnan sizhu* musician. Lu is also highly idiosyncratic: he plays more thirty-second notes and more trills than any of the other performers and favors an extreme tempo increase in the second cycle of the piece, an increase of thirty beats per minute as opposed to about six beats per minute for the other three performers.

The third cycle, played in two of the performances transcribed in example 6.2, is in many ways qualitatively different from the first two cycles: the tempo is usually more than doubled and the melody is simplified. This third cycle is almost never notated. Although a skilled player could conceivably play a melody similar to the first two cycles of the piece at this faster tempo, this would be aesthetically unacceptable. Instead, the performer must simplify the more elaborate melody through the process known as *jianzi,* or "subtracting characters (i.e., notes)." While most of the strong-beat notes in the third cycle of the piece are identical to those played in the first two cycles, in many cases the overall melodic shape and character is altered considerably (as in measures 115 and 119 of Cai's performance).

Example 6.3 shows the same excerpt from "Zhonghua Liuban" as played on the *erhu* by six different performers. While each rendition is unique, the playing of Yang Lixian (d) and Zhou Hao (f) is quite similar. In particular, both of these players move up into the second position from the middle of measure 28 until the end of measure 30, while all the other performers remain in the first position throughout. The similarity is not accidental, as Yang is Zhou's student. Thus, idiosyncratic choices found in Zhou's playing (such as the last beat of measure 31 where the seventh scale degree is emphasized) recur throughout Yang's rendition. This is an example of a performer whose playing clearly contains traces

EXAMPLE 6.3 "Zhonghua Liuban *(erhu)*: performed by a) Chen Yonglu, b) Liu Chengyi, c) Liu Yuehua, d) Yang Lixian, e) Zhao Yongping, and f) Zhou Hao

EXAMPLE 6.3 (continued)

Sources of recordings: a) November 19, 1985; b) December 6, 1985; c) February 4, 1985; d) March 4, 1985; e) December 12, 1985 (all field recordings); f) performer's home recording (no date)

of his teacher's style but also incorporates individual embellishment (Yang's rendition also differs from Zhou's notation for the piece).

The rendition played by Liu Yuehua (c) is a more complex case. Liu is the son of Liu Chengyi (b) and has also studied with Zhou Hao. While some figures played by Liu Yuehua and Zhou are shared, the two renditions are dissimilar enough that a genetic relationship could not be established by examining these excerpts. Similarities between the two Lius are somewhat more frequent, and a few idiosyncratic figures that they share, such as the third beat of measure 27, are not played by any of the other performers. However, their playing is still much more dissimilar than that of Yang and Zhou. Liu Yuehua's rendition is an example of a young performer who has transcended his influences to develop a style of his own.

VARIATION BY AN INDIVIDUAL PERFORMER

Continuing with the same excerpt from "Zhongua Liuban," example 6.4 contains transcriptions of Lu Chunling's *dizi* playing on six separate occasions. Only the first cycle of each performance is shown; the first line is a transnotation of the performer's own prescriptive notation. Lu clearly treats his notation as one possibility of many, rather than as a fixed standard; few of the on-beat notes are changed in any version, but a wealth of differences in detail can be found. In some cases, two basic possibilities exist (as in the last beat of measure 30); in others, additional notes played in performance embellish the notated figure without changing its shape (as in beat 2 of measure 27).

Each of the excerpts in examples 6.2 and 6.4 is unique; all share some commonalities, but those in example 4 share a degree of similarity that the various individual renditions in example 2 do not. By looking at many renditions by the same performer, we can begin to glimpse the individual style that acts as a kind of signature identifying the performer. In comparing example 6.2 with example 6.4, it is easy to identify which of the four renditions in the former is played by Lu Chunling: for example, the figures played on the second and fourth beats of measure 27 of example 6.2d.1 and 2d.2 are quite similar to several of Lu's other renditions but quite unlike anything played by the other three performers.

THE NATURE OF VARIATION

In his discussion of related yet distinct renditions of a song, Charles Seeger has spoken of "variants" and "versions" as a series of nesting boxes. Each individual rendition is a variant, similar variants are classes

EXAMPLE 6.4 "Zhonghua Liuban *(dizi):* a) notation, and b–g) as performed by Lu Chunling

EXAMPLE 6.4 (continued)

Sources: a) notation adapted from Lu (1982:48); b) January 11, 1985 (first version); c) January 11, 1985 (second version); d) November 1, 1984; e) March 3, 1985; f) November 18, 1985 (b–f are field recordings); g) cassette *Jiangnan Sizhu* 2 8026 L008 (1983)

of variants, and other similarities group songs progressively into versions, classes of versions, families, and repertory of the tradition as a whole (1977b:282). Seeger's paradigm provides a conceptual framework for investigating relationships among pieces. This framework has worked well for studying American folk song and, since it deals primarily with melody rather than text, can also be applied to the study of instrumental styles in any culture.

In Chinese instrumental music, the "boxes" into which a given musical item can be placed often are overlapping rather than nesting. It is perhaps most fruitful to simply list some of the boxes into which the musical examples studied here can be placed, without trying to determine which box fits inside of which. For example, within the large family of pieces based on "Lao Liuban," "Zhonghua Liuban" simultaneously belongs to several groups:

1. Variants of "Lao Liuban" played in *Jiangnan sizhu*
2. Variants of "Lao Liuban" that have sixty metrical units
3. Variants of "Lao Liuban" expanded by threefold doubling

At this general level, "Zhonghua Liuban" is grouped with some pieces in the *Jiangnan sizhu* repertory but separated from others. It is also closely tied structurally to some pieces having no connection to *Jiangnan sizhu*. With regard to the level of expansion, "Zhonghua Liuban" itself could be split to join two different categories, since the third cycle of the piece is actually a less expanded (or more compact) treatment of the musical material. Thus, a piece belongs to certain categories and subcategories according to its place as a member of an extended tune family and to other categories and subcategories according to its place in a regional tradition.

At a more particularized level, all variants of "Zhonghua Liuban" examined here are played by musicians who are resident in Shanghai and who, regardless of their occupation, participate in amateur *Jiangnan sizhu* clubs. Both of these facts could be used as criteria for classifying the variations they play as distinct from, for example, those played by participants in Hangzhou music clubs. Example 6.3 shows that student-teacher relationships can result in variants sharing enough in common to form a small subgroup. Further examination of the playing of the performers within a single club or of the students of a particular teacher could result in many such subgroupings of variants.

All the renditions played on the *dizi* clearly share elements that distinguish them from those played on the *erhu*. This is also the case for renditions played on other instruments, although variants played on instruments that produce sounds in a similar fashion (such as the *dizi* and *xiao*) tend to have more in common than, for example, those played on the *dizi* and *erhu*. At the most particularized level, all renditions by a given performer form a group of variants.

It is also likely that renditions played by the same individual on different instruments may be linked by that performer's conception of the piece, a conception expressed by preferences for certain notes or phrases regardless of the instrument played. This set of variants could be placed in a category that would overlap with classifications based on the instrument played. Ability to play several instruments is almost universal among *Jiangnan sizhu* musicians, and this affects both how the music is conceived and how the performers interact.

SEVEN

Texture

T he characteristic musical texture of *Jiangnan sizhu* is an example
of what Western scholars call heterophony, defined by Peter Cooke
as "simultaneous variation, accidental or deliberate, of what is
identified as the same melody" (1980:537). Most definitions of heterophony are compatible with Cooke's; William Malm, for example,
describes it as "music in which the different parts are performing the
same tune at the same time, but each part is making its own melodic or
rhythmic variants of it" (1977:10).

HETEROPHONY IN CHINESE MUSIC

Heterophony is present in many types of Chinese music, including opera
and narrative song as well as instrumental ensemble traditions, a fact
widely known and stated. Malm's survey of Asian and Oceanic music, for
example, mentions the heterophonic relationship between voice and accompaniment in *Kunqu* and Peking opera and includes a brief musical
example of the latter (ibid.:163, 165).

Surprisingly few Western-language studies of specific Chinese musical
traditions, however, include more than passing reference to texture or
analysis of multipart musical examples. Fredric Lieberman has presented
a complete two-part transcription of a *nanguan* piece, but his commentary avoids the word "heterophony," referring instead to an "effect of
rudimentary polyphonic stratification" (1971:3). Alan Thrasher's dissertation includes a two-part transcription of a different *nanguan* piece, but
he does not discuss the texture other than to state that "all performers
play the same melodic line heterophonically" (1980:134). Liang Mingyue
includes a four-part transcription of an excerpt from the *Jiangnan sizhu*
piece "Sanliu," but his only comment on it is that "heard vertically, the
combined lines present a multi-heterophonic texture" (1985:220).

Rulan Chao Pian has transcribed and analyzed a narrative song with *sanxian* accompaniment (1978; 1979–80). In her analysis, she includes many brief references to the relationship between the two melodic lines and sums up her observations as follows:

> As for the relationship between the instrument and the voice line, I have already mentioned in general terms the function of the instrumental part as a refrain, its use in providing rhythmic variety, as well as reinforcing the overall forward drive. Melodically, it has its own characteristic motifs, and at times it also echoes the vocal line . . . the combination of tones between the voice and the instrument, is most likely the result of independent melodic progression rather than an intentional manipulation of intervals, except the unison or octave relationship. (1979–80:22–24)

Nora Yeh's dissertation on *nanguan* includes a section on heterophony (1985:324–30) in which she discusses definitions of the term and Chinese musicians' changing attitudes toward multipart relationships. She observes that *nanguan*'s texture is largely attributable to the different functions and playing styles characteristic of each melodic instrument.

> Although not clearly spelled out, the type of heterophony found in *nanguan* music leaves the skeletal melody virtually unchanged. Rather, it enhances this melody. True, sometimes the secondary instruments seem to dominate the musical space. Yet ultimately the secondary and variable melodic instruments remain in their respective places, according to the instrumental hierarchy. (ibid.:327)

Yeh includes a four-part transcription of a musical excerpt and identifies the kinds of ornaments and embellishments played on each instrument (ibid.:330), but she does not elaborate on the relationship among the parts shown in the example. She does, however, indicate that the *pipa* line in *nanguan* is considered to be the skeleton melody, while the other parts are embellished variants of it.

Since the 1950s, some Chinese musicologists have turned their attention to the multipart relationships found in traditional Chinese music. In English, a useful overview of this scholarship is contained in an article by Robert Mok (1966). He discusses the kinds of Chinese music characterized as heterophonic, historical references to multipart Chinese music, and eleven musical examples drawn from a variety of vocal and instrumental traditions. At several points, Mok suggests some of the factors contributing to heterophony:

> When there is more than one part in the accompaniment, as when a group of instruments is used, it is found that the parts are to a great extent the result

of extemporization by each instrument according to the general pattern of the melody. There is a great deal of interplay, rhythmic variation and imitative figuration in the parts. The musicians rely on their innate musical sense and skill to create an interesting accompaniment. Although the harmony is simple, the overall effects are greatly enhanced by the tonal colours of the instruments. Since instruments of different timbres are used, each instrument tends to stand out against the others. (ibid.:18)

Heterophony in instrumental ensemble results when the players do not play in unison but extemporize on a given melody. The degree of heterophony effect is therefore determined to a large extent by the freedom and skill of the individual player in extemporization. Intervals that are created in this manner are mostly consonant, with dissonant intervals formed by passing or auxiliary notes. Parallel fourths and fifths which are not normally considered satisfactory in Western music sound not unpleasant in pentatonic music. (ibid.:20)

The term used by Chinese musicologists that corresponds most closely to heterophony is *zhisheng fudiao,* "branch sound polyphony," often explained as resembling small branches of a river that continually diverge from the main stream and then return to it. This term may have originated as the translation of a concept devised by musicologists in the Soviet Union, and it appears repeatedly in a Chinese translation of an influential Russian article on the types of multipart textures found in Chinese music (A'erzamanuofu 1962).[1] Li Minxiong defines *zhisheng fudiao* in some detail:

> In the textural form "branch sound polyphony," each instrumental part is a variation on a "mother tune"; each player, using the mother tune as a foundation, and staying within the restrictions of the [ensemble as a] whole, amply gives play to his individual performing skill and the characteristics of his instrument, and creates a distinctive individual musical part. Each individual instrumental part must flow smoothly in its horizontal melodic movement, and, in terms of the vertical texture,[2] must be coordinated harmoniously with the other instrumental parts. (n.d.:7)

The heterophonic texture is thus an integral part of the performance process. Li describes the heterophony resulting from collective semi-improvised variation as "spontaneous" *(zifa),* while a multipart texture written out in advance is described as "conscious" *(zijue).* He states that the latter type of heterophony is what we should be interested in (ibid.:10), and the musical examples he discusses are presumably composed rather than transcribed. Most other Chinese musicologists also focus their attention on prescriptive multipart notation rather than on transcriptions of actual performances. For this reason, their examples drawn from the *Jiangnan sizhu* repertory tend to be idealized and differ somewhat from the texture heard in a typical performance in a Shanghai music club. The analysis in the present study will be based on transcriptions of field and commercial recordings.

HETEROPHONY IN *JIANGNAN SIZHU*

At least four different factors contribute to the heterophonic texture characteristic of *Jiangnan sizhu:* 1) sounds are produced differently on each instrument, and each instrument has a different range and/or pitch vocabulary; 2) conventions have been established for the idiomatic style of playing each instrument; 3) most players have a unique way of realizing a piece on their instrument; and 4) each rendition of a piece by a single individual will vary somewhat from any other rendition, whether or not such variance is consciously sought.

Aphorisms are often used to describe the musical texture. Common expressions include "inlaying and making way" *(qiandang ranglu,* also pronounced *kandang ranglu)* and the paired statements "you simple and I complex; you complex and I simple" (the Chinese terms are *jian,* meaning "simple" or "sparse," and *fan,* meaning "complex" or "dense"). Both of these aphorisms refer to contrast in the melodic density of the musical lines and also imply that two performers should alternate playing the denser or sparser part. Thus, contrast in the music occurs both horizontally, in that no instrument should play at a constant density throughout, and vertically, in that different instruments are playing at different densities at any given moment.

"Tacit understanding" *(moqi),* referring to the intuitive communication developed by a group of musicians playing together over a long period of time, is another phrase encountered in writings on *Jiangnan sizhu.* This expression stresses the fact that the multipart texture in traditional *Jiangnan sizhu* is the result of interaction among individuals rather than the arrangement of a single individual, and each rendition of a piece is collectively realized or recomposed by the performers involved.

The *Jiangnan sizhu* performers I know use a different set of expressions to discuss the ensemble texture in their music. For example, they may refer to the "way of fitting together" *(peihefa)* the various melodic lines. Individual melodic lines are referred to as "parts" *(shengbu,* literally "sound parts"); a musician will speak, for example, of a recording in which all the parts can be heard clearly or may criticize a performance in which all the parts are too nearly identical. Parts may also be referred to as "notation" *(puzi);* a performance may be evaluated, for example, by how compatible the *dizi* and *erhu* "notations" are. It is difficult to determine how traditional such expressions are; references to parts and

notation may well have resulted from recent Western-influenced developments in Chinese music. However, some form of heterophony appears to
have long been a fundamental part of most traditional Chinese ensemble music, perhaps so fundamental that no special terms are required

Source of recording: early commercial recording (China Records?, no date)

EXAMPLE 7.1 "Zhonghua Liuban" *(xiao* and *erhu):* performed by a) Sun Yude
(xiao) and b) Chen Yonglu *(erhu)*

to indicate its presence. One term commonly used is *qizou,* meaning "playing together." Chinese musicologists now define *qizou* as playing in unison or in octaves; however, even such definitions may be qualified. Li Minxiong notes that literal unison rarely exists in Chinese instrumental ensemble music and that the concept of *qizou,* which he first defines as playing in unison or octaves, includes some divergence among the parts (n.d.:1). Thus, *qizou* might best be translated literally as "playing together," with the understanding that a degree of heterophony is assumed to be present.

Unlike *nanguan,* in *Jiangnan sizhu* no single instrument actually plays the skeleton melody; in fact, the leading instruments tend to play the most ornamented melodic lines. Unlike narrative singing or Chinese opera, there is no easy distinction to be made between the primary melodic line (i.e., the voice) and secondary ones. Analysis of texture in *Jiangnan sizhu* is thus problematical but also potentially revelatory. The logical place to begin an investigation is with duets. The duet, the most elemental *Jiangnan sizhu* ensemble, is sometimes referred to as *dandang,* "single fitting." Duets may or may not be played by one "silk" and one "bamboo" instrument; combinations such as *erhu* and *yangqin* or two *erhu* are common.

The excerpts examined here are, once again, from "Zhonghua Liuban." This passage (measures 9–22) is the second long phrase of the piece and is probably more representative of the typical multipart style than the piece's opening, since there is often some unsteadiness in the opening seconds of a performance as the players adjust to each other's senses of tempo and intonation.

Example 7.1 is a duet played on the *xiao* and *erhu* transcribed from a commercial recording, probably from the 1950s (I have worked from a cassette dubbing and have not had access to the disc), by Sun Yude and Chen Yonglu. Measure 10 is a good example of contrasting densities, with the *xiao* sustaining a note in the first half of the measure and then playing a melodically active passage in the second half. In other places (measure 18), both instruments play at the same density. Because the *erhu* stays within the first position, octave shifts provide contrast between the two parts even when both instruments are playing the same melody (as in the last half of measure 13, where the *erhu* changes octaves on the fourth beat). While most of the on-beat notes are unisons or octaves, sometimes the two instruments are a third or a sixth apart (last beats of measures 10 and 12), and even when they play the same on-beat notes, the two parts consistently contrast in the way these notes are elaborated. The frequent juxtapositions of E and F♯ (as in the first beats of measures 9 and 21) are the result of Chen's preference for *erhu* motives beginning with what might be thought of as an on-beat grace note, where the F♯

(clearly the tone of the skeleton melody) is delayed until the following sixteenth note. At the end of a beat, the two parts are often a step apart (as at the end of measures 10 and 11) but move immediately to a unison on the downbeat.

Example 7.2 is a duet played on the *erhu* and *yangqin*, transcribed from a field recording. The *erhu* player, Chen Yonglu, is the same as in

Source of recording: field recording November 19, 1985

EXAMPLE 7.2 "Zhonghua Liuban" *(erhu* and *yangqin):* performed by a) Chen Yonglu *(erhu)* and b) Zhang Zhengming *(yangqin)*

EXAMPLE 7.2 (continued)

the preceding example, and the similarity between the two renditions is strong. The *yangqin* part is the denser of the two throughout this excerpt, but there is considerable give and take between the parts, often achieved through shifts in register. The *erhu* is the louder instrument dynamically, but the *yangqin* part becomes dominant when it is played in its upper register (an octave higher than the *erhu*); so by playing a short phrase in the upper octave (as on the last beat of measure 13) and then moving down again, the *yangqin* part seems to emerge and then recede. In several places, the *yangqin* fills in with thirty-second notes while the *erhu* sustains an eighth or dotted eighth note (measure 10, beat 4, and measure 15, beat 3). Most of the on-beat notes are unisons or octaves, but occasional thirds (measure 21, beat 2), sixths (measure 12, beat 4), or thirds and sixths (when the *yangqin* plays octaves, as in measure 15, beat 2) occur.

Example 7.3 is also a duet played on the *erhu* and *yangqin* and is transcribed from the performers' home recording. Despite the great dissimilarity in the way the two instruments produce their sounds, there are many short phrases where the two parts follow each other closely (such as the last half of measure 16). Although there are places (measure 17) where the *erhu* part is much less dense than that of the *yangqin*, the two parts tend to become dense and sparse simultaneously rather than in alternation, as in the passage from the beginning of measure 14 through the middle of measure 15. While there are a fair number of on-beat thirds and sixths, there are only two instances (the third beat of measure 9 and the opening of measure 14) of the juxtaposition of E and F♯ found in the preceding two examples. The performers in this example, Zhou Hao and Zhou Hui, are brothers born in the 1920s who

Source of recording: performers' home recording (no date)

EXAMPLE 7.3 "Zhonghua Liuban" *(erhu* and *yangqin):* performed by a) Zhou Hao *(erhu)* and Zhou Hui *(yangqin)*

have been playing together most of their lives. The ensemble aesthetic suggested here is somewhat different from the ideals of contrast and exchange so common in writings on *Jiangnan sizhu.* Instead, there is a great deal of synchronization, and the periodic occurrence of unison passages (such as the last half of measure 16) seems to show a familiarity with each other's playing.

EXAMPLE 7.3 (continued)

Example 7.4 is a duet for *dizi* and *yangqin* transcribed from a commercial recording from about 1960. The *yangqin* plays an accompanying role in this example, for the most part maintaining a constant sixteenth-note density. Thus, contrasting densities occur, but these are primarily due to the *dizi* sustaining notes or filling in with rapid thirty-second-note passages. Especially toward the latter half of the excerpt, the *yangqin* line approaches being a paraphrase of the *dizi* melody, often following the same melodic curve but with a less ornamented melody. At no point does the *yangqin* part move to the forefront; a comparison of the opening measures of the *yangqin* line in examples 7.3 and 7.4, both played by Zhou Hui, shows example 7.4 to be a more reserved and restrained rendition of the piece.

Example 7.5 shows the melodic lines for *xiao, erhu,* and *pipa.* The *xiao* and *pipa* lines tend to change register at the same time, although the *xiao* is actually an octave lower throughout, but the *erhu,* following the convention of staying within the range of a major ninth, shifts back and forth between playing in the same register as the *pipa* and playing an octave below. The *pipa* part is punctuated with open-string notes, with the result that notes more than two octaves below the main melody line are inserted. In addition, jumps between the middle and upper octave are also featured. This can be seen, for example, in measures 13 and 14. All the instruments tend to play continuously at similar densities, with the *pipa* part slightly more dense than the other two. There is relatively little use of strong contrasts in which one or more instruments drop back while another fills in. The most striking contrast between this and all the previous examples is the strong concurrence in the choice of on-beat notes.

Source of recording: China Records *Yue Er Gao* M-2328 (no date; original recording 1960)

EXAMPLE 7.4 "Zhonghua Liuban" *(dizi and yangqin):* performed by a) Lu Chun-ling *(dizi)* and b) Zhou Hui *(yangqin)*

Even though there are three instruments instead of two, at most points all three play the same pitches on the beat.

The preceding chapter suggested that an individual's rendition of a piece on a given instrument varies from one performance to the next but that the scope of this variation is rather limited. The examples examined here further suggest that the unique heterophonic texture of each

EXAMPLE 7.4 (continued)

performance is more the result of the combination of individual renditions of the piece than of improvisation or spontaneous interaction
and that multiple renditions by the same group of players would show a
relatively high degree of similarity. Theoretically, one could recombine
parts transcribed from different recordings and produce a fair predic-
tion of what would occur if the individuals playing the parts performed
together. The *erhu* parts in examples 7.1 and 7.2, for example, could be
exchanged with little change in the overall musical texture of either
example.

An aesthetic of contrast is important in the horizontal realization of
the melodic line of each individual instrument, and vertical contrasts
naturally occur as these lines are juxtaposed. The simple/complex contrasts mentioned in aphorisms thus seem to be descriptions of a musical
result rather than of a process, and the constantly shifting musical
texture owes as much to differing individual styles as to conscious spontaneous interaction among the performers. Such interaction is extremely
important, however, with regard to tempo, intonation, and dynamics.
The relationship between register and dynamics has been noted above
(examples 7.2 and 7.5), and the contrasts and overlappings among the
various instruments in the ensemble are used to great effect by experienced performers. Further analysis of multipart examples may suggest
other principles of ensemble interaction that are not commonly articu-
lated by performers. Example 7.3, for instance, suggests that periodic
synchronization among the parts may be aesthetically desirable and an
indicator of a high degree of familiarity and communication among the
performers.

EXAMPLE 7.5 "Zhonghua Liuban" *(xiao, erhu,* and *pipa):* performed by a) Cai Cide *(xiao),* b) Liu Yuehua *(erhu),* and c) Shi Quan *(pipa)*

EXAMPLE 7.5 (continued)

Source of recording: field recording January 11, 1985

EIGHT

Aesthetics

Aesthetic issues have been touched upon in discussions of performance practice, learning the music, style of playing the instruments, variation, and heterophony. Here, more fundamental aesthetic principles are examined: the "traditional" values held by *Jiangnan sizhu* performers and scholars, the values that underlie attempts to "develop" the music, and the interplay of these sets of values as they affect the course of the music's preservation and/or change.

TRADITIONAL AESTHETIC PRINCIPLES

Before the middle of the present century, aesthetics in *Jiangnan sizhu,* as in most non-elite traditions, were rarely written about, at least not in published or publicly circulated form. However, in the last few decades, performers and scholars have begun to record some of these principles in print, and their aesthetic values can be grouped under several topics: general characteristics of the music, ornamentation, improvisation, and ensemble playing.

Since 1949, socialist—Marxist-Leninist and/or Maoist—aesthetic standards have affected all Chinese art forms, and performers, scholars, and educators in Shanghai have all been exposed to these standards. Published writings concerning traditional music must be compatible with the prevailing policies toward performing arts; even in lessons, interviews, or conversations, most musicians understandably try to avoid any statements that might be construed as counter progressive. I believe the principles discussed in this section are representative of values that predate 1949, and most are also applicable to pre-twentieth-century or earlier musical practices. However, it can be assumed that any current discussions or writings concerning *Jiangnan sizhu* will tend to emphasize those traditional values that are compatible with socialist ones. For example, recent writings often stress *Jiangnan sizhu*'s roots in the music of ordinary laborers and peasants while downplaying its associations with the elite or with "superstition" (i.e., religion).

General Characteristics of *Jiangnan Sizhu*

Descriptions of Chinese musical techniques tend to be relatively straightforward, but to the Western reader discussions of aesthetics may seem extremely vague. In the West, affective descriptions are widely viewed as being appropriate for music criticism but not for serious scholarship; in China, however, the vast majority of instrumental music is programmatic in nature, and scholars, critics, and performers all pay considerable attention to interpreting the extramusical associations of titles and subtitles. In discussing the style of a particular piece or of an entire tradition, musicians refer to natural phenomena, places, historical events, and subtle shades of mood and feeling that evoke the spirit or flavor of the music.

One of the most frequently quoted lists of *Jiangnan sizhu* characteristics is that of Jin Zuli (1961:1; also in Gao 1981; Li Minxiong 1982). These characteristics are *xiao,* "small," referring to the ensemble size; *qing,* "light" or "gentle," here used in the sense of "lively but graceful"; *xi,* "fine" or "detailed," referring to the meticulous playing style; and *ya,* "elegant," referring to the refined melodies.

Another important quality Jin cites (1961:2) is *pingwen,* "smooth" in the sense of "not jumpy" or "without rough edges," which is especially characteristic of the long pieces played through without any abrupt breaks or tempo changes. He stresses that even in pieces with different tempos for different sections, the changes should be gradual, from slow to moderate to fast. This latter value is widely held by *Jiangnan sizhu* aficionados. One knowledgeable listener praised a performance of "Xingjie" by the Tianshan Music Club, led by Jin Zuli, as resembling a "single thread" (*yitiao xian*) played from beginning to end, adding that this is a quality rarely found in contemporary *Jiangnan sizhu* playing (Teng Yongran, personal communication).

Water imagery is prominent in writings on *Jiangnan sizhu.* Zhou Dafeng variously describes the music as like "ripples on green water," "a clear small stream," and "a painting mirrored in the water" (1980:61). Sustained notes played with a gentle undulation on the *erhu* or *dizi* are known as "wave sounds" *(langyin),* and discussions of the music often refer to the multitude of rivers and lakes in the Jiangnan area. Although *Jiangnan sizhu* is in many ways an urban music, the recurrence of references to pastoral scenes indicates the importance of poetic imagination in the music.

The natural environment and the personality of the people who inhabit the Jiangnan area are often intertwined: "The beautiful pieces of *Jiangnan sizhu* reflect the Jiangnan people's frank, open, and optimistic personalities, their vigorous and ambitious mental outlook, and express their feelings of heartfelt love and praise for the green hills and beautiful waters of their countryside of fish and rice" (Cheng 1981:55). Such passages may at times border on doggerel, but a sense of regional character runs very deep in regional art forms, and phrases such as "land of fish and rice" and "heaven above, Suzhou and Hangzhou below" have long been used with pride to refer to Jiangnan.

Without denying the validity of affective descriptions, some scholars feel that to define "Jiangnan musical style," more concrete musical characteristics need to be identified. Chen Yingshi has suggested that temperament, scales, tonality, mode, meter, rhythm, melodic tendencies, formal structure, methods of embellishment, performance techniques, and the interaction among musical instruments are among the topics which should be examined (1985:33). Chinese scholars have discussed some of these issues with reference to *Jiangnan sizhu,* but the viewpoints of experts from within the tradition have rarely been published. Defining a regional style—often called *difang secai,* meaning "regional color"—is a complex task, but any attempt at definition should incorporate the perspectives of those who specialize in a regional tradition as well as those of scholars from outside the tradition.

Ornamentation, Improvisation, & Ensemble Playing

The type and extent of ornamentation or variation considered appropriate for playing *Jiangnan sizhu* involve several criteria: 1) idiomatic techniques that are related to the way a particular instrument is played; 2) conventions established for an individual instrument—in any regional style some techniques are preferred over others, as concepts of what "sounds good" on a particular instrument, such as preferred register, vary from one region to another; 3) tastes of an individual or a musical group. However, the ideal of interacting well musically with the other performers in the ensemble is often the overriding principle upon which both individual and collective performances are evaluated. Style (of playing each of the instruments), variation, and heterophony have been treated earlier as individual topics, but they are ultimately closely interrelated in *Jiangnan sizhu.*

Gan Tao of Nanjing stresses the uniqueness of each performance of a piece, which is collectively recomposed each time it is played. He states that although "on the surface" it seems that "each player performs freely, with improvised ornamentation," recomposition must be grounded in a thorough knowledge of the characteristics and expressive capabilities of each instrument. Even with this knowledge, a quality performance can only be achieved through playing together often with the same musicians. Through such individual and collective experience, a musician learns the principles of give and take (Gan 1978:96).

Gan is also one of the few scholars to clearly articulate the role of notation in *Jiangnan sizhu*. He claims that if you follow exactly what is written, the result may still sound good but will not be "authentic" *(zhenzheng) Jiangnan sizhu*. One reason is that even detailed notation does not indicate which notes are "primary" and "secondary" *(zhu* and *ci)* or which are "strong" and "weak" *(shi* and *xu)*. If a performer is not familiar with the piece played, his or her performance will betray such ignorance (ibid.). Gan goes on to stress the importance of being familiar with the styles of *Kunqu* and other opera traditions of Jiangnan. He observes that nowadays one often hears *Jiangnan sizhu* performed with none of the Jiangnan flavor and compares such flavorless performances to renditions of Chinese folk songs by foreign vocalists with no knowledge of Chinese music (ibid.:98).

Another principle of ensemble playing is the interaction of simple/sparse and complex/dense. In an expanded sense, this principle incorporates rhythmic contrast among the instrumental parts, and it should be observed especially in slow pieces or sections (Shanghai Qunzhong 1960:4). Li Minxiong sees the interaction between the *dizi* and *erhu* as being particularly important and speaks of the mutual simple/complex relationship between the melodic lines played on these two instruments (1982:53). Wu Yiqun stresses the importance of "fitting [the musical lines] together through tacit understanding" *(moqi de peihe)* among the musicians in the ensemble (1980:48).

When asked about the quality of a given performance, musicians will most often refer to how well it is blended or put together *(peihe)*. A performance that is well *peihe*-d may vary considerably in the degree of divergence of the individual parts: one performer described another club's playing as well-blended even while criticizing their tendency toward a musical texture close to unison. A different group is widely praised for their ensemble playing, yet the individual styles of some of its musicians are often denigrated. A performance felt to be poorly blended may be characterized as *luanqi bazao,* an aphorism literally meaning "disorderly sevens and rotten eights" and perhaps best translated as "chaotic." Again, the implication is that the total musical result is more significant than the individual parts—that is, in a chaotic performance the individual parts may be well played, but since they are not well integrated, little pleasure can be derived from hearing or participating in the ensemble.

Attitudes toward the learning process also reveal widely accepted aesthetic conceptualizations. The apprentice performer is often advised to "listen more and [play] together more" *(duo ting duo he)*. Several years after leaving Shanghai, I finally came to realize that this seeming cliché encapsulates several of the underlying principles of traditional *Jiangnan sizhu*. It is only through repeated listening over a long period of time that an individual can absorb the ways of ornamenting a melody, the sense of give and take between the various melodic lines, the gradual increases in tempo, and the ebb and flow of dynamic changes—in short, all the elements that make up the "flavor" of the music. He or she learns to hear not only the general characteristics that pervade the entire tradition but also the particularities of each piece in the repertory. It is only through listening that one internalizes the music, a process that is inevitably slower but more natural and less rigid than that of memorization. By playing together with others, a musician gains practical experience in applying what he has learned through listening, begins to appreciate the variety of individual styles, and learns to adapt to different senses of tempo and dynamics. Even negative experiences, such as losing one's place in the middle of a piece, contribute to the development of aural skills, since to recapture the thread of the music a performer must listen to instruments other than his own. Finally, because of the inward-directed physical arrangement of the instruments in *Jiangnan sizhu* ensemble, it is only when playing in a group that a musician is seated in the ideal location for listening.

Traditional Aesthetics in Other Genres

Over the past few centuries, the tradition of writing about musical aesthetics has been cultivated most assiduously by scholars and performers of *qin* zither music and *Kunqu* opera. In a sense, their writings serve as models for all discussion of Chinese musical aesthetics, so it is worthwhile to briefly compare them with *Jiangnan sizhu* aesthetics to see if there is evidence of pervasive values in traditional Chinese music.

Although the specific terms used by *qin* and *Jiangnan sizhu* scholars and performers in discussing aesthetics are somewhat different, some basic values are shared. Pastoral scenes play an important role in *qin* lore, and paintings depict players on mountain peaks surrounded by clouds or seated beside a stream. The titles and subtitles of many pieces describe such scenes, and some legendary players derived their fame from the ability to convey them to listeners. Such total immersion in nature is even given metaphysical value. On the significance of rural, pastoral scenes, R. H. Van Gulik states that "the contemplation of the beauty of streams and mountains may impart to the observer the vital forces that are inherent in nature, and thereby prolong his earthly life" (1968:58).

Several excerpts from a thirteenth-century *qin* handbook will serve to illustrate that the concerns of *qin* players are not unlike those of *Jiangnan sizhu* musicians. For example, on sound production it states:[1] "When producing sounds one should aim at simplicity and also at naturalness. Its wonderfulness lies in the correct shifting over from the light touch to the heavy, and in applying correctly ritardando and accelerando . . . [if one plays badly] the melody is spoilt and confused" (ibid.:74). And on performance demeanor it advises that "if while playing one changes one's mien and allows the eyes to wander, or worse, if the body is stooping, the feet put one atop the other, the head shaking, and the shoulders moving up and down, then an atmosphere of unelegance [*sic*] is created" (ibid.). On the limitations of musical notation, the handbook states: "one must understand the meaning of a tune. If one just plays the music as it is written, one will not be able to express the sentiments of the composer" (ibid.:75).

Of course, in many respects, *qin* music and *Jiangnan sizhu* are very different. Informal musical and social interaction are fundamental to the nature of *sizhu* musics, while for a *qin* player a noisy teahouse setting would be abhorrent, as would practices such as smoking and sipping tea while playing or conversing while others are performing.[2] However, writings about the *qin* and conversations with my teachers and performers from *sizhu* and other traditions all clearly indicate that most players of Chinese instruments have a complex and deep relationship with their instrument and the music played on it and that the summoning of poetic and natural imagery plays an important role in their performance and appreciation of the music.

Writings on *Kunqu* aesthetics are also concerned with some of the same issues as *Jiangnan sizhu*, but as with *qin* sources, the specific terms used tend to be different. These handbooks describe many subtle ornaments with names that translate as "repeated note," "tremolo," "stabilizing note," "carry-over note," "filling-in note," and "clarifying technique" (Strassberg 1976:51). Even though the terms are different, the practice of naming ornament types and placing high value on their proper execution is common to the two traditions. In both genres, careful attention is given to the treatment of long sustained notes, and the *Kunqu* preference for a "slightly wavy quality" corresponds to the *Jiangnan sizhu* "wave sounds." In general, *Kunqu* singing should stress "elegance, purity, urbanity, and smoothness," and long phrases should be "smooth and flowing" (Wei Liangfu 1977:7). Again, the terms differ, but the sentiments are similar.

Qin music is usually solo, although duets with a *xiao* or songs with *qin* accompaniment are also established traditions. Writings on *Kunqu* aesthetics focus on singing, not the ensemble accompaniment, so there are fundamental differences between these traditions and the *Jiangnan sizhu* ensemble, where the musical leadership is often shared by several instruments. In *qin* music and *Kunqu*, musical notation is melodically very specific and includes many symbols for ornamental nuances. *Qin* players are free to choose their own rhythm and tempo or even change some of the notated pitches (discussed in Yung 1984 and 1985), and *Kunqu* singers differ in their realizations of the notation, but neither tradition encourages improvisation to the extent of *Jiangnan sizhu*. However, even in an ensemble tradition a musician's primary experience of the music is through his or her own instrument, so the aesthetics of sound quality, timbre, and expressiveness are important to musicians in all three traditions.

Surveys of Chinese instrumental music often include generalized lists of *sizhu* aesthetics, but an examination of intensive studies of individual *sizhu* genres indicates that the differences among these traditions may be as important as their similarities. In her dissertation on *nanguan*, Nora Yeh has noted some of the features that distinguish it from other *sizhu* traditions:

> In *nanguan*, a loud volume and percussive melodic playing are absent . . . rather, the ensemble strives for an extremely delicate balance in sound, a relatively low tessitura, and a quiet mood. Even the liveliest and the fastest passages have a tendency to strive for a controlled and solemn state. Tempos are kept slow or moderate, in keeping with the generally tranquil and restrained ideal of sound. (1985:90–91)

Many of the positive values attributed here to *nanguan*— "delicate," "quiet," "controlled," "tranquil"—apply to *Jiangnan sizhu*, but it is also true that loud and fast passages, percussive melodic playing, high tessitura, and pieces that are far from being "solemn" or "restrained" are essential parts of the latter tradition's aesthetics. Many attempts at overviews of *sizhu* aesthetics take one genre as a standard, with the result that other genres may seem to deviate from it. Gao Houyong (1981:79–83), for example, uses *Jiangnan sizhu* as the most representative *sizhu* genre, and the preceding quotation from Yeh is in response to Gao's discussion of *sizhu* aesthetics. Alan Thrasher, in his dissertation on aesthetics in Chinese music, uses *nanguan* as the primary standard and emphasizes slow tempos, low volume, and a sparse texture (1980:134). Based on this, *Jiangnan sizhu* would appear to be the atypical tradition, with its prominent fast and loud passages and a "saturated" texture, with many instruments of similar timbre and range filling up the same sonic space.[3] On a general level, *Jiangnan sizhu* is more similar to *Guangdong Yinyue* and *Chaozhou xianshi* than to *nanguan,* which is never as loud or fast as the other three traditions. Generalizations about the characteristics common to *sizhu* genres might well be followed by qualifications stating which traditions are exceptions to the rule, and we should keep in mind the great diversity among *sizhu* musics as well as their commonality.

DEVELOPMENT & CHANGE

In 1964, the faculty and students of the Chinese music theory department of the Shanghai Conservatory undertook a major field study of *Jiangnan sizhu* in Shanghai. At the conclusion of their work, they reached a consensus on three problems the tradition faced at that time (summarized from Li Minxiong 1982:51–52):

> 1. A lack of new pieces (the repertory had not changed since 1911) and a decline in the size of the active traditional repertory; "Man Sanliu," "Man Liuban," and "Sihe Ruyi" were rarely played, and the latter piece was believed to be on the verge of extinction
> 2. A lack of organized leadership; only one of the four groups they investigated had a regular leader; the others played together without any direction, organizing their activity only in preparation for rare public performances
> 3. A lack of successors to the tradition; very few young people were involved in the music clubs studied

My own research in the 1980s indicates that changes have occurred since the 1964 survey. In the repertory, although "Man Sanliu" and "Man Liuban" are still played relatively infrequently, "Sihe Ruyi" is among the most-performed pieces, and most *Jiangnan sizhu* musicians can play it without notation. Although some music clubs have a small repertory, the total number of pieces played among the various clubs is rather large. Some groups make concerted efforts to learn pieces unfamiliar to most of their members; however, new or recent compositions are still rare. Few of the clubs are actually directed by a single leader, although they all have a leader in name, but their activity could not be considered directionless, and several groups are conscientious in their weekly meetings which are treated more as serious rehearsals than as social gatherings. With regard to successors to the tradition, older players still predominate, but a significant number of young performers are regular participants, and two clubs are composed primarily of younger members.

The problems pointed out in the 1964 survey are representative of three major issues pertinent to discussion of change and development in *Jiangnan sizhu*: 1) how to expand the repertory, through new composition or revival of neglected or forgotten traditional pieces; 2) how—or whether—to organize musical activity; and 3) how to recruit and train younger musicians to perpetuate the tradition. These issues are of concern to all who take an active interest in *Jiangnan sizhu*, including scholars, educators, and amateur and professional musicians, but these diverse groups often have divergent views on the relative importance of the problems and the appropriate solutions for them. Among the topics relevant to discussion of development and change are repertory, group organization and leadership, perpetuation of the tradition, performance style, and musical instruments and temperament.

Repertory

Changes in repertory include modifying existing pieces and composing new ones. Modification is the subject of much discussion in Shanghai *Jiangnan sizhu* circles. For example, it is widely recognized that much of the *Jiangnan sizhu* repertory includes greatly expanded treatments of short *qupai*, but some scholars and performers believe that there have been cases where pieces have become too expanded.

> When speaking of the characteristics of performance, at the same time we must point out one place where traditional performance still awaits improvement: if there is excessive "making slow and adding flowers," it causes the music to verge on a kind of purely technical showing off; if [the principle of] slow-moderate-fast (meaning slow, moderate, and fast variations of the same musical material) is used to create a tediously long musical structure, it often causes people to experience an oppressive, weighted down, and tired feeling, [a feeling of] lopsided and plodding repetition of one note after the other, and the loss of a sense of treating the piece as an entirety, to the point where the performance clearly becomes fragmented and lacking in terseness; this unnatural seeking after a leisurely and meticulous style causes harm to the piece's simple true nature. We can say that the production of these weaknesses is the result of a tendency for *Jiangnan sizhu* to gradually leave real life in the last few decades. Because of this, we believe that we must guard against this kind of tendency developing any further from now on. (Shanghai Qunzhong 1960:5)

Although rarely expounded upon at such length, this view is also shared by other scholars, and Li Minxiong (1982:50) cites the pieces "Man Sanliu" and "Man Liuban" as particularly problematical in this regard. It would be an oversimplification, however, to see statements such as the above passage as nothing more than ideologically motivated attempts by non-performers to change the *Jiangnan sizhu* repertory. The two pieces cited by Li are those least often played by amateur music clubs, and this must be attributed in part to their slow tempo and highly expanded structure, which increases the difficulty of learning them. While scholars may criticize these pieces for being esoteric and detached from ordinary life, performers' relative neglect of them is also a form of implicit criticism. One reason these pieces are seldom played is that relatively few musicians know them, even though notation and recordings are available. Two other long and complicated pieces, "Xingjie" and "Sihe Ruyi," are frequently played.[4] It could be that musicians do not learn "Man Sanliu" and "Man Liuban" because they do not like them, but it can also be suggested that they do not learn them because they are not played often enough; since aural familiarity plays an important role in learning *Jiangnan sizhu*, infrequently performed pieces require the student to make a conscious effort to become familiar with them through memorization or listening to recordings.

Among the other longer pieces, a structurally edited version of "Xingjie" has become standard in professional circles. In the notation for the piece, which is contained in Shanghai Qunzhong (1960), the final section is played only once, with the slow and medium cycles omitted. This is the structural arrangement of the piece taught in conservatories, found in virtually all published notation, and played on most commercial recordings. However, in the amateur music clubs, the complete (slow-moderate-fast) version is still standard and was the one played in the great majority of performances of "Xingjie" that I heard during my fieldwork. The editing of "Xingjie" is a suggested reform which, more than two decades later, has not found acceptance among the primary carriers of the tradition. The amateur groups' adherence to the longer version of the piece clearly sets them at odds with professional circles, an ideological separation compounded by the fact that a musician who learns the shorter version will not be able to play with Shanghai's *Jiangnan sizhu* clubs unless he or she makes the effort to learn—by necessity, largely aurally—the additional cycles of the piece. Beyond the rejection implicit in not playing the "revised" shorter version, some amateur musicians feel strongly that the deletions abandon the traditional principle of gradual acceleration in favor of an aesthetic (possibly Western influenced) of sharp contrast in tempo: the "essence" (*jinghua*) of the entire piece is cut out, leaving nothing but "a head and a tail."

Chen Yingshi also expresses distaste for pieces that have become overly expanded. He believes that if such pieces were played on stage the results would be "dreadful to contemplate" and suggests that such repertory was appropriate to a social context that no longer exists. In the past, *Jiangnan sizhu* was to a great extent a type of "ceremonial" *(yishi)* music, whereas today it has moved to the concert stage and mass media (1985:35). Long, slow, static pieces are appropriate as accompaniment for primarily nonmusical activities, such as a wedding banquet; when they become the sole focus of attention, listeners may become bored or restless.

Chen's point is important, but it is also true that aside from accompanying such ceremonial or ritual functions, *Jiangnan sizhu* has traditionally been a type of chamber music played for purely recreational purposes and intended primarily for the entertainment of the musicians themselves. The amateur music club is an institution with many precedents in Chinese music, but in contemporary China music is expected to "serve the masses," and playing for the enjoyment of a select group has connotations of elitism and selfishness. Until the middle of the present century, there was no tradition of performing Chinese instrumental music on stage (except in the sense that opera accompanists sit at one side of the stage and somtimes perform instrumental interludes; in this sense, narrative singers or their accompanists may also perform instrumental overtures "on stage"). In contemporary professional circles, the prevailing view is that if music is "good," it will be appreciated when performed in a concert setting. By the same logic, if a piece or genre is not appreciated when played in such a setting, it is lacking in quality or vitality and should either be abandoned or reworked. This has led to the widespread editing of traditional repertory and an emphasis on faster, louder, and more dramatic pieces or treatments.

Many *Jiangnan sizhu* musicians oppose tampering with existing repertory; however, there is little resistance—at least in principle—to new *sizhu* composition. I believe that most would agree with the following statement: "A great many folk performers are also composers at heart, and they are the ones who are most familiar with the musical language of *Jiangnan sizhu*. I hope that professional and amateur composers can go forward hand in hand to create pieces having both the *Jiangnan sizhu* style and the spirit of the times" (Wei Zhongle 1985:18).

The performance of a new piece in a teahouse described in chapter 2 shows the importance of cooperation between composer and performers, but amateur-professional collaboration on composition remains an unrealized ideal. Although it may seem to some progress-oriented individuals that the amateur *Jiangnan sizhu* community stubbornly clings to the past, this is not necessarily the case. Within the repertory commonly played today, there are already pieces from three different historical periods: adaptations of "ancient" *pipa* pieces, the Eight Great Pieces of presumably more recent origin, and several Cantonese pieces composed in the early twentieth century. Since repertory of widely varying longevity already coexists in *Jiangnan sizhu*, there is no reason why new or recent pieces cannot be similarly assimilated.[5]

The primary issue seems to be one of musical quality: that is, new pieces are not shunned because they are "new" but because they are "bad." Several musicians have also expressed reservations about the relative worth of some of the forgotten pieces that have recently been reconstructed from notation, including those pieces their own group performs. Even Li Minxiong, an ardent advocate of development, acknowledges that few of the new or newly revived pieces measure up to the Eight Great Pieces, and if new composition is not done well it can only injure the "historical status and social function" of *Jiangnan sizhu* (1985:27).

Notwithstanding *Jiangnan sizhu* musicians' presumed willingness to play "good" new pieces, barriers impeding their assimilation do exist. Published notation is not available for most recent compositions due to the complexities of the state-run publishing industry and the difficulty of getting anything to press within a reasonable time period. Also, some performers and ensembles value having exclusive access to music that others cannot play, and Chinese musicians in general are reluctant to share notation with other than close acquaintances. Furthermore, most new compositions or arrangements tend to have fixed parts for each instrument. In traditional practice, each musician is free to realize his or her own part, either by embellishing a skeletal melody or by freely varying a learned version, and this self-expression is highly valued by many performers. When each part is rigidly prescribed, their enjoyment may be decreased, resulting in a lack of enthusiasm for playing such music.

Group Organization & Leadership

For many amateur *Jiangnan sizhu* performers, music making is as much a social as a musical activity and is not intended to be listened to or appreciated by a larger audience. A player's level of accomplishment is not the sole or even the primary determinant of who plays which instrument in a music club. Some older musicians who were once brilliant performers are now barely competent, with their playing marred by shortness of breath or poor intonation. Visitors from another music club or from out of town, accustomed to playing with an entirely different group of musicians, may have trouble blending well with the group they are visiting. Some players who have never achieved a high degree of musical competence are treated deferentially because of their long-term participation in a group. Beginners are encouraged to participate even though their playing may still be substandard. In an amateur music club, it would be almost unthinkable for a leader to discourage any of these musicians from joining in the music making.

There is little doubt that by assigning musical parts to the individuals who are most accomplished on each instrument and playing a piece repeatedly with this same arrangement of players the quality of ensemble playing will improve. In preparation for performances intended for a large live or radio audience, even the most traditional music clubs hold rehearsals where players are assigned to specific instruments and pieces are carefully rehearsed. Traditional aesthetics stress the value of repeatedly playing with the same group of musicians, and some musicians express frustration at the difficulty of trying to improve group performance in the noisy teahouse settings where the performers change from week to week. A few musicians who regularly participate in the public teahouses have also formed splinter groups of a more select nature, where a small group of performers attempt to achieve a more satisfying level of ensemble playing. One such group consists of older musicians who specialize in playing *guqu* and meet irregularly at one performer's home. A group of young musicians led by Dong Kejun formed another splinter group in 1985; they rehearsed in the evenings, specialized in relatively virtuosic (and fast) renditions of traditional pieces, and had the stated intention of cultivating the performance of new repertory.[6]

It thus appears that attempts at systematic organization of amateur music clubs would in many ways be contrary to the purposes and conventions of their music making and that such organization might well alienate some of the music's devotees. However, the formation of new groups with a more musical and less social orientation is a practical way to cultivate ensemble playing skills.

Perpetuation of the Tradition

In both amateur and professional circles, there is widespread concern about the scarcity of young people who are seriously interested in *Jiangnan sizhu* music. Wei Zhongle sees a need to integrate the music more closely with people's life-styles and to disseminate it more widely (1985:16). An obvious step in this direction would be to expose more people to the music through performances and broadcasts, as only after becoming familiar with the repertory and style can one begin to enjoy and appreciate it. New venues of performance can be considered: composer Hu Dengtiao mentions having heard *koto* and *shakuhachi* (Japanese zither and end-blown flute) played at a scenic spot in Japan and suggests that *Jiangnan sizhu* would be highly appropriate in Shanghai's Yu Gardens

(1985:21). His own arrangements of *Jiangnan sizhu* pieces, while contro-
versial, have succeeded in arousing the interest of young professional
performers.

There is little chance that *Jiangnan sizhu* will die out completely as a
musical tradition in the near future, although the relative scarcity of
accomplished younger players indicates that the number of active performers may well decrease. The widespread availability of notation and
recordings has enabled musicians outside of the Jiangnan area to perform the music. The May 1987 *Jiangnan sizhu* competition included
performing groups from many parts of China and from as far away as
Singapore, and *Jiangnan sizhu* ensembles also exist in North America.
Geographically diverse interest in the music bodes well for its future survival, but it does bring up an important aesthetic question: which are the
essential and which the peripheral elements of a musical tradition? To
many *Jiangnan sizhu* musicians, aural assimilation and individual recomposition or variation are crucial to the spirit of the music. From this
perspective, groups that merely memorize notated or recorded versions
of the repertory might be labeled as "so-called" *Jiangnan sizhu* ensembles.
Already, young players from Shanghai, who have at least heard "authentic" *Jiangnan sizhu* performances, are often faulted for playing the notes
without having grasped the essence of the musical style; mastering the
style is even more difficult for performers who are geographically and/or
culturally distant from the living tradition.

Performance Style

There is relatively little agitation in either professional or amateur circles
for major changes in the traditional performance style of *Jiangnan sizhu*.
However, the treatment of musical dynamics and the deportment of the
performer are two aspects of performance that should be touched upon
in a discussion of musical change.

Changes in dynamic levels are important in most traditional Chinese
music, but they tend to be subtle, involving the dynamic shape of a single
sustained note or contrast between repetitions of an identical phrase. In
Jiangnan sizhu, accomplished traditional performers who play together
regularly pay attention to refining their treatment of dynamics, and the
traditional aphorism "inlaying and making way" implies dynamic interplay as well as contrast in melodic density. In professional circles it is
often suggested that increased attention to dynamic changes is one way
to bring new interest to old repertory in *Jiangnan sizhu,* as well as in other
traditional musics.

The amateur musicians I know all believe that dynamic changes are an
important part of *Jiangnan sizhu,* but they also stipulate that such changes

should not be exaggerated. On more than one occasion, when I mentioned one well-known performer's avowed interest in developing the dynamic aspect of *Jiangnan sizhu*, other musicians sang a convincing parody of his playing, followed by a rejoinder that such exaggeration has no place in the music. The implication is that dynamic contrasts should evolve naturally from the music itself and through interaction among the players rather than being arbitrarily imposed. Attitudes toward dynamics are undoubtedly affected by the fascination with nineteenth-century Western art music (since the early twentieth century and still continuing today) that has led to the widespread acceptance of a "late romantic" aesthetic in professional music circles. Most recent compositions for Chinese instruments emphasize extreme contrasts in volume, as well as in tempo, tonality, technique, and other elements.

Conservatory students usually learn a few pieces in each important regional style. To facilitate the students' learning, many educators have attempted to distill the important features of regional playing styles and to pass these on through their teaching, writing, and annotated or arranged repertory. These attempts are of undeniable value, but when not supplemented by conscientious listening they may encourage superficial interpretations bordering on parody, where the liberal application of a few characteristic ornaments is assumed to be sufficient to bring out the correct regional "flavor." This superficiality largely stems from using descriptive characterizations of stylistic elements in a prescriptive manner, somewhat akin to indiscriminately employing whole-tone scales and parallel thirteenth chords to "write like Debussy" or "bending" third and seventh scale degrees to "play the blues." These analogies may exaggerate the problem, but it is clear that a major reason for *Jiangnan sizhu* specialists' criticism of many professional performers' and composers' attempts to play or write in the style of their music is that these nonspecialists may "know" many of the special stylistic characteristics of the tradition but have not developed a sense of how, when, or how often to apply them.[7]

Traditionally, *Jiangnan sizhu* musicians rarely use extraneous motions or exaggerated facial expression while playing. In fact, in a series of photographs that I took of a group of performers, the prints appeared to be identical until I noticed that the performers' hands were in different positions on their instruments in each photograph. Such restraint is not forced or tense, and the need for restraint is rarely mentioned by *sizhu* musicians; it is simply that in traditional Chinese music, emotion is expressed through the music itself. Musicians have no need to "act out" their playing, and there is no audience to entertain.

As previously mentioned, the deportment of most modern professional Chinese musicians is quite different. They have been strongly influenced by extroverted Western art musicians; in addition, the duty of artists to "serve the masses" encourages musicians to help the audience understand the mood of the music by providing extramusical cues. Since the performance of Chinese instrumental music on the concert stage is a recent phenomenon, models for such performance had to be sought elsewhere; it is hardly surprising that the most influential models for performance behavior have been the Western or Western-inspired traditions that have also been most influential musically in this century.

However, even in professional circles, voices of protest can be heard. Some teachers and students at the Shanghai Conservatory strongly oppose overemphasizing the visual component of what is essentially an aural form of artistic communication. An outstanding young *qin* player complained to me repeatedly about having her performance grades lowered for failing to use "expressive" movements. Qin Pengzhang, a highly respected conductor and *pipa* player, wrote the following critique of a young *pipa* player's exaggerated choreography:

> The external movements during a performance should be natural, and properly reflect one's internal state. But often one notices that her right hand fingers would precede the plucking techniques with some preparatory gestures; these might involve movements of her head, shoulders, arms, elbows, and wrists, singly or in combination. Also noticeable are frequent shaking of head, raising of shoulders, sudden glare of eyes, swaying of body, and so forth. These external movements match the phrasing and accented notes of the music, and appear to be consciously designed to be so. Some of these external movements are not visually pleasing; they seem merely to impress upon the audience the seriousness of the performer. On the contrary, they tend to distract the audience's concentration on the music. Other movements appear to be aimed at purely visual effects. (1982:40; translation courtesy of Bell Yung)

Musical Instruments & Temperament

In recent years, silk strings have been increasingly rarely played in the PRC. High quality silk strings are difficult to obtain, so even players who prefer them may be forced to use strings made of other materials. However, the change to other materials has also involved elements of practicality and aesthetics. Steel strings and nylon-steel strings are durable, hold their pitch better than silk, and, most important, produce a significantly louder sound than pure silk.

The change in strings has also affected the balance of instruments in the *Jiangnan sizhu* ensemble, especially between steel-stringed "silk" and unchanged "bamboo" instruments. The *xiao* is now barely audible in any but the smallest ensemble and is now rarely used as the leading wind instrument, except in pieces in which the *dizi* is never played. The *yang-qin* played in *Jiangnan sizhu* has bronze strings, but the traditional instrument has a small resonator and is played with light, flexible beaters. It is relatively equal in dynamic level to the silk-stringed *pipa* and *erhu* but noticeably softer than the same instruments played with metal strings. The ideal material used for strings in *Jiangnan sizhu* is still a subject for discussion. Wei Zhongle has suggested that the study of the capabilities of musical instruments can contribute to the development of *Jiangnan sizhu* (1985:16) and that research on strings should be given high priority by those concerned with the tradition's future (ibid.:19).

The traditional *Jiangnan sizhu* ensemble is an example of what Liang Mingyue calls "polytemperament" (1985:23), in which different instruments in the same ensemble are tuned or constructed according to different principles of sound production. In recent decades the ensemble has become even more "poly." The equal-tempered *pipa* has become standard in amateur *Jiangnan sizhu* clubs, but the equidistant-hole *xiao* and *dizi* are usually retained. This contrast is a fundamental one, since the other important instruments are all tunable (*yangqin* and, to a lesser extent, *sheng*) or can play any gradation of pitch (*erhu, sanxian*). However, other than the controversy over which type of flute is appropriate for *Jiangnan sizhu,* the issue of temperament is rarely discussed by performers or scholars. (A "seven-tone equidistant" scale is sometimes mentioned but has little basis in reality, and may well be a concept devised to find an indigenous "folk" counterpart to the twelve-tone equal-tempered scale.) More important is being "in tune" within the group, with the intonation of the *yangqin*—the most difficult stringed instrument to retune—usually taken as the standard to which the instruments capable of adjusting their intonation must adapt.

MODERNIZATION & WESTERNIZATION

The influence of Western music on non-Western traditions has been a prominent theme in much recent literature in the field of ethnomusicology. Numerous studies of specific musical traditions have described or discussed such influence, and scholars such as Bruno Nettl (1978) and Margaret Kartomi (1981) have attempted to categorize the various types of responses to Western music and musical values. One of Nettl's books (1985) is an extended look at many of the ways in which musical cultures have been influenced by the West and the ways in which they have changed—and are changing—as a result of this influence. Central to discussions of musical change are syncretism, modernization, and Westernization; Nettl's definitions of these concepts—which, as he himself points out, are understood in very different ways by different scholars—will serve as a useful starting point for the present discussion. Summarizing the "heuristic concept of syncretism" developed by Melville Herskovits, Richard Waterman, and Alan Merriam, he describes it as "the confluence of similar or compatible culture traits to create new, mixed forms" (1985:19). Syncretism usually refers to a synthesis of elements drawn from two different cultures or from two different areas or ethnic groups within a culture. Contemporary *Jiangnan sizhu* can be viewed as a merging of the "popular" and "refined" streams of ensemble music native to the Jiangnan area, but since these streams both emanate from the same cultural-linguistic region, the music is not syncretic in the sense that the term is commonly used (although other traditions such as the Modern Chinese Orchestra and the Eight Model Works of the Cultural Revolution are clearly examples of musical syncretism).

The concepts of modernization and Westernization are much more pertinent to the present study:

> Modernization may be described as the incidental movement of a system or its components in the direction of Western music and musical life, without, however, requiring major changes in those aspects of the non-Western tradition that are central and essential. Westernization is the substitution of central features of Western music for their non-Western analogues, often with the sacrifice of essential facets of the tradition. (ibid.:20)

Scholars outside of the field of music have also employed these terms to describe cultural changes that do not actually involve the incorporation of Western elements but that are inspired or provoked by contact with Western culture. In his discussion of the role of the treaty ports in China's development, Rhoads Murphey has suggested that modernization be understood as

> a term that should connote not merely economic changes such as were involved in the emergence of a national market and the beginning of a technological revolution in production and transport, but institutional, organizational, and ideological adjustments to a new order, and the early emergence of Asian nationalism. Although these developments all involved something more than and different from Westernization, they were set in train primarily through the presence and actions of Westerners in Asia, and are appropriately viewed as Asian responses to Western stimuli. (1974:18)

Nettl's and Murphey's definitions are quite different in their language and scope, but they can be viewed as compatible, and together they describe several of the fundamental issues that need to be addressed before we can begin to evaluate the types of changes occurring in a specific tradition—musical or cultural. Some criteria need to be established for identifying "major changes," "central features," and "essential facets" of a tradition; in the case of China, we must determine which developments have been "set in train primarily through the presence and actions of Westerners."

Among *Jiangnan sizhu* musicians and scholars, there is much disagreement concerning the essential features of the tradition. The issue of Western influence on Chinese music is an extremely complex one. While direct Western influence on *Jiangnan sizhu* has been minimal, indirect influence has occurred. Western musicians and composers (regardless of whether they have been physically present in China) have been highly respected and imitated and have had a considerable impact on some types of Chinese music and on music education, affecting attitudes toward notation, improvisation, and the visual aspects of performance.[8] Amateur *Jiangnan sizhu* musicians have not adopted these new attitudes, and this puts them at odds with the policies of the professional musical community. The fact that they feel compelled to defend their traditional perspectives can be viewed as a type of ideological adjustment indirectly provoked by Western influence.

In much of contemporary Chinese music and culture, identifying which traits or concepts are Chinese and which are Western or non-Western–non-Chinese is a complex task. China has a long history of assimilating foreign objects and ideas, often using them in ways so undeniably Chinese that their foreign origin becomes irrelevant: most of the musical instruments in the *Jiangnan sizhu* ensemble, often treated as icons representing Chinese culture, evolved from prototypes not indigenous to China. This process of "Sinicization" continues today in all aspects of Chinese culture: socialist ideology, which Chinese refer to as "Marxism-Leninism," is a European system of thought, but Mao Zedong reshaped it for his own purposes, and his principles on aesthetics laid out at the Yanan forum are tailored to fit Chinese culture.[9] The emphasis placed on controlling the arts is an acknowledgement of their power to influence and change society; this concept has much stronger roots in Confucianism than in any form of Western philosophy. The idea of music originating from and serving "the masses" is tied to socialist ideals of antielitism and egalitarianism, yet it also can be traced to the Confucian belief that the music heard throughout a well-governed state should be "healthy" and reflect the order and harmony ideally found at all levels of social and political organization.

Many of the phenomena found in Chinese music today are neither as "Western" nor as "modern" as they may seem at first glance. The modern conservatory for training musicians has borrowed heavily from its Western counterpart in both pedagogy and curriculum, yet China has had institutions for training performers since antiquity. Attempts to establish an orthodoxy with standards—in instrument design, tuning, and "official" versions of repertory—to be followed by all may seem to be the product of an authoritarian regime or a response to the influence of Western art music, yet throughout Chinese history, new dynasties have been concerned with establishing their own musical standards. The promotion of the equal-tempered scale in China today is related to a widespread admiration for the Western music associated with equal temperament, yet the scale was invented in China.[10] Similarly, the institution of the Modern Chinese Orchestra may resemble the Western symphony, but large and diverse orchestras of Chinese musical instruments dating from well over two millennia ago have been historically documented and excavated. The attitudes toward musical notation prominent in professional circles today are undoubtedly influenced by Western art music, yet sophisticated indigenous notational systems were developed in China at an early date. In other words, the music conservatory, standardization of instruments and repertory, equal temperament, the large orchestra, and musical notation, all elements whose presence is often cited as evidence of Western influence on non-Western musical traditions, existed in China well before the presence and activities of Westerners in the last two centuries.

The existence of historical precedents within China, however, does not necessarily mean that contemporary developments are actually descended from these indigenous musical practices or conventions. The music played by Modern Chinese Orchestras has little relationship to that of ancient Chinese ensembles: it has been composed, for the most part, by individuals whose primary training is in Western art music, and common-practice harmonic principles and late-romantic aesthetics are central to most works written for this ensemble. The notion of a composer writing highly specific parts for each player is a rather Western one, as is that of a conductor who is not a player but leads the ensemble with gestures. The equal-tempered scale remained an intellectual curiosity for centuries in China and was not widely adopted until musicians began to admire foreign musics using it. Similarly, interaction between so-called "great" (orthodox, centralized, elite, refined) and "little" (heterodox, regional, folk, popular) traditions has shaped many aspects of Chinese culture, but the current push to modify and adapt little traditions and to bring them to the conservatory and concert stage can be viewed as an attempt to make indigenous Chinese music competitive with that of the West.

China has such a long and diverse musical history that virtually any musical feature can be identified as having been part of some tradition at some time somewhere in China. In many of the examples cited above, the Western impact is largely one of influencing the selections made concerning which indigenous musics, features, or concepts are admired, promoted, or emphasized in China today. Recently, extinct traditions or instruments have been reconstructed and reintroduced, developments often prompted by a desire to develop an indigenous tradition analogous or superior to one well-known in the West.

This influence on musical choices can also be seen in the neglect or deemphasis of indigenous musics or musical features for which a highly valued foreign counterpart does not exist. Long, slow, and static pieces are not widely admired in China today, but if "minimalist" or "new age" musics were to become popular, the status of Chinese repertory with similar musical features might change. Improvisation is rarely viewed as a legitimate musical art in Chinese professional musical circles, and this condescension is consistent with the fact that traditions from other cultures which prize improvisation or spontaneous recomposition by performers (such as India, the Middle East, Indonesia, and Africa) are generally relegated to the category of "primitive music," while jazz is still widely regarded as decadent dance music.

Many of the recent trends in Chinese music—conservatories, standardization, large orchestras, prescriptive notation—are based on principles that have existed in Chinese culture for centuries, but the modern application of these principles is heavily influenced by Western art music. Still, it must be remembered that all of these developments are still in their infancy. Because of this, their "foreignness" is often disturbingly obvious to people who value traditions that are indigenous to China or whose foreign origins have been obscured by centuries of Sinicization. Undoubtedly, Chinese educators, composers, and performers will continue to seek out ways to apply Western musical concepts to create results that are uniquely Chinese and complementary to preexisting Chinese musical concepts and traditions.

Epilogue

This study is intended to be a multifaceted introduction to the musical tradition *Jiangnan sizhu*. It is multifaceted in that various aspects of the music, its environment, and the ideology associated with it have been examined, and that perspectives and values held by professional performers, amateur performers, and musicologists (both Chinese and Western) have been considered. It is an introduction in that much research still remains to be done.

Each chapter concerns a discrete topic, but many of these topics are interlinked. A recurring theme is the interplay of individuality and commonality, which is a key to both the tradition's musical style and to its interpersonal dynamics. A *Jiangnan sizhu* musician shares a common tradition with a large number of other players with whom he or she interacts musically and socially on a regular basis and may also share a more specialized tradition with a smaller group in which the interaction involves a more intimate level of communication. As has been shown, through participation in a *Jiangnan sizhu* music club an individual belongs both to a small community in Shanghai society, those who know and play the music, and to a more exclusive one, the club. A player of a specific instrument is expected to follow many stylistic conventions in order to perform in the *Jiangnan sizhu* style appropriate for that instrument, but is also expected to develop a unique and recognizable style. In the repertory of *Jiangnan sizhu*, widely known pieces are juxtaposed with those known only to a select few. All of the musical parts share a common skeleton melody, yet some diversity among these parts is essential to the ensemble style, with the aesthetic ideal a harmonious, seamless blending in which the individual parts continually diverge and converge, emerging from the collective musical texture and receding back into it.

The *Jiangnan sizhu* musician thus exists in an environment in which he or she must maintain a balance between individual and collective identity. The music club serves both to affirm collective identity and to assert a uniqueness that distinguishes its members from all other such clubs. An individual is expected to be able to perform adequately in conjunction with any other group of musicians who know the music, yet aesthetic standards repeatedly stress the cultivation of an ensemble in which the same performers play together repeatedly over a long period of time.

Phenomena such as the balance between individuality and commonality and the presence of insider/outsider distinctions made at several different levels of exclusivity may be highly idiosyncratic, reflecting the society and musical environment of Shanghai. They may also be a manifestation of fundamental principles underlying the concept of the ensemble in Chinese music. Much more detailed information concerning the musical environments of other ensemble traditions is needed before we can begin to establish the particularity or universality of the musical and social characteristics found in Shanghai *Jiangnan sizhu*.

In many ways, the *Jiangnan sizhu* tradition has split into two branches, one amateur and one officially sponsored. The former is played in music clubs by individuals for whom the music is an avocation, while the latter is perpetuated by professional performers from Modern Chinese Orchestras and conservatories. At present, the best-known *Jiangnan sizhu* performing ensemble, which has made numerous commercial recordings of the music, is a quartet consisting of Lu Chunling, Ma Shenglong, Zhou Hao, and Zhou Hui.[1] All have been or are associated with the Shanghai Chinese Orchestra, but they have also played *Jiangnan sizhu* for most of their lives, and all except Ma are very active in the amateur music clubs. Among younger professional performers, however, few, if any, of those who perform or record *Jiangnan sizhu* have a strong background in the tradition. On several occasions while I was in Shanghai, the conductor of a Modern Chinese Orchestra in Singapore arranged to hear or videotape the quartet mentioned above. When one or more of the players were not available, Liu Yuehua and Lu Dehua, both factory workers, were recruited to complete the group.

At the official level, *Jiangnan sizhu* is a form of Chinese music being avidly promoted, as evidenced by the national and international coverage given to the 1987 competition in Shanghai. While amateur groups are still included in this type of competition, the fact that they were not awarded any of the prizes indicates that what is being promoted is a revisionist version of the tradition in which the more traditional groups are an anachronism. A newspaper article on this competition quoted the head of the composition department of the Shanghai Conservatory's observations on the event:

I am quite pleased with what I have heard in the competition. . . . The overall level of *Jiangnan sizhu* music, both the composition and the performance skills, has been raised. Some Western musical means of presentation are adopted in playing the music, such as the contrast of *forte* and *piano*. Polyphony and harmony are used in composition and the music no longer sounds simple and monotonous. (Qiao and Kong 1987)

The perspective of the judges for the competition was probably similar. All four of the top awards went to a team from the Central Conservatory in Beijing. Shanghai groups mentioned as receiving awards were the teams from the Shanghai Chinese Orchestra and the Shanghai Conservatory and the Six-Nation University Students' Orchestra (ibid.).[2] None of the amateur Shanghai *Jiangnan sizhu* clubs are included in the list of winners. The present study notwithstanding, the official school will most likely become the *Jiangnan sizhu* known to the Chinese musical community at large, while the amateur groups will continue to play for themselves and the occasional ethnomusicologist.[3] It is also likely that the two branches of the music will enrich each other and the tradition as a whole, and that their combined activities will result in increased awareness of and appreciation for a unique musical tradition.

Translation of the Regulations of the China National Music Ensemble

GENERAL PRINCIPLES

The China National Music Ensemble is a voluntary academic research organization for those who are involved in professional music work and for amateur music lovers who possess a definite level [of musical skill] (formerly the Purple Sounds National Music Club and China National Music Ensemble). Its purpose is to promote our country's socialist and realist people's new musical culture; [and to] serve as a helping hand for our Party's literary and artistic undertakings.

The China National Music Ensemble supports the literary and artistic policies of the Chinese Communist Party, upholds the directing of literature and arts toward the service of workers, peasants, and soldiers and actively participates in the people's revolutionary struggle. Through the methods of cooperative study and intensive individual research, [we will] continuously raise our level of playing (and singing), theoretical research, and musical composition.

The duties of the China National Music Ensemble are:

(1) To unite those who have a high level of specialized musical training and proficiency in the performance of Chinese or Western instruments, those whose work is in vocal music, researchers of music theory, and composers, to collectively research and mutually discuss various questions for study relating to the art of music: for example, instrumental and vocal performance techniques, compositional techniques, orchestration (including Chinese music, symphonic music, and orchestration combining Chinese and Western music), music criticism, research in music theory, musical aesthetics, reform of musical instruments, phonetics, and conducting.

(2) To organize members' study of Marxist and Leninist literary and artistic theory, to study literary and artistic principles and policies of the Party, to thoroughly study vocational and artistic skills, and to deeply par-

ticipate in the people's life of struggle. Unceasingly raising our level of ideological understanding and artistic training will cause music to greater serve the masses of the people.

(3) To organize members' study and research into our country's various ethnic groups' ancient music, song and dance music, theatrical music, folk music, *Jiangnan sizhu,* the outstanding revolutionary pieces dating from "May Fourth" [the May Fourth Movement of 1919] on, and foreign "music of the people," in order to "make the past serve the present" and "make foreign things serve China"; to industriously struggle to promote the cause of our country's music.

(4) To actively rehearse repertory and participate in performances, to satisfy the needs of the masses for music, and to promote the development and improvement of instrumental and vocal performing arts and composition.

(5) To organize performances or publications of the results of the group's research and to record outstanding performance repertory in order to expand the influence and usefulness of music in society. To preserve them properly so as to serve as documentation of this group's long-term intensive study and to serve as a contribution to our country's musical cause.

(6) To increase exchange activities with our brother musical organizations and with foreign musical organizations in order to enrich the content of our research and to widen our field of vision.

MEMBERSHIP

(1) All musical artists who have a high degree of specialized musical training and proficiency (no matter whether they are professional musicians or amateur music lovers with a high level of skill) and who endorse this group's regulations may apply to become members of the group.

(2) All those who wish to become members of this group must first submit an application to the group's business council and must attach documents which can indicate the applicant's musical and social activities; after undergoing examination and approval by the group's business council, they can become a member of the group.

(3) New members entering the group must pay a new member's fee; all members must pay a regular membership fee set by the group's business council.

(4) All members who are in one of the following situations, after undergoing examination by the group's business council, may be expelled or have their membership suspended:

1. Those who have been stripped of their citizen's right to vote.

2. Those who violate the national interest and people's interests through reactionary political actions or speech.

3. Those who violate this group's regulations or do harm to the work of the group.

4. Those who do not participate in rehearsals, instrumental or vocal performances, or compositional and theoretical activities for a long period of time.

ORGANIZATION

(5) The group's highest administrative organization is the plenary session of the membership. When a plenary session is not held, the business council elected by the membership is the highest administrative organization and is responsible for managing daily affairs.

(6) The business council is comprised of a president, a vice-president, a secretary, a performance organizer, a general affairs organizer, and an assistant organizer, who are responsible for planning and handling various activities.

(7) All repertory performed outside [the club] (including pieces composed or arranged by this group's members) or publications of compositions or theoretical articles which are done in the name of this group should first have the approval of the business council. Then they may be performed or published. Individuals' performing activities or published writings which are not in the name of this group are not covered by this regulation.

(8) A plenary session of the membership will convene once every six months, the business council will meet once a month, and unscheduled meetings may be convened by the president when necessary.

FUNDS

(9) The sources of the group's funds and operating expenses are:

1. Members' dues.

2. For all income derived from performances or publications in the name of this group, 60 percent should be put into the group's operating expense fund.

3. Other assistance.

SUPPLEMENTARY ARTICLES

These regulations will become effective after approval of a plenary session of the group's members; revisions must be similarly approved.

[The group's address is here.]

Approved July 1984

An Introduction to Cipher Notation

As used in *Jiangnan sizhu,* cipher notation uses the numerals one through seven to represent the seven degrees of (approximately) a major scale. At the beginning of a notated piece, the key is indicated by stating that "1 = D" (or E♭, E, etc.). A dot above or below a numeral indicates, respectively, a higher or lower octave. A numeral standing by itself is a quarter note. A single line beneath a numeral makes it an eighth note, a double line a sixteenth note, and so on (analogous to the number of beams attached to a note in staff notation). A hyphen indicates that the previous note is sustained for the time value assigned to the hyphen. A zero indicates a rest. Time values are assigned to sustained notes (hyphens) and rests (zeros) in the same manner as for pitches (numerals). A brief excerpt from an instrumental transition commonly played in the folk song "Moli Hua" will illustrate these principles.

Source: Traditional Jiangsu folk-song melody

"Moli Hua" (instrumental transition)

Notes

PREFACE

1. Since the late 1980s, several American graduate students in ethnomusicology have produced Ph.D. dissertations based on fieldwork in the PRC, including Terence Liu, Sue Tuohy, Daniel Ferguson, Francesca Ferguson (all 1988), and Frederic Lau (1991). The journal *CHINOPERL* has published many accounts of fieldwork in China and other articles (e.g., Pian 1984–85) which discuss music in Chinese society, and the *Association for Chinese Music Research Newsletter* and *CHIME* (the newsletter of the European Foundation for Chinese Music Research) include reports on fieldwork and other recent research. Alan Thrasher (1990) and Stephen Jones (forthcoming) have written monographs based on intensive fieldwork in China.

2. Many Chinese musicologists, including my teachers, have had extensive fieldwork experience, but have rarely written about performance context or musical behavior. In contrast to Western ethnomusicology, anthropology has had virtually no influence on Chinese musicology. This situation is now changing, and some influential Chinese scholars, especially those working with Chinese minority traditions, are beginning to focus on contextual and social issues.

3. Relatively brief but significant exceptions were Liang Mingyue (1971) and Lieberman (1971).

4. An administrator at the Shanghai Conservatory told me that there had been several students from Eastern Europe in the 1950s and 1960s. When I went to Shanghai in 1981, Rafaella Gallio, from Italy, and Odette Sanchez, from France, had already been studying at the conservatory.

5. I went to China under the auspices of the Committee on Scholarly Communication with the People's Republic of China, a U.S. government–sponsored organization supporting graduate and postdoctoral research in all fields of study. In the final weeks before my planned departure for China, the CSCPRC informed me that they had just learned that I would be assigned to the Shanghai Conservatory instead of, as originally planned, the Central Conservatory in Beijing. My assignment to Shanghai was thus unexpected; in light of the present study, it was also auspicious.

6. A *danwei* is one's place of work or study. While in China, my *danwei* was the Shanghai Conservatory.

7. It was not feasible to establish an ongoing student-teacher relationship with any of these amateur musicians, not only because I had "official" teachers at the conservatory, and it would have been inappropriate for others to usurp their role, but also because I was a foreigner. Despite the relative freedom of activity allowed to foreign students at the time I was

in China, limitations did exist, and many Chinese were understandably hesitant about establishing long-term unauthorized relationships as intimate as that of teacher-student.

8. At first, the amateur musicians only offered polite compliments about my playing. It was not until I had learned one of the more difficult pieces in the repertory, "Xingjie," that I began to receive serious criticism and advice on performance.

9. This is a Hong Kong reprint of the 1962 Shanghai Wenyi Chubanshe edition. A different Shanghai Wenyi Chubanshe edition from later in the 1960s omits several of the pieces associated with *Jiangnan sizhu*.

10. By "extended" I mean a year or more. Alan Thrasher's recent monograph on the Yi people of Yunnan province is based on relatively short—but obviously quite productive—fieldwork in China: a summer and a "brief but intense" follow-up (1990:11). Stephen Jones's book (forthcoming) is based on numerous relatively short research trips. Some of the authors of the dissertations mentioned in note 1 are in the process of writing books based on their fieldwork in China.

PROLOGUE

1. The character *da* can mean "large," "great," or even "serious" depending on the context. "Great" is closest to the sense of *da* as used in *Ba Da Mingqu*.

2. In Hong Kong, many pieces from the repertory of *Guangdong Yinyue* (the Cantonese *sizhu* tradition) are familiar to musicians and to much of the populace at large. *Nanguan* (another regional *sizhu* tradition) plays a relatively prominent role in the musical lives of communities in both Taiwan and Fujian. *Jiangnan sizhu* would seem to be a smaller part of the musical landscape in Shanghai than is either of these related traditions in their native environments.

1. HISTORICAL BACKGROUND & INTERGENRE RELATIONSHIPS

1. In one sense, *dou* means "grading" or "judging"; in another, "competition." *Chashan douyue* was performed as part of a festival celebrating the collection and grading of tea leaves. In addition, according to He, elements of competitiveness were part of the performances taking place at the event. Since both senses of *dou* may be implied, I have left the word untranslated.

2. In recent years *guanxian* has been applied to the Western symphony orchestra; historically, the term indicates an ensemble of string and wind instruments of unspecified type.

3. Mackerras (1972:7) translates *guan* as "single-reed *guan*." It is my understanding that all *guan* are double-reed instruments; that is, the mouthpiece is a double reed. Mackerras's intent may have been to distinguish this instrument from the *shuang guan* that uses two pipes, each with its own double reed.

4. Chinese musicologists often categorize instrumental ensemble genres combining winds and percussion as *chuida*, "blowing and striking," music, and *shifan gu* and *shifan luogu* are sometimes collectively referred to as *Sunan chuida*, "*chuida* music from southern Jiangsu." However, the labeling of these genres as *chuida* is somewhat misleading for at least two reasons: first, most *chuida* traditions feature double-reed wind instruments, but such instruments are only occasionally found in Jiangsu string-wind-percussion music; and second, stringed instruments are rarely featured in most *chuida* musics but are central to *shifan* music. For other reasons, Yang Yinliu has also suggested that the term *"chuida"* is not appropriate for describing these traditions (Yang Yinliu and Cao 1982:2; here, Yang explains

why he changed the title of a collection of notation from *Sunan Chuida*, as it appeared in an earlier addition, to *Sunan Shifan Guqu* [Sunan *shifan* drum pieces]).

5. The recordings to which I had access were made with a *shifan* expert playing the lead drum, accompanied by other musicians reading from notation. The tendency toward unison playing on these recordings may be due in part to the fact that some of the players were not thoroughly familiar with the music. I was not able to find any evidence that *shifan* music is still performed in China outside of the conservatories, and on a brief research trip to Wuxi, Li Minxiong and I found no *shifan* musical activity. However, *shifan* music is still played by Taoists in Suzhou (Tsao Pen-yeh, personal communication), and is also performed in Changshou (Chou Chun-yi, personal communication).

6. It should be noted that in this context *sizhu* is a designation of the instrumentation used in an ensemble and does not imply any direct connection among these geographically dispersed genres.

7. The early history of *Jiangnan sizhu* is still poorly documented. To date, the most authoritative account is a short article by Jin Zuli with Xu Ziren. A complete translation of this article is contained in Witzleben (1987b:201–15).

8. I am grateful to Stephen Jones for suggesting the phrase "is deemed superior" (personal communication).

9. According to former Datong member Qin Pengzhang (personal communication), the piece's five movements were adapted from traditional repertory: 1) "Nao Ge" (Cymbal song), a Qing dynasty ensemble piece; 2) "Zhuangtai Qiusi" (At the dressing table, thinking of autumn), a section from the *pipa* piece "Saishang Qu" (Song of the frontier); 3) "Jiangjun Ling" (The general leads his troops), a *pipa* piece; 4) an excerpt from the *pipa* piece "Yue Er Gao" (The moon is high); and 5) an excerpt from the *pipa* piece "Bawang Xie Jia" (The hegemon king sheds his armor).

10. This is a large ensemble of Chinese instruments arranged in "families," like a Western symphony orchestra, led by a conductor. These ensembles are called *minzu yuetuan*, "people's orchestras," in the PRC; different names are used in Taiwan, Hong Kong, and Singapore. "Modern Chinese Orchestra" is Han Kuo-huang's English term for this type of ensemble; although not a literal translation of any of the Chinese names, it is a concise and accurate description of this type of ensemble (see Han 1979).

11. As has been pointed out, the term *"sizhu"* has been in use for centuries, and Shanghai musicians have colloquially referred to their music as *sizhu;* the addition of the term *"Jiangnan"* clarifies the tradition's locale and distinguishes it from other regional traditions that are now often referred to as types of *sizhu* ensembles. Today, the expression *"Jiangnan sizhu"* is widely used by the performers in Shanghai music clubs.

12. Although I have never witnessed such a procession in Shanghai, I have observed Chaozhou musicians playing in a procession in Hong Kong. Instruments normally played while seated, such as the *erhu*, were propped against the performer's hip, and the *yangqin* was placed in a sedan chair that was carried by two men while a third played the instrument as he walked along. Although the softer-sounding instruments are inaudible from a distance, spectators can hear each instrument clearly as the players walk by.

13. To a Westerner like myself, the title suggests the metaphor of a bridge joining husband and wife or two families, but I found no support for this interpretation among Chinese musicians or scholars.

14. *Jiangnan sizhu* may sometimes be heard in variety shows featuring many types of Chinese and Western musics, but this type of contextual relationship does not indicate any significant relationships among the traditions so juxtaposed.

15. It is interesting to note that the *siming nanci* variant of this latter piece, while different from the *Jiangnan sizhu* version, has many similarities to the version for *zheng* solo

transmitted by Wang Xunzhi as taught to me by Sun Wenyan. As Wang was originally from Hangzhou, this may indicate that there is a regional Zhejiang version of this piece related to, but distinct from, that played in Shanghai.

16. Miao and Qiao also discuss mode, melodic framework, phrase patterns, and other topics that may have implications for the further study of *Jiangnan sizhu*. Alan Thrasher has suggested that the folk song "Moli Hua," the *Jiangnan sizhu* piece "Huanle Ge," the Cantonese piece "Pinghu Qiuyue," and the *pipa* solo (also adapted for Cantonese ensemble) "Hangong Qiuyue" form a type of tune family that apparently includes repertory from both the Jiangnan and Cantonese areas: "I believe that their ["Hangong Qiuyue" and "Pinghu Qiuyue"] stylistic similarities with *Moli Hua* and *Huanle Ge* are more than just coincidence. Because of their common modal characteristics, melodic cliches, and overall structures, these pieces belong to a particular melody family of central eastern China" (1985:253).

17. A recording of Shanghai Taoist music *(Ying Xian Ke)* names "Xiao Baimen" as one of the *qupai* in a medley. Listening to the recording, I found no apparent relationship to the *Jiangnan sizhu qupai* of the same name, but detailed analysis may well establish that the two tunes are musically related. See chapter 5 for a discussion of the "Xiao Kaimen"/"Xiao Baimen" tune complex.

2. *JIANGNAN SIZHU* IN SHANGHAI, 1981–1985

1. Bonnie Wade has used these terms to describe audiences for classical Indian music: a listener is "a person who is focusing primary attention on the music-making," while a hearer is "a person who is hearing music while focusing primary attention on something other than the music" (1984:14, 47n.5). Music that can either be listened to attentively or ignored is certainly also widespread in contemporary Western society, from folk and jazz clubs to restaurants and cocktail lounges.

2. In practice, the solos are most often combined into groups of three instruments playing at a time. Informants state that this is a time-saving measure, as the piece is already quite long. I suspect that it may also serve as a face-saving measure: when I heard the piece played with individual solos, some players almost invariably became nervous and lost their place.

3. The music clubs' statements of purpose are rarely available to nonmembers, and I cannot yet ascertain if this document is typical.

4. These included the *Jiangnan sizhu* music clubs, amateur and professional Modern Chinese Orchestras, children's groups, and students and teachers from the Shanghai Conservatory.

5. The linguistic shortcomings of a foreigner or overseas Chinese who cannot speak the Shanghai dialect are somehow more readily tolerated.

6. Some of the conservatory's foreign students have had extensive contact with the *Jiangnan sizhu* clubs, but they cannot be considered a permanent part of Shanghai's musical community.

7. One student told me that his teacher assigned him to memorize "Zhonghua Liuban" for the next lesson. When the student found this task impossible, the teacher admitted that he could not memorize the piece either.

8. Cantonese Music is often cited as a *sizhu* tradition that has maintained its integrity while expanding its repertory and enlarging its audience. It should be noted that the most influential composers and innovators in Cantonese Music, such as Lü Wencheng, have had a strong background in performing Cantonese Music and Cantonese opera, so their compositions are deeply rooted in the traditional Cantonese style.

9. In one of my lessons, Zhou did criticize me for mixing his arrangement with that of another musician, a published version that I had previously learned. This indicates that

even though he wanted me to be able to depart from his notated version, I was expected to thoroughly master it first, and my own additions should be compatible with his artistic conception of the piece.

3. INSTRUMENTS

1. In English, overviews can be found in entries in *The New Grove Dictionary of Musical Instruments* (Lui 1984; Thrasher 1984a–i) and *The New Grove Dictionary of Music and Musicians* (Liang 1980; Lui 1980; and Mackerras 1980), all of which include substantial bibliographies. In Chinese, *Zhongguo Yueqi* (1978) and Zheng Deyuan (1984) are comprehensive surveys of musical instruments. Hu (1982), a manual for orchestration with Chinese instruments, includes information such as the range and pitch vocabulary of each instrument. Chinese music dictionaries (notably Miao Tianrui, Ji, and Guo 1984) include entries, often illustrated, for individual instruments, and a survey of musical instruments of China's minority peoples (Yuan Bingchang and Mao 1986) includes many photographs of instruments related to those of the Han Chinese. Among the writings on specific instruments, the following include detailed descriptions of the instruments and playing techniques: for *dizi*, Thrasher (1978), Zhao (1985), and Lau (1991); for *xiao*, Sun (1977); for *sheng*, Miller (1983); for *erhu*, Qian (1982), Yu (1985), and Terence Liu (1988); for *pipa*, Addison (1974) and Myers (1987; 1992); for *yangqin*, Ng (1980) and Le (n.d.).

2. A player who has mastered these four instruments is sometimes referred to as a *quanshou*, literally a "complete hand." A few experts can play all of the instruments in the ensemble, but such comprehensive ability is rare among younger players and almost unheard of in contemporary professional circles.

3. The nomenclature for pitch register is a modification of the Helmholtz system, substituting superscript Arabic numerals for apostrophes. Thus, low C, bass C, middle C, treble C, and high C are written respectively as C, c, c^1, c^2, and c^3 rather than as C, c, c', c", and c'". Each octave begins with a C, so that the note below middle C (c^1) is b and the note above it is $c\sharp^1$. When discussing keys or scale degrees, no specific octave is implied unless so indicated.

4. In the examples notated here, some of the symbols designating types of ornaments are those that *Jiangnan sizhu* musicians themselves use. However, for symbols that are difficult to read when adapted to staff notation, I have chosen my own symbols. In these illustrative examples, when a special symbol is used, the first measure of the example shows the symbol and the following measure gives an approximate indication of the musical result. When no special symbol is used (as in example 3.1b), no explanatory measure is added.

5. I gave a copy of the recording *Chinese Classical Instrumental Music*, made in the United States in the late 1940s by Shanghai musicians including Sun Yude, to Sun Wenyan, his daughter and my *zheng* teacher. She commented that the performers were obviously using silk-stringed instruments, the sound of which is so different from what is commonly heard today.

6. Stopping the strings with different parts of the finger also gives the performer different kinesthetic sensations. Playing with the pads of the fingers is said to produce a "thicker" sound, and this quality is undoubtedly experienced tactilely as well as aurally. See Bell Yung's article on the *qin* (1984) for a discussion of kinesthetics in Chinese instrumental performance.

7. This statement does not apply to the pieces in the Additional Repertory called *guqu*. These have been adapted from solo *pipa* repertory, and the techniques found in the original solo versions are retained in the ensemble *pipa* part.

4. REPERTORY

1. Attempting to define musical style reveals the inherent limitations of using speech to describe nonverbal phenomena, a problem Charles Seeger has addressed in many of his writings. The article "Speech, Music, and Speech about Music" (1977a) is a concise introduction to his ideas on this issue.

2. In many cases, only part of the club's playing session was observed and documented, so both the total number of pieces played and the numbers of performances of some individual pieces were actually higher than the figures given. My own presence may have influenced the choice of repertory played, and the fact that I visited some clubs more frequently than others gives disproportionate weight to the repertory favored by certain groups.

3. Two music clubs changed their locale while I was in Shanghai. Changes in location result in a somewhat different combination of musicians, which may well influence the repertory chosen. I have counted the repertory played by these clubs in their old and new locations separately, so some pieces are listed as being played by as many as eleven different music clubs.

4. The English word "florid" is somewhat different in its implications. A florid melody may be ornate, but all of the notes are written into the music or are inseparable from the melody itself. The Chinese term implies notes which are added, often spontaneously, to a skeletal melody.

5. A collection of the *pipa* music of Ju Shilin (1796–1819) contains both "Lao Baban" and a set of ten variations entitled "Liuban" (transnotated in Lin 1983). This manuscript was hand copied and recopied before being published, so it is impossible to verify if it does indeed contain versions of these pieces which predate those of Rong Zhai.

6. I am not aware of any Chinese term used to categorize the performance characteristics I have called "soft style." The usage of this term in reference to *Jiangnan sizhu* refers to instrumentation and volume. It should not be confused with the "soft" and "hard" string ensembles in Cantonese Music, which differ mainly in the string instruments played, nor with the terms "soft" and "hard" in Kejia (Hakka) music, which refer to different scales or modes.

7. These pieces are "old" in the sense that detailed musical notation from nineteenth-century collections has survived and that some of their titles are found in literary references that predate surviving notation by several centuries. Some of the Eight Great Pieces or the "mother tunes" on which they are based may well predate some of the *guqu*.

8. I have, however, heard one recording made by *Jiangnan sizhu* musicians on which small bells or bowls are played for a performance of "Pu'an Zhou," probably to invoke the atmosphere of Buddhist music. Arrangements of these pieces for Modern Chinese Orchestra may also add percussion.

9. Their performance of "Xunyang Yeyue" can be heard on the recording *Hangong Qiuyue*. An abbreviated version of the piece is also included on *Chinese Classical Instrumental Music*.

10. One other recent composition was heard in a music club (the performance of "Jiangnan zhi Chun" discussed in chapter 2), but is not included in the table as I was not documenting the repertory played on that occasion. The repertory played in the 1985 festival is also excluded, since the table represents repertory played by *Jiangnan sizhu* music clubs in their customary performing environments.

11. "Pipa Guqu" may simply be a generic term rather than a title. "Yu Furong" is the subtitle of the last section of the *pipa* piece "Hangong Qiuyue," and the title may refer to this section played by itself. At the time I heard these performances, I was not yet familar enough with the repertory to be able to identify these pieces other than by the titles that were given to me.

5. FORM

1. My understanding of this and other terms and concepts discussed in this chapter is largely based on my studies at the Shanghai Conservatory with Li Minxiong in 1981-82 and 1984–85, and much of the analysis which follows is the result of his guidance. Li's textbook (1982) is the most complete collection of his writings. A large portion of that material has appeared in his collection of analyses of forty instrumental pieces (1983) and in other publications and manuscripts (1981; 1987; n.d.). A large body of writing exists concerning the theory and analysis of Chinese instrumental music: among the recent books by other scholars are Gao (1981), Ye (1983), Li Xi'an and Jun Chi (1985), and Yuan Jingfang (1987). Structural elements of some of the Eight Great Pieces are discussed in these sources and also in Thrasher (1985). The "Asian Music Theory" issue of the journal *Asian Music* (1989; articles by Gao, Han, Huang, Jones, Thrasher, and Tsao) includes discussion of formal structures and *qupai* in various genres of Chinese music.

2. For example, many *zheng* pieces from Henan and Shandong provinces are variants of "Lao Baban" that adhere strictly to a sixty-eight-beat metrical structure. The melodies in these variants, however, often diverge considerably from the original tune, at times only preserving the opening phrase of "Lao Baban." Chaozhou and Kejia musical traditions also make much use of metrically strict expansion (see Thrasher 1988).

3. *Zi* literally means "character" or "word," but since in traditional Chinese *gongchepu* notation ideographs are used to represent scale degrees, the implication in this context is that of a musical note.

4. In a sense, this type of shift is a modulation, as the basic anhemitonic pentatonic scale changes from 1 2 3 5 6 to 7 2 3 5 6, which can be rearranged as 5 6 7 2 3. If in the original scale 1 were equivalent to C, the latter scale could be rewritten as 1 2 3 5 6 with 1 as G. However, since the original heptatonic pitch vocabulary does not change, the latter scale would have a lowered seventh degree (F natural), as in the mixolydian mode. For this reason, Chinese musicologists view the process of *jiezi* as being different from modulation. It should be noted that in contemporary Chinese music theory, equal temperament is assumed, so that the microtonal changes in intervallic relationships which traditionally characterize different keys are not taken into account. The principle of *jiezi* is discussed at length in Li Minxiong's writings.

5. Another common explanation is that the opening phrase was originally six beats long and was later expanded to eight beats (see Huang 1982; Thrasher 1985:243-44). Since the earliest notated sources all contain the eight-beat opening, as do all the *Jiangnan sizhu* variants whose titles include the word "six," I consider Shen's explanation to be more credible.

6. The meaning of *"yaopian"* in this context is obscure. In *Kunqu* opera, it refers to the treatment in which a *qupai* is followed by a variant of itself; rather than repeat the name of the *qupai* in the notation, the term *"yaopian"* is written as an indicator of this treatment. Since the musical material in the so-called *yaopian* in "Man Sanliu" is not a variant of the preceding section or of any other part of the piece, this explanation of the term cannot apply here.

7. Li Minxiong treats this passage as an extension of the previous B section in his analysis of "Sanliu" (1982:318).

8. The scheme for "Sanliu" is basically that of Li Minxiong (1982:318); the scheme for "Meihua Sannong" was a collaboration between Li and myself, based on transnotation from the original Li Fangyuan collection.

9. Li Minxiong's analysis of the many derivatives of "Kaimen" (an unpublished study that I was able to examine), for example, involves considerable creative imagination in reconciling seeming discrepancies among the various pieces.

10. The traditional order of solos is *dizi, sanxian, sheng, fanhu, qinqin, xiao, pipa, yangqin,* and *erhu.* At present, the solo passages are usually condensed into three groups of three instruments each, with the groupings following this same order.

11. The correspondence is so close that in at least one notated version of "Sihe" (Gan 1985:334–38) the opening section is subtitled "Man Sanliu," and the third section (the end of "Yu Elang") is subtitled "Sanliu." Although accomplished *Jiangnan sizhu* performers are well aware of this and other interrelationships, most Chinese scholars writing on *Jiangnan sizhu* have ignored this and other "Sihe"/"Sanliu" connections. Alan Thrasher has made note of the "Sihe"/"Sanliu" relationships and their implications for our understanding of the repertory as a whole (1985:257–58).

6. VARIATION

1. "Zhonghua Liuban" is the piece most frequently performed by Shanghai *sizhu* groups and is clearly representative of the tradition as it exists today, so it has been selected for the analyses in chapters 6 and 7.

2. Because of the incomplete nature of the repeat, the measure numbers of corresponding points in the three cycles are separated by the number 44 rather than 60.

3. At least two cycles are almost always played in Shanghai *Jiangnan sizhu* clubs. The choice of whether or not to play the third cycle lies largely with the *dizi* player; on almost every occasion that I heard these performers play the piece, Cai and Lu played the third cycle while Dong and Jin did not.

7. TEXTURE

1. This term does not appear in the earlier articles cited by Mok (Shen Zhibai 1958; Chen Mingzhi 1959). Although Mok's use of the English term "heterophony" is appropriate for describing the musical examples in his article, the original sources are terminologically less clear. The title of Chen's article, for example, which Mok translates as "The Heterophonic Factor in Chinese Music," is literally closer to "A Preliminary Discussion of Polyphonic Elements in My Country's Folk Music."

2. In the past, Chinese notation—like ordinary Chinese writing—was written in vertical columns, but for contemporary musicologists, "vertical" texture refers to the relationship between sounds occurring simultaneously, a concept referring to notes as they appear in Western staff or cipher notations.

8. AESTHETICS

1. This and the following two quotations are Van Gulik's translations of the handbook. Both the translations and original Chinese texts are included in the reference cited.

2. I am speaking here of the idealized *qin* performance aesthetics that are expressed in handbooks for that instrument. While contemporary *qin* players would not think of performing their instrument in a teahouse environment, I know several *qin* players who enjoy listening to *Jiangnan sizhu,* and some musicians are accomplished in playing both traditions.

3. The concept of saturation has been described by Lewis Rowell in his comparison of Indian and Japanese music and aesthetics, with the Indians preferring a saturated sound spectrum (1983:193, 196).

4. The preceding quotation from Shanghai Qunzhong does not mention any specific pieces; in fact, the statement is part of an introductory essay for a collection of notation that includes a score for an unedited "Man Liuban." The criticism may be directed at the slow sections of "Xingjie," which the collection presents in the edited version discussed below.

5. Barbara Smith has provided some insightful observations in response to my interpretation, and her comments deserve repeating:

> I might ask if, for the older players, playing *Jiangnan sizhu* is a stable (even if fluid) point of respite from other kinds of recent—and forced—changes in the social milieu; that is, they may have comfortably at hand as much repertory as they have time to enjoy, and they may have so many other challenges and social adjustments to make that they do not seek more kinds of challenges (other than participating in "good" performances) in their *Jiangnan sizhu* activity. As I remember the "concert piano scene" when I was young [in the 1920s–1930s], the active piano repertory in recitals in the US included Bach (although the pieces had been composed for harpsichord or clavichord they were a basic part of "piano literature"—perhaps analogous to the *pipa* pieces assimilated into *Jiangnan sizhu*?), Mozart/Beethoven, the "Germanic romantic composers" and the "French impressionist composers" (the latter being about as close to "contemporary" as was common in recitals/concerts, although these composers had died some decades before). Admittedly, for the older concert pianists of that period, the impressionist compositions were composed during their lifetimes—though by composers who were older than they. The exception to this statement was Rachmaninoff who played his own pieces (much as Beethoven, Chopin and Liszt had played their own pieces), but at the time (so far as I remember) other pianists of Rachmaninoff's age-group did not play Rachmaninoff's pieces—it was pianists of a younger generation who included his pieces on their programs, and a still younger generation who began to program American and other more contemporary music. (Incidentally, these younger pianists played quite differently from the old-timers—even in playing the standard "classics"). (personal communication, May 2, 1990)

It must be admitted that even the most progressive *Jiangnan sizhu* devotees are close to the conservative end of the spectrum of musical activity in contemporary China, and many of the values expressed by playing or appreciating *Jiangnan sizhu* are out of step with modern society and music. In the early twentieth century the tradition was rapidly evolving and changing, and musicians may well have been much readier to embrace recently composed Cantonese repertory than musicians today would be to accept contemporary compositions.

6. The former group can be heard on the recording *Hangong Qiuyue,* and the latter group is featured on *Huanle Ge* and *Jie Xinniang.*

7. I am using the word "specialists" to denote musicians whose primary area of musical expertise is *Jiangnan sizhu.* They may or may not be professionals; in fact, few professionals are *Jiangnan sizhu* specialists.

8. Terence Liu, in his dissertation on the development of the solo *erhu* tradition (1988), includes considerable discussion of performers' changing attitudes toward tradition, modernization, and "development." He also discusses the effects of political events on performers' careers and on the fluctuating popularity of repertory and styles.

9. McDougall (1980) is an annotated translation of these talks.

10. See Needham and Robinson (1962:220-28) for a discussion of the development of twelve-tone equal temperament in China.

EPILOGUE

1. Several of this quartet's recordings, including *Popular Jiangnan Music,* are listed in the Selected Discography.

2. The recordings *Hanjiang Canxue* and *Suti Manbu* are selections from this competition.

3. The *Shanghai Jiangnan Sizhu Xuehui* (Shanghai Society for the Study of *Jiangnan Sizhu* Research) was established in 1987, and published a journal the following year (Shanghai Jiangnan 1988). However, according to Zhou Hao and Zhou Hui, no further issues of the journal have been produced (as of 1993), and much of the situation described in this book remains the same: in particular, very few young professional musicians or conservatory students are actively involved with the amateur music clubs (personal communication). However, the quartet of the Zhou brothers, Lu Chunling, and Ma Shenglong has performed in England and (with Lu replaced by a local *dizi* player) in Hong Kong, so international awareness of *Jiangnan sizhu* music continues to grow. Frederick Lau (1993) has some insightful comments on recent developments in *Jiangnan sizhu*.

Character List & Glossary

PERSONAL NAMES

A Bing	阿炳	*erhu* player and composer (real name Hua Yanjun)
Bai Juyi	白居易	Tang dynasty poet
Cai Cide	蔡慈德	*Jiangnan sizhu dizi* player
Cao Song	曹松	Tang dynasty poet
Chen Dacan	陳大燦	Taoist *erhu* player
Chen Liansheng	陳蓮笙	Taoist priest and musician
Chen Yonglu	陳永祿	*erhu* and *pipa* player and conservatory teacher
Chen Yongnian	陳永年	*Jiangnan sizhu* musician
Chen Zijing	陳子敬	*pipa* player
Chuan Jiafu	傅家福	*Jiangnan sizhu* musician
Dong Kejun	董克鈞	*Jiangnan sizhu dizi* player
Du Lian'gen	杜連根	*Jiangnan sizhu dizi* player
Gan Tao	甘濤	*erhu* player and conservatory teacher
Gao Houyong	高厚永	musicologist
He Baoquan	何寶泉	*zheng* player and conservatory teacher
Hou Shiquan	候世泉	*Jiangnan sizhu sheng* player
Hua Yanjun	華彥鈞	*erhu* player and composer (known as A Bing)
Jin Minggao	金鳴皋	Taoist musician
Jin Zuli	金祖禮	*Jiangnan sizhu* musician and scholar
Li Fangyuan	李芳園	compiler of 1895 collection of *pipa* notation

Li Minxiong	李民雄	musicologist, performer, and composer
Li Tingsong	李廷松	*pipa* player
Lin Shicheng	林石城	*pipa* player and scholar
Liu Chengyi	劉成乙	*Jiangnan sizhu erhu* player
Liu Tianhua	劉天華	*erhu* and *pipa* player and composer
Liu Yuehua	劉躍華	*Jiangnan sizhu erhu* player
Lu Chunling	陸春齡	*dizi* player
Lu Dehua	陸德華	*Jiangnan sizhu pipa* player
Lü Wencheng	呂文成	Cantonese musician and composer
Lui Pui Yuan (Lü Peiyuan)	呂培源	*pipa* and *qin* player
Ma Shenglong	馬聖龍	*pipa* player and conductor
Qin Pengzhang	秦鵬章	*pipa* player and conductor
Ren Huichu	任悔初	*yangqin* player and instrument maker
Rong Zhai	榮齋	compiler of notation for *Xiansuo Beikao*
Shao Xiaoxian	邵孝賢	*siming nanci* musician
Shen Duomi	沈多米	*erhu* player
Shen Fengquan	沈鳳泉	*erhu* player
Shi Quan	石泉	*Jiangnan sizhu pipa* player and composer
Song Jinglian	宋景濂	*xiao* player
Sun Wenyan	孫文妍	*zheng* player and conservatory teacher
Sun Yude	孫裕德	*xiao* and *pipa* player and conservatory teacher
Tan Weiyu	潭謂裕	*xiao* and *dizi* player and conservatory teacher
Teng Yongran	滕永然	musicologist
Wang Yuting	汪昱庭	*pipa* player
Wang Xunzhi	王巽之	*zheng* player
Wei Liangfu	魏良輔	Ming dynasty *Kunqu* singer
Wei Zhongle	衛仲樂	*pipa* and *qin* player and conservatory teacher
Wu Zhimin	吳之珉	*erhu* player and conservatory teacher
Xu Qingyan	許青彥	musicologist and composer
Xu Xingfa	許興法	*Jiangnan sizhu pipa* player
Yang Lixian	楊立賢	*Jiangnan sizhu erhu* player
Yin Xiaoxiang	尹校翔	*Jiangnan sizhu* musician

Zhang Zhengming	張徵明	*Jiangnan sizhu yangqin* player
Zhang Zupei	張祖培	*pipa* player and conservatory teacher
Zhao Yongping	趙永平	*Jiangnan sizhu erhu* player
Zheng Jinwen	鄭覲文	founder of the Datong music club
Zhou Hao	周皓	*Jiangnan sizhu erhu* player and teacher
Zhou Hui	周惠	*Jiangnan sizhu yangqin* player and teacher
Zhou Shaomei	周少梅	*erhu* player and teacher

MUSICAL INSTRUMENTS

ban	板	clapper; also a technical term
bangzi	梆子	woodblock
biqi gu	荸薺鼓	"water chestnut drum," double-headed frame drum
daqin	打琴	struck zither (hammer dulcimer)
di	笛	transverse bamboo flute
diangu	點鼓	double-headed frame drum
dizi	笛子	transverse bamboo flute
dongxiao	洞簫	end-blown bamboo flute
fanhu	反胡	two-stringed bowed lute, the lower-pitched cross *erhu*
erhu	二胡	two-stringed bowed lute (fiddle)
guan	管	double-reed aerophone
Guangdong bangzi	廣東梆子	woodblock ("Cantonese" woodblock)
guban	鼓板	"drum" and "clapper," both played by the same musician
guqin	古琴	seven-stringed plucked zither
huaigu	懷鼓	double-headed frame drum
hudie yangqin	蝴蝶揚琴	"butterfly *yangqin*," struck zither
huqin	胡琴	two-stringed bowed lute (generic name)
paiban	拍板	clapper
pengling	碰鈴	bronze concussion bells
pipa	琵琶	four-stringed plucked lute
qiaoqin	敲琴	struck zither (hammer dulcimer)
qin	琴	seven-stringed plucked zither

qinqin	秦琴	two- or three-stringed plucked lute
qinxiao	琴簫	end-blown bamboo flute
qudi	曲笛	*"Kunqu dizi,"* transverse bamboo flute
ruan	阮	four-stringed plucked lute
sanxian	三絃	three-stringed unfretted plucked lute
sheng	笙	free-reed mouth organ
shuangguan	雙管	double-pipe double-reed aerophone
shugu	書鼓	double-headed frame drum
suona	嗩吶	double-reed aerophone
tiqin	提琴	two-stringed bowed lute
tongsiqin	銅絲琴	struck zither (hammer dulcimer)
xiao	簫	end-blown bamboo flute (a different character from the term meaning "small")
yangqin	揚琴	struck zither (hammer dulcimer)
yueqin	月琴	four-stringed plucked lute
zheng	箏	thirteen- to twenty-one-stringed plucked zither; also called *gu zheng*

OTHER NAMES, TERMS, & TITLES

Aihaozhe	愛好者	"Music Lovers," name of a *Jiangnan sizhu* music club
Ba Da Mingqu	八大名曲	"eight great famous pieces," *Jiangnan sizhu* repertory
Ba Da Qu	八大曲	"eight great pieces," *Jiangnan sizhu* repertory
baisha xiyue	白沙細樂	"white sand delicate music," *sizhu* genre from Yunnan province
Baiyunguan	白雲觀	"White Cloud Temple," Taoist temple in Shanghai
ban	板	"beat" or "measure"; also a percussion instrument
banyan	板眼	"beats" and "eyes," pattern of strong and weak beats
"Bawang Xie Jia"	霸王卸甲	"The hegemon king sheds his armor," title of a piece

bayin	八音	"eight sounds," an ancient system of instrument classification
"Changhen Ge"	長恨歌	"Lament everlasting," title of a poem by Bai Juyi
chanyin	顫音	"shaking note," *dizi* technique
Chaozhou xianshi	潮州絃詩	"Chaozhou string poetry," *sizhu* genre from Guangdong province
chashan douyue	茶山斗樂	"*dou* music from the tea hills," ancient musical genre
"Chezi Kaimen"	尺字開門	"*Chezi* [a scale degree] open the gate," title of *qupai*
chuanqi	傳奇	"marvel tales," historical genre of Chinese opera
chuida	吹打	"blowing and striking," wind and percussion music
"Chun Man Pujiang"	春滿浦江	"Spring is full on the Pu River," title of a piece
"Chun Zao"	春早	"Spring morning," title of a piece
"Chunfeng Chui Jiangnan"	春風吹江南	"The spring wind blows in Jiangnan," title of a piece
chunhou	淳厚	"mellow and rich"
"Chunhui Qu"	春輝曲	"Spring brightness tune," title of a piece
Chunjiang	春江	"Spring River," name of a *Jiangnan sizhu* music club
"Chunjiang Hua Yueye"	春江花月夜	"Spring, river, flowers, moon, and evening," title of a piece
ci	次	"secondary"
"Da Kaimen"	大開門	"Large open the gate," title of a *qupai*
daiyin	帶音	"leading note," *erhu* technique
dandang	單檔	*Jiangnan sizhu* played by only two instruments
dantanlun	單彈輪	"single plucked roll," *yangqin* technique

danwei	單位	one's place of work or study in China
"Dao Baban"	倒八板	"Inverted eight beats," title of a piece
"Dao Chun Lai"	到春來	"The coming of spring," title of a piece
Datong	大同	"Great Togetherness," name of an early Shanghai music club
dayin	打音	"struck note," *dizi* technique
"Dengyue Jiaohui"	燈月交輝	"Moon and lanterns mutually shining," title of a piece
di san bian	第三遍	"the third time"; here, third cycle of a piece
dianzhi huayin	墊指滑音	"padded finger sliding note," *erhu* technique
difang secai	地方色彩	"regional color," characteristics of a regional style
duo ting duo he	多聽多合	"listen more, (play) together more," aphorism
errentai paiziqu	二人台牌子曲	sizhu genre from Inner Mongolia
fan	繁	"complex" or "dense"
"Fan Wang Gong"	凡忘工	"*Fan* [a scale degree] obliterates *gong* [a scale degree]," title of a piece
fangman jiahua	放慢加花	"making slow and adding flowers," technique of structural expansion
fengge	風格	"style"
"Fenghuang Sandiantou"	鳳凰三點頭	"The phoenix nods its head three times," title of a section of the piece "Sihe Ruyi"
gaochao	高潮	"high tide" or "climax"
gongchepu	工尺譜	notational system using Chinese characters
gu	古	"old"

Guangdong Yinyue	廣東音樂	"Cantonese music," *sizhu* genre from Guangdong province
Guangxi wenchang	廣西文場	narrative song genre from Guangxi province
guanxian	管絃	"winds and strings," type of ensemble music
gudian	古典	"old" or "classical"
"Guomin Dale"	國民大樂	"Great happiness for the nation's people," title of a piece
Guoyu	國語	national Chinese spoken dialect
Guoyue	國樂	"national [Chinese] music"
Guoyuehui	國樂會	"national music club"
Guoyueshe	國樂社	"national music club"
guqu	古曲	"old pieces," subgenre of *Jiangnan sizhu* repertory
"Hangong Qiuyue"	漢宮秋月	"Han palace and autumn moon," title of a piece
"Hantian Lei"	旱天雷	"Thunder on a dry day," title of a piece
"Hao Jiangnan"	好江南	"Jiangnan is good," title of a piece
hen xiang	很像	"resembles very much"
Henan quzi	河南曲子	narrative song genre from Henan province
hetou	合頭	"together," refrain in the piece "Sanliu"
Hezhong	合眾	"United," name of *Jiangnan sizhu* music club
hua	花	"ornament" or "ornamented," literally "flower"
"Hua Liuban"	花六板	"Ornamented six beats," title of a piece
"Hua Sanliu"	花三六	"Ornamented three six," title of a piece

"Huaban Sihe"	花板四合	"Ornamented *ban* four together," title of a piece
"Huahua Liuban"	花花六板	"Double ornamented six beats," title of a piece
"Huaigu"	懷古	"Cherishing the past," title of a piece
"Huanle Ge"	歡樂歌	"Song of joy," title of a piece
Hudong	滬東	name of a *Jiangnan sizhu* music club; name of an area in Shanghai
huihuayin	回滑音	"returning sliding note," *erhu* technique
Huju	滬劇	genre of Chinese opera from Shanghai
jiahua	加花	"add flowers," to ornament a melody
jian	簡	"simple"
jian chang	見長	"to be deemed superior" or "seems long"
"Jiangjun Ling"	將軍令	"The general leads his troops," title of a piece
Jiangnan	江南	name of a *Jiangnan sizhu* music club; name of a region to the south of the lower Yangtze
Jiangnan sizhu	江南絲竹	"silk and bamboo" music from the Jiangnan region
"Jiangnan zhi Chun"	江南之春	"Jiangnan's spring," title of a piece
jianpu	簡譜	"simple notation," a notational system (cipher notation)
jianzi	減字	"subtract notes," to simplify a melody
jiao	轎	sedan chair used in traditional Chinese wedding processions
Jiaochuan zoushu	蛟川走書	narrative singing genre from Zhejiang province

"Jiaoshi Mingqin"	蕉石鳴琴	"Sounding the *qin* on a rock [among the] bananas," title of a piece
jiezi	借字	"borrowed note," technique of tonal alteration
jinghua	精華	"essence"
Jinling	金陵	"Golden Mound" (the old name for the city of Nanjing), name of a *Jiangnan sizhu* music club
Jinshu	晉書	[Book of the Jin (Dynasty)], title of a book
jiubuji	九部伎	"nine kinds of music" in the Tang dynasty
jixing jiahua	即興加花	improvised ornamentation ("flowers")
"Kongque Kaiping"	孔雀開屏	"The peacock opens its tail," title of a piece
"Kuai Liuban"	快六板	"Fast six beats," title of a piece
"Kuaihua Liu"	快花六	"Fast ornamented six," title of a piece
"Kuailede Nongcun"	快樂的農村	"Happy villages," title of a piece
Kunqu	崑曲	"songs of Kun," genre of Chinese opera
kuochong	擴充	"to expand"; here, expansion of musical form
langyin	浪音	"wave sound," *erhu* technique
"Lao Baban"	老八板	"Old eight beats," title of a piece
"Lao Liuban"	老六板	"Old six beats," title of a piece
"Lianhuankou"	連環扣	"Interlocking chain," title of a piece
"Liuban"	六板	"Six beats," title of a piece
liupai	流派	a "school" or regional tradition of performance practice

"Liuqing Niang"	柳青娘	"Willow woman," title of a piece
luanqi bazao	亂七八糟	"disorderly sevens and rotten eights," chaotic
lunzhi	輪指	"rolling fingers," *pipa* technique
"Luogu Sihe"	鑼鼓四合	"Gongs and drums, four together," title of a string, wind, and percussion piece from the Shanghai area
madeng	馬燈	"horse lantern" dance from the Wuxi area
mai	賣	"to sell"; here, name used in titles of the solo sections in the piece "Sihe Ruyi"
mai guai	賣乖	"to show off one's talent"
"Man Liuban"	慢六板	"Slow six beats," title of a piece
"Man Sanliu"	慢三六	"Slow three six," title of a piece
"Meihua Sannong"	梅花三弄	"Three playings of plum blossoms," title of a piece
menyin	悶音	"covered note," *erhu* technique
minjian	民間	"folk" or "not officially sponsored," literally, "among the people"
minzu yuetuan	民族樂團	Modern Chinese Orchestra
"Moli Hua"	茉莉花	"Jasmine flower," title of a song
moqi	默挨	"tacit understanding"
moqi de peihe	默挨的配合	"fitting together through tacit understanding," description of ensemble interaction
muqu	母曲	"mother tune," archetypal tune or piece on which other pieces are based

Nanbeipai Shisan Datao Pipa Xinpu	南北派十三大套琵琶新譜	[New notation for thirteen northern and southern school *pipa* suites], collection of notation for *pipa*
nanguan	南管	"southern pipes," *sizhu* tradition from Fujian province and Taiwan
nanxi	南戲	"southern plays," historical genre of Chinese opera
nanyin	南音	"southern sound," *sizhu* tradition from Fujian and Taiwan
"Nao Ge"	鐃歌	"Cymbal song," title of a piece
"Nichang Qu"	霓裳曲	"Rainbow clothing tune," title of a piece
peihe	配合	"fit together"; here, refers to the parts in an ensemble
peihefa	配合法	"method of fitting together"; here, in an ensemble
"Pinghu Qiuyue"	平湖秋月	"Calm lake and autumn moon," title of a piece
pingtan	評彈	genre of narrative song from Suzhou
pingwen	平穩	"smooth"
pinyin	拼音	romanization system for the Chinese language
"Pipa Guqu"	琵琶古曲	"Old tune for *pipa*," title of a piece
pipa taoqu	琵琶套曲	"*pipa* suites," category of repertory
"Piying Diao"	皮影調	"Leather shadow melody," title of a piece
piying xi	皮影戲	"leather shadow theater," shadow puppet theater
"Pu'an Zhou"	普庵咒	"Buddhist chant," title of a piece
Pudong	蒲東	school of *pipa* playing from the Shanghai area

putong hua	普通話	national Chinese spoken language
putong qu	普通曲	"ordinary" or "common" tunes or pieces
puzi	譜子	musical notation
qiandang ranglu	嵌擋讓路	"inlaying and making way," the give and take between musical parts
"Qiao"	橋	"Bridge," title of a piece
qing	輕	"light" (not heavy)
qingke chuan	清客串	type of nineteenth-century instrumental group
"Qinglian Yuefu"	青蓮樂府	"Green lotus ballad," title of a piece
qingshang yue	清商樂	Han dynasty musical genre
qingxi	清晰	"bright and clear"
qiyue qupai	器樂曲牌	"instrumental titled tune"
qizou	齊奏	"playing together"
quanshou	全手	"full hand," name given to a *Jiangnan sizhu* expert
qupai	曲牌	"titled tune," an archetypal tune or tune type
quyi	曲藝	"song arts," general term for narrative song
sai	賽	"to compete"; here, name used in titles of the solo sections in the piece "Sihe Ruyi"
"Saishang Qu"	塞上曲	"On the frontier," title of a piece
"Sanhualiu"	三花六	"Triple ornamented six," title of a piece
"Sanliu"	三六	"Three six," title of a piece
"Sanliuban"	三六板	"Three six beats," title of a piece
sao	掃	"sweep," *pipa* technique
Shandong qinshu	山東琴書	narrative song genre from Shandong province

Shanghai Jiangnan Sizhu Xuehui	上海江南絲竹學會	Shanghai Society for the Study of Jiangnan Sizhu
"Shanghai Matou"	上海碼頭	"Shanghai wharf," title of a song
shanghuayin	上滑音	"ascending sliding note," *erhu* technique
Shenbao	申報	name of Shanghai newspaper
shengbu	聲部	"sound part," the musical part played by an instrument or voice
shi	實	"strong"
shibuji	十部伎	"ten kinds of music" in the Tang dynasty
shifan gu	十番鼓	string, wind, and percussion genre from Wuxi
shifan luogu	十番鑼鼓	string, wind, and percussion genre from Wuxi
"Shiliuban"	十六板	"Sixteen beats," title of a piece
"Shuang He Feng"	雙合鳳	"A pair of phoenixes," title of a piece
"Shuang Qiao"	雙橋	"Double bridge," title of a piece
shuangtanlun	雙彈輪	"double plucked roll," *yangqin* technique
shuochang	説唱	"speech-song," general term for narrative song
Sichuan yangqin	四川揚琴	narrative song genre from Sichuan province
"Sihe"	四合	"Four together," title of a piece; also, designation for a multisection piece
"Sihe Ban"	四合板	"Four together beats," title of a piece
"Sihe Ruyi"	四合如意	"Four together, as you please," title of a piece
siming nanci	四明南詞	genre of narrative song from Ningbo

sizhu	絲竹	"silk and bamboo," string and wind instrumental ensemble music
su	俗	"popular" or "vulgar"
Sunan chuida	蘇南吹打	wind and percussion music from southern Jiangsu province
"Suyang Qiao"	蘇楊橋	"Su[zhou] and Yang[zhou] bridge," title of a piece
tanci	彈詞	genre of narrative song from Suzhou
"Tanci Sanliu"	彈詞三六	"*Tanci* three six," title of piece
tangming gong	堂名宮	*Kunqu* singing in the style of *xiaotangming*
tao	套	a set of something, as in *taoqu*
taoqu	套曲	a multisection piece
Tianshan	天山	"Heavenly Mountains," name of *Jiangnan sizhu* music club
"Tou Mai"	頭賣	first solo section in the piece "Sihe Ruyi"
touyin	透音	"appearing note," *erhu* technique
tuanzhang	團章	list of regulations for a music club or other organization
tui	推	"push," *pipa* technique
wanquan yiyang	完全一樣	"completely the same"
"Wen Jiangjun"	文將軍	"Refined *jiangjun*," title of piece
Wenming Yashe	文明雅社	"Refined Brightness Elegant Society," name of an early Shanghai music club
"Wudai Tongtang"	五代同堂	"Five generations in the same hall," title of a multisection piece
"Wuxi Jing"	無錫景	"Wuxi scenery," title of a song
"Wuzi Kaimen"	五字開門	"*Wuzi* [a scale degree] open the gate," title of a *qupai*

xi	細	"detailed"
xiandai liuxing Zhongguo yinyue	現代流行 中國音樂	"modern popular Chinese music"
xianghe ge	相和歌	"harmonious songs," Tang dynasty musical genre
xiangtong	相同	"similar" or "identical"
xiansheng	先生	"sir," a form of address
Xiansuo Beikao	弦索備考	[A reference appendix for strings], title of a collection of notation
Xiansuo Shisantao	弦索十三套	[Thirteen pieces for strings], alternate title for *Xiansuo Beikao*
xiao	小	"small" (a different character from the name of the instrument)
"Xiao Baimen"	小拜門	"Small worshiping at the gate," title of a *qupai*
"Xiao Kaimen"	小開門	"Small opening the gate," title of a *qupai*
"Xiao Liuban"	小六板	"Small six beats," title of a piece
"Xiao Yue Er Gao"	小月兒高	"Small the moon is high," title of a piece
xiaodiao	小調	genre of urban song
xiaotangming	小堂名	type of nineteenth-century instrumental group
"Xiaotao Hong"	小桃紅	"Small red peach," title of a piece
Xiaozhao	霄霓	name of an early Shanghai music club
Xiju	錫劇	regional opera tradition from Wuxi
"Xingjie"	行街	"Street procession," title of a piece
"Xingjie Kuaiban"	行街快板	"Street procession, fast *ban*," title of a section of the piece "Xingjie"

"Xingjie Sihe"	行街四合	"Street procession, four together," title of a piece
Xinsheng	新聲	"New Sound," name of *Jiangnan sizhu* music club
xitong	系統	"system"; here, a set of pieces which are interrelated
xu	虛	"empty"
xu chanyin	虛顫音	"empty" or "false" "shaking note," *dizi* technique
"Xuhua Luo"	絮花落	"Catkin flowers falling," title of a piece
"Xunfeng Qu"	薰風曲	"Fragrant wind tune," title of a piece
xunhuan qu	循環曲	"circulating piece," type of formal structure
"Xunyang Yeyue"	潯陽夜月	"Xunyang River, evening moon," title of a piece
ya	雅	"refined"
yan	眼	"eye," a secondary beat
"Yangba Qu"	陽八曲	"*Yang* eight tune," title of a piece
Yangzhou Huafang Lu	楊州畫舫錄	[The Yangzhou painted pleasure-boat record], title of a book
yaopian	么篇	title of a section of the piece "Man Sanliu"
"Yidian Jin"	一點金	"One drop of gold," title of a piece
"Yinhe Hui"	銀河會	"Meeting at the silver river [Milky Way]," title of a piece
yishi	儀式	"ceremonial," as in ceremonial music
yitiao xian	一條弦	"a single thread"
yiyin	倚音	"leaning note," *dizi* technique
Yongju	甬劇	regional opera tradition from Ningbo
you guanxi	有關係	"is related to"
"Yu Da Bajiao"	雨打芭蕉	"Rain striking the bananas," title of a piece

"Yu Elang"	玉娥郎	"Jade moth," title of a *qupai*
"Yu Furong"	玉芙蓉	"Jade lotus," title of a piece
"Yuanban Sanliu"	原板三六	"Original *ban* three six," title of a piece
"Yuanban Sihe"	原板四合	"Original *ban* four together," title of a piece
"Yue Er Gao"	月兒高	"The moon is high," title of a piece
Yuelin	樂林	"Music Forest," name of a Shanghai music club
"Yuge"	漁歌	"Fisherman's song," title of a piece
Yunhe	雲和	"Cloud Harmony," name of an early Shanghai music club
"Yunqing"	雲慶	"Cloud celebration," title of a piece
"Yushun Xunfengcao"	虞舜薰風曲	"Fragrant winds of [the emperors] Yu and Shun," title of a piece
zaju	雜劇	"miscellaneous plays," an ancient genre of Chinese opera
Zenghouyi	曾候乙	the Marquis of Zeng, whose tomb contained musical instruments
zengyin	贈音	"presenting note," *dizi* technique
"Zhaojun Yuan"	昭君怨	"Zhaojun's resentment," title of a piece
Zhedong luogu	浙東鑼鼓	genre of wind and percussion music from eastern Zhejiang province
"Zhegu Fei"	鷓鴣飛	"Partridges flying," title of a piece
zhenzheng	真正	"authentic"
zhisheng fudiao	支聲復調	"branch sound polyphony," heterophonic musical texture
"Zhongban"	中板	title of a piece (contraction of "Zhonghua Liuban")

"Zhongban Hua Lao Liuban"	中板花老六板	"Medium tempo ornamented old six beats," implied title of "Zhonghua Liuban"
Zhongguo	中國	"China," name of a *Jiangnan sizhu* music club
Zhongguo Yinyuejia Xiehue	中國音樂家協會	Chinese Musicians' Association
"Zhonghua Liuban"	中花六板	"Medium ornamented six beats," title of a piece
Zhouli	周禮	[Rituals of Zhou], title of a book
zhu	主	"primary"
Zhuangtai Qiusi	妝台秋思	"At the dressing table, thinking of autumn," title of a piece
zi	字	"character" or "syllable"; a note in *gongchepu* notation
zifa	自發	"spontaneous"
zijue	自覺	"conscious" or "deliberate"
"Zizhu Diao"	紫竹調	"Purple bamboo melody," title of a piece
"Zouma"	走馬	"Running horses," title of a piece
zuoceyin	左側音	"left-side note," *erhu* technique

References Cited

Addison, Don
    1974   "Elements of Style in Performing the Chinese P'i-p'a." *UCLA Selected Reports* 2(1):118–39.

A'erzamanuofu, Fu 弗　阿爾紮瑪諾夫 (F. Arzamanov)
    1962   "Lun Zhongguo Duoshengbu Yinyue de Mouxie Tedian" 論中國多聲部音樂的某些特點 [Discussion of a few characteristics of Chinese multipart music]. *Yinyue Yicong* 音樂譯叢 [Collection of Translations on Music] 1:100–160.

Asian Music
    1989   20(2) (Chinese Music Theory). Articles by Gao Houyong, Han Kuo-Huang, Huang Jinpei, Stephen Jones, Alan R. Thrasher, and Tsao Pen-Yeh.

Association for Chinese Music Research Newsletter
    1987–   (biannual)

Becker, Judith
    1980   "A Southeast Asian Musical Process: Thai *Thǎw* and Javanese *Irama*." *Ethnomusicology* 24(3):453–64.

Chen Chien-tai
    1978   "Chaochou (South China) Instrumental Style: Transcriptions and Analyses of Two Representative Works." Master's thesis, Kent State University.

Chen Mingzhi
    1959   "Dui Woguo Minjian Yinyue zhong Fudiao Yinsu de Chubu Tantao" 對我國民間音樂中復調因素的出步探討 [Preliminary discussion of polyphonic elements in my country's folk music]. *Yinyue Yanjiu* 音樂研究 [Music Research] no. 4:2–16.

Chen Yingshi 陳應時
    1985   "Jiangnan Sizhu Chu Yi" 江南絲竹雛議 [Beginning investigations on *Jiangnan sizhu*]. *Shanghai Yinxun* 上海音訊 [Shanghai Music Report] no. 1:32–35.

Cheng Yuanmin 程源敏
    1981   "Youmei de Jiangnan Sizhu" 優美的江南絲竹 [Beautiful *Jiangnan sizhu*]. In *Minzu Qiyue Guangbo Jiangzuo* 民族器樂廣播講座 [Broadcast

discussions on instrumental music], ed. Zhongyang Renmin Guangbo Diantai Wenyi Bu Yinyue Zu 中央人民廣播電台文藝部音樂祖 [Music Department of the Culture and Arts Ministry of the Central People's Broadcasting Station]. Yinyue Chubanshe 人民音樂出版社 [People's Music Publishing]. 54–60.

CHIME (Newsletter of the European Foundation for Chinese Music Research)
  1990–   (biannual)

CHINOPERL Papers (The Conference on Chinese Oral and Performing Literature)
  1969–   (annual or biennial)

Cooke, Peter
  1980   "Heterophony." In *The New Grove Dictionary of Music and Musicians*, ed. Stanley Sadie. London: Macmillan. 8:537–38.

De Francis, John
  1976   *Beginning Chinese Reader*. New Haven: Yale University Press.

DeWoskin, Kenneth
  1982   *A Song for One or Two: Music and the Concept of Art in Early China*. Ann Arbor: University of Michigan Center for Chinese Studies.

Dolby, William
  1976   *A History of Chinese Drama*. London: Paul Erek.

Dujunco, Mercedes
  1994   *Tugging at the Native's Heartstrings: Nostalgia and the Post-Mao "Revival" of Xian Shi Yue String Ensemble Music of Chaozhou, South China*. Ph.D. dissertation, University of Washington.

Ferguson, Daniel
  1988   *A Study of Cantonese Opera: Musical Source Materials, Historical Development, Contemporary Social Organization, and Adaptive Strategies*. Ann Arbor: University Microfilms International.

Ferguson, Francesca
  1988   *Dualistic Relationships in Northern Chinese Narrative Arts*. Ann Arbor: University Microfilms International.

Frankel, Ch'ung-ho Chang
  1976   "The Practice of *K'un-ch'u* Singing from the 1920's to the 1960's." *CHINOPERL Papers* no. 6:82–92.

Gan Tao 甘濤
  1978   "Guanyu Jiangnan Sizhu Yanzou Yishu de Jidian Tihui" 關於江南絲竹演奏藝術的幾點體會 [A few points on the performance art of *Jiangnan sizhu*]. *Nanyi Xuebao* 南藝學報 [Journal of the Nanjing Arts Institute] no. 11 (Nov.): 95–98.
  1985   *Jiangnan Sizhu Yinyue* 江南絲竹音樂 [The music of *Jiangnan sizhu*]. Nanjing: Jiangsu Renmin Chubanshe 江蘇人民出版社 [Jiangsu People's Publishing Company].

Gao Houyong 高厚永
  1981   *Minzu Qiyue Gailun* 民族器樂概論 [Survey of instrumental music]. Nanjing: Jiangsu Renmin Chubanshe 江蘇人民出版社 [Jiangsu People's Publishing Company].
  1989   "On *Qupai*." Translated by Zhou Li. *Asian Music* 20(2):4–20.

Guofeng Yinyueshe 國鳳音樂社 [National Phoenix Music Club]
  1939   *Xiandai Liuxing Zhongguo Yinyuepu* 現代流行中國音樂譜 [Notation for contemporary popular Chinese music]. Shanghai: Guoguang Shudian 國光書店 [National Brightness Bookstore].
Han Kuo-Huang
  1979   "The Modern Chinese Orchestra." *Asian Music* 11(1):1–43.
  1989   "Folk Songs of the Han Chinese: Characteristics and Classifications." *Asian Music* 20(2):107–28.
He Changlin 何昌林
  1985   "Liang Zhou Sizhu Hui Cha Shan: Tan Tangdai de 'Cha Shan Dou Yue'" 兩州絲竹會茶山 — 談唐代的茶山斗樂 [*Sizhu* of two regions meeting at Cha Shan: a discussion of *Cha Shan dou* music from the Tang dynasty]. *Shanghai Yinxun* [Shanghai Music Report] no. 1:39–45.
Hu Dengtiao 胡登跳
  1982   *Minzu Guanxian Yuefa* 民族管絃樂法 [Method for Chinese orchestra]. Shanghai: Shanghai Wenyi Chubanshe 上海文藝出版社 [Shanghai Literature and Arts Publishing Company].
  1985   "Rang Jiangnan Sizhu Geng Jingzhi, Duocai" 讓江南絲竹更精致, 多彩 [Let *Jiangnan sizhu* become more exquisite and colorful]. *Shanghai Yinxun* 上海音訊 [Shanghai Music Report] no. 1:20–21.
Huang Jinpei
  1982   "Concerning the Variants of 'Lao Lioban' [*sic*]." Translated by Alan Thrasher. *Asian Music* 13(2):19–30.
  1989   "*Xipi* and *Erhuang* of Beijing and Guangdong Operas." *Asian Music* 20 (2):152–95.
Jiang Yuanlu 姜元祿 and Yan Zhu 燕竹, eds.
  1989   *Jiangnan Sizhu (Zongpu)* 江南絲竹（總譜）[*Jiangnan sizhu* (Ensemble scores)]. 2 vols. Beijing: Renmin Yinyue Chubanshe 人民音樂出版社 [People's Music Publishing Company].
Jin Zuli 金祖禮
  1961   "Jiangnan Sizhu Gaishu" 江南絲竹概述 [Overview of *Jiangnan sizhu*]. Mimeographed. Shanghai: Shanghai Conservatory of Music.
Jin Zuli 金祖禮 and Xu Ziren 徐子仁
  1983   "Shanghai Minjian Sizhu Yinyue Shi" 上海民間絲竹音樂史 [History of folk *sizhu* music in Shanghai]. *Zhongguo Yinyue* 中國音樂 [Chinese Music] no. 3:28–31.
Jones, Stephen
  1989   "The Golden-Character Scripture: Perspectives on Chinese Melody." *Asian Music* 20(2):21–66.
  forthcoming   *Folk Music of China: Living Traditions of Instrumental Music.* Oxford: Clarendon Press.
Kartomi, Margaret J.
  1981   "The Processes and Results of Musical Culture Contact: A Discussion of Terminology and Concepts." *Ethnomusicology* 25(2): 227–50.
Kishibe, Shigeo
  1960–61   *A Historical Study of the Music in the T'ang Dynasty* (in Japanese,

summary in English). 2 vols. Tokyo: University of Tokyo Press. English Summary: 2:1–45.

Lau, Frederic

1991 *Music and Musicians of the Traditional Chinese Dizi*. Ann Arbor: University Microfilms International.

1993 "Little Great Tradition: Recent Developments in *Jiangnan Sizhu*." Paper presented at the Annual Meeting of the Association for Asian Studies, Los Angeles.

Le Si 樂思

n.d. *Yangqin Yanzoufa* 揚琴演奏法 [Method for performing the *yangqin*]. Hong Kong: Xianggang Hongye Shuju Chuban 香港宏業書局出版 (Won Yin Book Company).

Lee Yuan-yuan

1980 "The Music of the Zenghou *Zhong*." *Chinese Music* 3(1):3–15.

Levy, Harold S.

1971 *Translations from Po Chu-i's Collected Works*. 2 vols. New York: Paragon Book Reprint Corporation.

Li Fangyuan 李芳園

1895 *Nanbeipai Shisan Datao Pipa Xinpu* 南北派十三大套琵琶新譜 [New notation for thirteen northern and southern school *pipa* suites].

Li Guangzu 李光祖, ed.

1982 *Li Tingsong Yanzoupu* 李廷松演奏譜 [Li Tingsong's performance notation]. Beijing: Renmin Yinyue Chubanshe 人民音樂出版社 [People's Music Publishers].

Li Minxiong 李民雄

1981 "Chuantong Minzu Qiyue de Xuanlü Fajan Shoufa" 傳統民族器樂的旋律發展手法 [Techniques of melodic development in traditional Chinese instrumental music]. *Zhongyang Yinyue Xueyuan Xuebao* 中央音樂學院學報 [Journal of the Central Conservatory of Music] (1):19–30.

1982 *Minzu Qiyue Gailun* 民族器樂概論 [Survey of Chinese instrumental music]. Mimeographed. 1st ed. 1978. Shanghai: Shanghai Conservatory of Music.

1983 *Chuantong Minzu Qiyuequ Xinshang* 傳統民族器樂曲欣賞 [Appreciating traditional Chinese instrumental repertory]. Beijing: Renmin Yinyue Chubanshe 人民音樂出版社 [People's Music Publishing Company].

1985 "Ting Jiangnan Sizhu Jiaoliu Yanchu You Gan" 聽江南絲竹交流演出有感 [It was moving to hear the exchange performance of *Jiangnan sizhu*] *Shanghai Yinxun* 上海音訊 [Shanghai Music Report] no.1:26–28.

1987 *Minzu Qiyue Zhishi Guangbo Jiangzuo* 民族器樂知識廣播講座 [Broadcast lectures on understanding Chinese instrumental music]. Beijing: Renmin Yinyue Chubanshe 人民音樂出版社 [People's Music Publishing Company].

n.d. "Minjian Qiyue Hezou de Zhiti Xiefa" 民間器樂合奏的織體寫法 [Method for composing ensemble texture in Chinese instrumental music]. Mimeographed. Shanghai: Shanghai Conservatory of Music.

Li Xi'an 李西安 and Jun Chi 軍馳
  1985   *Zhongguo Minzu Qushi: Minge, Qiyue Bufen* 中國民族曲式: 民歌, 器樂部
         分 [Musical structure in Chinese music: section on folk song and
         instrumental music]. Beijing: Renmin Yinyue Chubanshe 人民音樂出
         版社 [People's Music Publishing Company].
Liang Mingyue (Liang Ming-yueh, David Ming-yueh Liang)
  1971   *Shantung Traditional Music.* New York: Performing Arts Program of the
         Asia Society.
  1980   "China V.3. *Hu-ch'in.*" In *The New Grove Dictionary of Music and
         Musicians,* ed. Stanley Sadie. London: Macmillan. 4:270–71.
  1985   *Music of the Billion.* New York: Peters Publications.
Lieberman, Fredric
  1971   Liner notes for *The Music of China II: Traditional Music of Amoy.*
         Anthology Records.
Lin Shicheng 林石城
  1982   "Pudong Pai Pipa Chutan" 蒲東派琵琶初探 [Preliminary discussion of
         the Pudong school of *pipa*]. *Guangzhou Yinyue Xueyuan Xuebao* 廣州音樂
         學院學報 [Journal of the Guangzhou Conservatory of Music] no. 1:66–
         76.
  1983   *Ju Shilin Pipa Pu* 鞠士林琵琶譜 [*Pipa* notation of Ju Shilin]. Beijing:
         Renmin Yinyue Chubanshe 人民音樂出版社 [People's Music
         Publishing Company].
Liu, Terence M.
  1988   *Development of the Chinese Two-Stringed Bowed Lute Erhu Following the New
         Culture Movement (c. 1915–1985).* Ann Arbor: University Microfilms
         International.
Lu Chunling 陸春齡
  1982   *Lu Chunling Dizi Quji* 陸春齡笛子曲集 [Collection of Lu Chunling's *dizi*
         pieces]. Beijing: Renmin Yinyue Chubanshe 人民音樂出版社 [People's
         Music Publishing Company].
Lui, Tsun-yuen
  1980   "China V.4. *P'i-p'a.*" In *The New Grove Dictionary of Music and Musicians,*
         ed. Stanley Sadie. London: Macmillan. 4:271–72.
  1984   "Pipa." In *The New Grove Dictionary of Musical Instruments,* ed. Stanley
         Sadie. London: Macmillan. 3:115–16.
McDougall, Bonnie
  1980   *Mao Zedong's "Talks at the Yan'an Conference on Literature and Art": A
         Translation of the 1943 Text with Commentary.* Ann Arbor: The University
         of Michigan Center for Chinese Studies.
Mackerras, Colin P.
  1972   *The Rise of the Peking Opera 1770–1870.* New York: Oxford University
         Press.
  1980   "China V.5. Other Instruments." In *The New Grove Dictionary of Music
         and Musicians,* ed. Stanley Sadie. London: Macmillan. 4:272–78.
  1983   *Chinese Theater: From Its Origins to the Present Day.* Honolulu: University
         of Hawaii Press.

Malm, William P.
  1977   *Music Cultures of the Pacific, the Near East, and Asia.* 2d ed. Englewood
          Cliffs, N.J.: Prentice-Hall, Inc.
Mark, Lindy Li
  1983   "Tone and Tune in *Kunqu.*" CHINOPERL *Papers* no. 12:9–60.
Miao Jing 苗晶 and Qiao Jianzhong 喬建中
  1987   *Lun Hanzu Minge Jinse Secai Qu de Huafen* 論漢族民歌近似色彩區的劃
          分 [A discussion on differentiating "similar color areas" in the folk
          songs of the Han Chinese]. Beijing: Wenhua Yishu Chubanshe 文化藝
          術出版社 [Culture and Arts Publishing Company].
Miao Tianrui 繆天瑞, Ji Liankang 吉聯抗, and Guo Nai'an 郭乃安, eds.
  1984   *Zhongguo Yinyue Cidian* 中國音樂辭典 [Chinese music dictionary].
          Beijing: Renmin Yinyue Chubanshe 人民音樂出版社 [People's Music
          Publishing Company].
Miller, Terry E.
  1983   "The Chinese Sheng in Modern Times." *Chinese Music* 6(3):43–48.
Mok, Robert T.
  1966   "Heterophony in Chinese Folk Music." *Journal of the International Folk
          Music Council* 18:14–23.
Murphey, Rhoads
  1974   "The Treaty Ports and China's Modernization." In *The Chinese City
          Between Two Worlds*, ed. Mark Elvin and G. William Skinner. Stanford:
          Stanford University Press. 17–71.
Myers, John E.
  1989   *Nanbei Erpai Miben Pipapu Zhenquan—A Critical Study of a
          Nineteenth-Century Handbook for the Chinese Pipa Lute.* Ann Arbor:
          University Microfilms International.
  1992   *The Way of the Pipa: Structure and Imagery in Chinese Lute Music.* Kent,
          Ohio: Kent State University Press.
Needham, Joseph, and Kenneth Robinson
  1962   "Sound." In *Science and Civilization in China*, ed. Joseph Needham.
          Cambridge: Cambridge University Press. vol. 4, 1:220–28.
Nettl, Bruno
  1978   "Some Aspects of the History of World Music in the Twentieth
          Century: Questions, Problems, and Concepts." *Ethnomusicology* 22(1):
          123–36.
  1985   *The Western Impact on World Music: Change, Adaptation, and Survival.* New
          York: Schirmer Books.
Ng, Josephine
  1980   "The Chinese Dulcimer: *Yang-ch'in.*" Master's thesis, University of
          Washington.
Pian, Rulan Chao
  1978   "The Courtesan's Jewel Box, a Medley Song—Text and Musical
          Transcription." CHINOPERL *Papers* no. 8:161–206.
  1979–80 "Musical Analysis of the Medley Song, 'The Courtesan's Jewel
          Box.'" CHINOPERL *Papers* no. 9:9–31.

1984–85 "The Autobiography of the Drum Singer, Jang Tsueyfenq (as told to Liou Fang)." Translated by Pian. *CHINOPERL Papers* no. 13:7–99.

Qian Zhihe 錢志和
  1982 "Jiangnan Erhu Yanzou Shang de Jidian Tese" 江南絲竹二胡演奏上 的幾點特色 [A few special characteristics of *Jiangnan erhu* playing]. *Yi Yuan* 藝苑 [Garden of the Arts] no. 3:88–90.

Qiao Minhua and Kong Zhiqiang
  1987 "Old Music Regains Popularity." *China Daily*, May 19.

Qin Pengzhang 秦鵬章
  1982 "Ting He Shufeng Pipa Duzouhui You Gan" 聽何樹鳳琵琶獨奏會有 感 [Feelings about hearing He Shufeng's solo *pipa* recital]. *Renmin Yinyue* 人民音樂 [People's Music] no. 6:38–40.

Renmin Ribao Haiwaiban 人民日報海外版 (People's Daily, Overseas Edition)
  1987 "Haineiwai Minyuetuan Ju Hu Bi Gaoxia: Jiangnan Sizhu Yanzou Chuangzuo Jie Fenxiao" 海內外民樂團聚滬比高下: 江南絲竹演奏創作 揭分曉 [Competition of Chinese and overseas instrumental ensembles in Shanghai; results of the *Jiangnan sizhu* performance and composition competition]. May 19. 4.

Renmin Yinyue Chubanshe Bianjibu 人民音樂出版社編輯部 [Editorial Department of People's Music Publishing Company]
  1983 *Youxiu Erhu Quxuan* 優秀二胡曲選 [Selection of outstanding *erhu* pieces]. 2 vols. Beijing: Renmin Yinyue Chubanshe 人民音樂出版社 [People's Music Publishers].

Rowell, Lewis
  1983 *Thinking About Music.* Amherst: University of Massachusetts Press.

Schimmelpenninck, Antoinet
  1990 "Report on Fieldwork—Jiangsu Folk Song." *CHIME* no. 1:16–29.

Seeger, Charles
  1977a "Speech, Music, and Speech About Music." *Studies in Musicology*. Berkeley: University of California Press. 16–30.
  1977b "Versions and Variants of the Tunes of 'Barbara Allen.'" 1966. Reprinted in *Studies in Musicology*. Berkeley: University of California Press. 273–320.

Shanghai Jiangnan Sizhu Xuehui Huikan 上海江南絲竹學會會刊 [Journal of the Shanghai Jiangnan Sizhu Research Society]
  1988 (inaugural issue)

Shanghai Qunzhong Yishu Guan 上海群眾藝術館 [Shanghai People's Art Institute]
  1960 *Shanghai Minjian Qiyue Qu Xuanji* 上海民間器樂曲選集 [Selection of Shanghai folk instrumental pieces]. Shanghai: Shanghai Wenyi Chubanshe 上海文藝出版社 [Shanghai Arts Publishing Company].

Shanghai Shi Wenxue Yishu Jie Lianhe Hui 上海市文學藝術界聯合會 [United Arts Association of Shanghai City]
  1956 *Minzu Qiyue Quji* 民族器樂曲集 [Collection of Chinese instrumental pieces], vol. 3. Shanghai: Shanghai Wenhua Chubanshe 上海文化出版 社 [Shanghai Cultural Publishing Company].

Shanghai Yinxun 上海音訊 [Shanghai Music Report]
    1985   No. 1 (issue on *Jiangnan sizhu*).

Shen Fengquan 沈鳳泉
    1982   *Jiangnan Sizhu Yuequ Xuan* 江南絲竹樂曲選 [Selection of *Jiangnan sizhu*
           pieces]. Hangzhou: Zhejiang Renmin Chubanshe 浙江人民出版社
           [Zhejiang People's Publishing Company].

Shen Sin-yan
    1979   "Foundations of the Chinese Orchestra (1)." *Chinese Music* 2(3):32–36.

Shen Zhibai 沈知白
    1958   "Zhongguo Yinyue, Shige yu Hesheng" 中國音樂, 詩歌與和聲
           [Chinese music, sung poetry and harmony]. *Yinyue Yanjiu* 音樂研究
           [Music Research] no. 3:26–44.

Skinner, G. William
    1977   "Cities and the Hierarchy of Local Systems." In *The City in Late Imperial
           China*, ed. G. William Skinner. Stanford: Stanford University Press.
           275–351.

Strassberg, Richard E.
    1976   "The Singing Techniques of *K'un-ch'u* and their Musical Notation."
           CHINOPERL *Papers* no. 6:45–81.

Sun Yude 孫裕德
    1977   *Dongxiao Chuizoufa* 洞簫吹奏法 [Method for playing the *dongxiao*]. 1962.
           Reprint (Shanghai: Shanghai Wenhua Chubanshe 上海文化出版社
           [Shanghai Cultural Publishing Co.]) Hong Kong: Xianggang Shudian
           香港書店 [Hong Kong Bookstore].

Sutton, Richard Anderson
    1982   *Variation in Javanese Gamelan Music: Dynamics of a Steady State*. Ann
           Arbor: University Microfilms International.

Thrasher, Alan R.
    1978   "The Transverse Flute in Traditional Chinese Music." *Asian Music*
           10(1):92–114.
    1980   *Foundations of Chinese Music: A Study of Ethics and Aesthetics*. Ann Arbor:
           University Microfilms International.
    1981   "The Sociology of Chinese Music: an Introduction." *Asian Music* 12(2):
           17–53.
    1984a–c   "Ban," "Di," and "Erhu." In *The New Grove Dictionary of Musical
           Instruments*, ed. Stanley Sadie. London: Macmillan. 1:119, 563–64,
           717.
    1984d–i   "Paiban," "Sanxian," "Sheng," "Shugu," "Xiao," and "Yueqin." In
           The New Grove Dictionary of Musical Instruments, ed. Stanley Sadie.
           London: Macmillan. 3:3–4, 293, 371–72, 379, 867–68, 887.
    1985   "The Melodic Structure of *Jiangnan Sizhu*." *Ethnomusicology* 29(2):
           237–63.
    1988   "Hakka-Chaozhou Instrumental Repertoire: An Analytic Perspective
           on Traditional Creativity." *Asian Music* 19(2):1–30.
    1989   "Structural Continuity in Chinese *Sizhu*: The *Baban* Model." *Asian
           Music* 20(2):67–106.

1990   *La-Li-Luo Dance Songs of the Chuxiong Yi, Yunnan Province, China.*
       Danbury: World Music Press.
1993   "Bianzou—Performance Variation Techniques in Jiangnan Sizhu."
       CHIME no. 6:4–20.

Tsao Pen-Yeh
1989   "Structural Elements in the Music of Chinese Story-Telling." *Asian Music* 20(2):129–51.

Tuohy, Sue Mary Clare
1988   *Imagining the Chinese Tradition—The Case of Hua'er songs. Festivals and Scholarship.* Ann Arbor: University Microfilms International.

Van Gulik, R. H.
1968   *The Lore of the Chinese Lute.* 1940. Reprint. Tokyo: Sophia University and Charles E. Tuttle Co.

Wade, Bonnie
1984   "Performance Practice in Indian Classical Music." In *Performance Practice: Ethnomusicological Perspectives*, ed. Gerard Behague. Westport, Conn.: Greenwood Press. 13–52.

Wang, Ying-fen
1986   "Structural Analysis of *Nanguan* Vocal Music: A Case Study of Identity and Variance." Master's thesis, University of Maryland.
1992   *Tune Identity and Compositional Process in Zhongbei Songs: A Semiotic Analysis of Nanguan Vocal Music.* Ann Arbor: University Microfilms International.

Wang Yuhe 汪毓和
1984   *Zhongguo Jinxiandai Yinyue Shi* 中國近現代音樂史 [A history of modern Chinese music]. Beijing: Renmin Yinyue Chubanshe 人民音樂出版社 [People's Music Publishing Company].

Wei Cipeng 韋慈朋 (J. Lawrence Witzleben)
1985   "Jiangnan Sizhu Xuexi Baogao" 江南絲竹學習報告 [Report on research on *Jiangnan sizhu*). Mimeographed. Shanghai: Shanghai Conservatory of Music.

Wei Liangfu 魏良輔
1977   "Qu Lü" 曲律 [Principles of *kunqu* singing]. Translated by Fu-yin Chen. *Asian Music* 8(2):4–25.

Wei Zhongle 衛仲樂
1985   "Fanrong Jiangnan Sizhu Fajan Jiangnan Sizhu" 繁榮江南絲竹發展江南絲竹 [Make *Jiangnan sizhu* glorious, develop *Jiangnan sizhu*]. *Shanghai Yinxun* 上海音訊 [Shanghai Music Report] no. 1:16–19.

Witzleben, J. Lawrence
1983a "Cantonese Instrumental Music in Hong Kong: An Overview with Special Reference to the Role of the *Gou Wuh (Gao Hu)*." Master's thesis, University of Hawai'i at Manoa.
1983b "Form and Texture in *Jiangnan Sizhu*." Paper presented at the Annual Meeting of the Society for Ethnomusicology, Tallahassee.
1987a "*Jiangnan Sizhu* Music Clubs in Shanghai: Context, Concept, and Identity." *Ethnomusicology* 32(2):240–60.

1987b   *Silk and Bamboo: Jiangnan Sizhu Instrumental Ensemble Music in Shanghai.*
        Ann Arbor: University Microfilms International.
1989   "Musical System and Inter-genre Relationships in Hong Kong." Paper
        presented at the Annual Meeting of the Society for Ethnomusicology,
        Cambridge, Mass.

Wu Yiqun 吳逸群
1980   "Tantan Shanghai Diqu de Jiangnan Sizhu" 談談上海地區的江南絲竹
        [Discussion of *Jiangnan sizhu* in the Shanghai area]. *Yinyue Aihaozhe* 音
        樂愛好者 [Music Lover] no. 1:47–48.

Wu Yuan 吳苑, ed.
1920   *Gongche Daguan* 工尺大觀 [Great survey of *gongche* notation], vol. 4.
        Beijing: Beijing Xinhua Shudian 北京新華書店 [Beijing New Culture
        Bookstore].

Xu Qingyan 許青彥
1983   "Cong Shifan Luogu dao Jiangnan Sizhu" 從十番鑼鼓到江南絲竹
        [From *shifan luogu* to *Jiangnan sizhu*]. *Zhongguo Yinyue* 中國音樂
        [Chinese Music] no. 3:32–33.

Xu Wei 徐渭
1959   "Nan Ci Xulu" 南詞敘錄 [A commentary on southern *ci* poetry]. In
        Zhongguo Gudian Xiqu Lunzhu Jicheng 中國古典戲曲論著集成 [Collected
        essays on ancient Chinese operatic music], ed. Zhongguo Xiqu
        Yanjiuyuan 中國戲曲研究院 [Research Institute for Chinese Operatic
        Music]. Beijing: Zhongguo Xiju Chubanshe 中國戲劇出版社 [Chinese
        Drama Publishing Company]. 3:235–56.

Yang Jingming 楊競明
1958   *Yangqin Quxuan* 揚琴曲選 [Selection of *yangqin* pieces], vol. 1. Beijing:
        Yinyue Chubanshe 音樂出版社 [Music Publishing Company].

Yang Yinliu 楊蔭瀏
1980   *Shifan Luogu* 十番鑼鼓 [*Shifan* gongs and drums]. Beijing: Renmin
        Yinyue Chubanshe 人民音樂出版社 [People's Music Publishing
        Company].
1981   *Zhongguo Gudai Yinyue Shigao* 中國古代音樂史稿 [Outline history of
        ancient Chinese music]. 2 vols. Beijing: Renmin Yinyue Chubanshe 人
        民音樂出版社 [People's Music Publishing Company].

Yang Yingliu 楊蔭瀏 and Cao Anhe 曹安和
1979   *Xiansuo Shisantao* 絃索十三套 [Thirteen pieces for strings]. 3 vols.
        Beijing: Renmin Yinyue Chubanshe 人民音樂出版社 [People's Music
        Publishing Company].
1982   *Sunan Shifan Guqu* 蘇南十番鼓曲 [Sunan *shifan* drum pieces]. Beijing:
        Renmin Yinyue Chubanshe 人民音樂出版社 [People's Music
        Publishing Company].

Ye Dong 葉棟
1983   *Minzu Qiyue de Ticai yu Xingshi* 民族器樂的體裁與形式 [Genres and
        form in Chinese instrumental music]. Shanghai: Shanghai Wenyi
        Chubanshe 上海文藝出版社 [Shanghai Literature and Arts Publishing
        Company].

Yeh, Nora
    1985   *Nanguan Music in Taiwan: A Little Known Classical Tradition.* Ann Arbor: University Microfilms International.

Yu, Siu Wah
    1985   "Three Er-hu Pieces from 'Jiangnan.' " Master's thesis, Queen's University of Belfast.
    1989   "Annotated Autobiography of Lui Pui Yuan." Unpublished manuscript.

Yuan Bingchang 袁炳昌 and Mao Jizeng 毛繼增, eds.
    1986   *Zhongguo Shaoshu Minzu Yueqi Zhi* 中國少數民族樂器志 [Musical instruments of the minority peoples of China]. Beijing: Xin Shijie Chubanshe 新世界出版社 [New World Publishing Company].

Yuan Jingfang 袁靜芳
    1987   *Minzu Qiyue* 民族器樂 [Chinese instrumental music]. Beijing: Renmin Yinyue Chubanshe 人民音樂出版社 [People's Music Publishing Company].

Yung, Bell
    1984   "Choreographic and Kinesthetic Elements in Performance on the Chinese Seven-String Zither." *Ethnomusicology* 28(3):505–17.
    1985   " 'Da Pu': The Recreative Process for the Music of the Seven-string Zither." In *Music and Context: Essays in Honor of John Ward*, ed. Ann Shapiro. Cambridge: Cambridge University Press. 370–84.

Zhao Songting 趙松庭
    1985   *Diyi Chunqiu* 笛藝春秋 [Spring and autumn of the art of *di*]. Hangzhou: Zhejiang Renmin Chubanshe 浙江人民出版社 [Zhejiang People's Publishing Company].

Zheng Deyuan 鄭德淵
    1984   *Zhongguo Yueqixue* 中國樂器學 (Chinese instrumentation). Taipei: Shengyun Chubanshe 生韻出版社 (Art-tune Publishing Company).

Zheng Jinwen 鄭覲文
    1924   *Xiaodi Xinpu* 簫笛新譜 [New notation for *xiao* and *di*]. Shanghai: Shanghai Wenming Shuju 上海文明書局 [Shanghai Literary Brightness Bookstore].

Zhongguo Yinyue Xueyuan 中國音樂學院 [China Conservatory of Music] and Zhongyang Yinyue Xueyuan 中央音樂學院 [Central Conservatory of Music]
    1983   *Minzu Yueqi Chuantong Duzou Quji: Erhu, Banhu Xuanji* 民族樂器傳統獨奏曲選集: 二胡, 板胡專輯 [Selected compilation of traditional Chinese instrumental solo pieces: *erhu* and *banhu* edition]. Beijing: Renmin Yinyue Chubanshe 人民音樂出版社 [People's Music Publishing Company].

Zhongguo Yueqi Jieshao 中國樂器介紹 [Introduction to Chinese musical instruments]
    1978   Beijing: Renmin Yinyue Chubanshe 人民音樂出版社 [People's Music Publishing Company].

Zhou Dafeng 周大風

1980   "Minzu Qing Yinyue: Jiangnan Sizhu" 民族輕音樂 : 江南絲竹 [Folk
         "light music": *Jiangnan sizhu*]. *Xihu* 西胡 [West Lake] (May):61–62.

Zhou Hao 周皓

1985   "Jiangnan Sizhu Yanzou Shang Yishu Jiagong Chutan" 江南絲竹演奏
         上藝術加工初探 [Preliminary discussion of artistic development in
         performing *Jiangnan sizhu*]. *Shanghai Yinxun* 上海音訊 [Shanghai Music
         Report] no. 1:36–38.

Zhou Hui 周惠, Zhou Hao 周皓, and Ma Shanglong 馬聖龍, eds.

1986   *Jiangnan Sizhu Chuantong Ba Da Qu* 江南絲竹傳統八大曲 [The
         traditional eight great pieces of *Jiangnan sizhu*]. Shanghai: Shanghai
         Wenyi Chubanshe 上海文藝出版社 [Shanghai Literature and Arts
         Publishing Company].

Selected Discography

Unless noted otherwise, all recordings are cassettes. Some have also been released on LP and/or other record labels.

Chinese Classical Instrumental Music
  The Chinese Cultural Theater Group. 1992 [1950]. New York: Folkways Records. Notes by Henry Cowell. Recorded in San Francisco. Performers include Sun Yude 孫裕德, Zhu Wenyi 朱文頤, and Zhou Hui 周惠.

Dengyue Jiaohui 燈月交輝 (Moon and lanterns)
  Shanghai Minzu Yuetuan 上海民族樂團 [Shanghai Chinese Orchestra]. 1981. Hong Kong: Baili Changpian Gongsi 百利唱片公司 (Bailey Record Company) NS-61. Performers include Zhou Hao 周皓 (*erhu*) and Zhou Hui 周惠 (*yangqin*).

Hangong Qiuyue 漢宮秋月 (The autumn moon over the Han palace)
  Shanghai Lao Chenghuang Miao Huxin Ting Yuedui 上海老城隍廟湖心亭樂隊 (The Traditional Ensemble of the Lake Pavilion of the Shanghai Old Emperor Temple). 1988. Hong Kong: 博藝製作有限公司 (Pop Art Production Company) PA-881. Notes in Chinese and English. *Guqu*, performed by members of the Hezhong music club.

Hanjiang Canxue 寒江殘雪 (The remaining snow on the winter rivers)
  Shoujie Haineiwai Jiangnan Sizhu Chuangzuo yu Yanzou Bisai 首屆海內外江南絲竹創作與演奏比賽 (一) (The First Competition of String-and-Wind Music of Southern Yangtse for Compositions and Performers at Home and Abroad). Vol. 1. 1987. Shanghai: 中國唱片 (China Record Co.) HL-539. Notes in Chinese and English.

Huanle Ge 歡樂歌 (Song of joy)
  Shanghai Lao Chenghuang Miao Huxin Ting Yuedui 上海老城隍廟湖心亭樂隊 (The Traditional Ensemble of the Lake Pavilion of the Shanghai Old Emperor Temple). 1988. Hong Kong: 博藝製作有限公司 (Pop Art Production Company) PA-882. Notes in Chinese and English. Performers include Dong Kejun 董克鈞.

Jiangnan Sizhu 江南絲竹
  Chen Yonglu 陳永祿 (*erhu*), Lin Shicheng 林石城 (*pipa*), and Lu Chunling 陸春齡 (*dizi* and *xiao*). 2 vols. 1987. Beijing: Huang He 黃河 [Yellow River] 8026 L007 and 華彩 [Bountiful China] 8026 L008.

Jiangnan Sizhu Ba Da Qu 江南絲竹八大曲 (The eight grand Jiangnan Chinese classics)

Shanghai Yinyue Xueyuan Jiangnan Sizhu Xiaozu 上海音樂學院江南絲竹小組 (Shanghai Conservatory Jiangnan Chinese Classical Ensemble). 2 vols. 1992. (Singapore?): Huang He 黃河 (Yellow River) compact disc 82024 and 82025. Notes in Chinese and English.

Jiangnan Sizhu he Guqu 江南絲竹和古曲 [*Jiangnan sizhu* and *guqu*]

Zhejiang Sheng Gewutuan 浙江省歌舞團 [Zhejiang Province Song and Troupe]. N.d. Beijing: Zhongguo Luyin Luxiang Gongsi 中國錄音錄像公司 [China Recording and Video Company] 8402. Notes in Chinese. Performers include Song Jinglian 宋景濂 (*dizi* and *xiao*), Shen Fengquan 沈鳳泉 (*erhu*), and Shen Duomi 沈多米 (*erhu*).

Jiangnan Sizhu Mingqu 江南絲竹名曲 (Famous south Yangzi string and pipe ensemble)

Various performers from Shanghai. 1981. Shanghai Yinxiang Gongsi 上海音像公司 (Shanghai Audio and Video Company) YAC-2. Notes in Chinese.

Jiangnan Sizhu Mingqu Jingxuan 1 江南絲竹名曲精選 (一) [Special collection of famous *Jiangnan sizhu* pieces 1] Lu Chunling 陸春齡, Ma Shenglong 馬聖龍, Zhou Hao 周皓, and Zhou Hui 周惠. 1991. Zhongguo Changpian 中國唱片 (China Record Company) HL-641. Notes in Chinese.

Jie Xinniang 接新娘 (Welcoming the bride)

Shanghai Putuo Shiyan Yuedui 上海普陀實驗樂隊 [Shanghai Putuo Experimental Orchestra]. Taipei: Tang Shan Yueji 唐山樂集 [Tang Mountain Music Collection] TS-216. N.d. Notes in Chinese. Directed by Dong Kejun 董克鈞.

Popular Jiangnan Music

Lu Chunling 陸春齡, Ma Shenglong 馬聖龍, Zhou Hao 周皓, and Zhou Hui 周惠. 1986. Hong Kong: Hong Kong Records compact disc 8.880015. Notes by Lai Kin (Chinese) and Keith Anderson (English).

Suti Manbu 蘇堤漫步 (Strolling along the Su Causeway)

Shoujie Haineiwai Jiangnan Sizhu Chuangzuo yu Yanzou Bisai 首屆海內外江南絲竹創作與演奏比賽 (二) (The First Competition of String-and-Wind Music of Southern Yangtse for Compositions and Performers at Home and Abroad). Vol. 2. 1987. Shanghai: 中國唱片 (China Record Company) HL-540. Notes in Chinese and English.

Yang Chun 陽春 [Sunny spring]

Zhejiang Sheng Gewutuan 浙江省歌舞團 [Zhejiang Province Song and Troupe]. 1983. Beijing: Beijing Shi Yinxiang Chubanshe 北京市音像出版社 [City of Beijing Recording Publishing Company] YY 3013. Performers include Song Jinglian 宋景濂 (*dizi* and *xiao*), Shen Fengquan 沈鳳泉 (*erhu*), and Shen Duomi 沈多米 (*erhu*).

Ying Xian Ke: Zhongguo Daojiao Yinyue, Shanghai Juan 迎仙客: 中國道教音樂, 上海卷 [Welcoming celestial guests: Chinese Taoist music, Shanghai volume] Taoist musicians from the Baiyunguan Temple. 1986. Zhongguo Changpian 中國唱片 (China Record Company) HL-508. Notes in Chinese and English by Chen Dacan 陳大燦.

Yue Er Gao 月兒高 (The moon is high)
Various artists, including Lu Chunling 陸春齡, Zhou Hui 周惠, and the
Shanghai Minzu Yuetuan 上海民族樂團 [Shanghai Chinese Orchestra]. N.d.
Beijing: Zhongguo Changpian 中國唱片 (China Record Company) 10" long
playing disc M-2328.

Zhongguo Fanyue 中國梵樂 (Buddhist music in China)
Zhongguo Shanghai Fojiao Xiehui 中國上海佛教協會 [Buddhist Association
of Shanghai, China]. 1987. Beijing: Zhongguo Changpian 中國唱片 (China
Record Company) SL-282. Notes in Chinese and English. Arranged and
directed by Dong Kejun 董克鈞.

Zhongguo Xuanlü 3: Jiangnan Sizhu 中國旋律（三）: 江南絲竹 (Chinese melody 3:
music of southern Yangtze)
Shanghai Minzu Yuetuan 上海民族樂團 (Shanghai Traditional Orchestra).
1986. Zhongguo Changpian 中國唱片 (China Record Company) HL-466.
Notes in Chinese.

Index

A Bing, 21
Additional repertory, 58, 63–69
Aesthetics: in Chinese music in general,
    xi, xvi; in *Jiangnan sizhu*, xii, 11, 25–27,
    29, 34–36, 40, 69, 89, 96, 103, 107–9,
    112, 115, 118–38, 139–41; in *Kunqu*,
    122–24; in *nanguan*, 124–25; in *qin*
    music, 122–24; in *sizhu* musics in gen-
    eral, 124–25; socialist, 118, 133, 136, 142
Aihaozhe Music Club, 23, 31

Ba Da Mingqu. See Eight Great Pieces
Ba Da Qu. See Eight Great Pieces
"Baban," 61, 62, 89
Bai Juyi, 7
Baisha xiyue, 9
Balungan, 72
Ban (musical instrument), 2, 53, 54, 56
Ban (musical term), 61, 75
Bangzi, 2, 56
Banyan, 75
Bayin, 5
Biqu Gu, 2, 54, 55, 56
Buddhist music, 20

Cai Cide, 93–96, 116–17
Cantonese Music, viii–ix, xxii, 9, 56, 67,
    68, 125, 129, 147 (Prologue) n.2,
    149nn.16, 8
Cantonese opera, 56, 149n.8
Cao Song, 6
Central Conservatory of Music, 8, 141
Chaozhou music, 9, 67, 68, 125, 148n.12
Chaozhou xianshi. See Chaozhou music
Chashan douyue, 6
Chen Liansheng, 20
Chen Yingshi, 58, 120, 127–28
Chen Yonglu, 13, 44, 65, 98–99, 108–11
Chen Yongnian, 55

Chen Zijing, 13
"Chezi Kaimen," 79
China National Music Ensemble. *See*
    Zhongguo (China) Music Club
Chinese Musicians' Association, 27, 28
Chinese opera, 7, 17–18, 27, 109, 128. *See
    also* Cantonese opera; *Huju; Kunqu;*
    Peking opera; *Xiju; Yongju*
Chuida music, 20–21. *See also Shifan* music
Chuanji, 7
"Chun Man Pujiang," 67
"Chun Zao," 67
"Chunfeng Chui Jiangnan," 67
"Chunhui Qu," 67
"Chunjiang Hua Yueye," 14, 66
Chunjiang Music Club, 23, 27
Cooke, Peter, 104
Cultural revolution, 14, 28, 32, 135

"Da Kaimen," 79
Dandang, 109
"Dao Baban," 63
"Dao Chun Lai," 67
Daqin, 50
Datong Music Club, 13–14, 66
"Dengyue Jiaohui," 65
Diangu, 54–55
Difang secai. See Identity, regional
Dizi: in *Jiangnan sizhu* ensemble, 2, 11,
    12, 24, 25, 37, 57, 65, 83, 107, 121, 134;
    key and temperament, 38–39, 47, 134;
    in *Kunqu,* 7–8, 17, 20; musical
    examples of, 40–41, 56, 74, 76, 79–80,
    94–95, 100–101, 114–15; notation for,
    xvi, 3, 14, 40–41, 73, 99, 100–101; in
    other ensemble musics, 8, 9, 18, 20,
    67; performers of, 4, 18, 29, *39;*
    playing, variation in, 92–96, 99,
    100–103; playing techniques, 38–41;
    solo tradition, 66, 68, 80;

"Silk and Bamboo" Music in Shanghai

was composed in 10/12 ITC New Baskerville
on a Macintosh system with Linotronic output
by Books International of Norcross, Georgia,
and the Character List and Glossary,
References Cited, and Selected Discography
were composed in 10/12 Baskerville
by Central Typographers of Hong Kong.
It was printed by sheet-fed offset
on 50-pound Glatfelter Supple Opaque Natural acid-free stock,
notch case bound with 88' binder's boards
covered in Holliston Roxite Vellum Finish cloth
by Thompson-Shore, Inc., of Dexter, Michigan.
It was designed by Diana Gordy,
and published by

THE KENT STATE UNIVERSITY PRESS
KENT, OHIO 44242